SEASONS OF MY LIFE

The Kenny Hibbitt Story

SEASONS OF MY LIFE

The Kenny Hibbitt Story

SEASONS OF MY LIFE

By Kenny Hibbitt, with Tim Nash

First published in Great Britain in 2018 by
Geoffrey Publications, Kingswinford, West Midlands.

ISBN 978-1-9996719-2-1

Cover design by Ruth Bartosik

Printed and bound by T. J. International Ltd.,
Trecerus Industrial Estate,
Padstow, Cornwall. UK. PL28 8RW.

Acknowledgements

When the idea was first mooted about writing this book, it was 1990 and I had just been appointed as Walsall manager. Chris Smith, the highly respected Saddlers correspondent for the *Express & Star*, came up with the idea. But although the idea was right, the timing wasn't. I was only 39 and I was just into my first managerial job, putting all of my efforts into that, as well as trying to juggle a family life. Some 28 years on, my children Kelly and Rod are grown up and I now have grandchildren of my own. Having lost my own grandparents at a very young age or sadly not known them at all, I was very keen for my grandkids to not only share my life as much as possible but also to leave them with a legacy, something they could hopefully look back on with pride in years to come. This was how the idea of writing a book was resurrected, and three and a half to four years ago, Chris and I started working together again to try to bring it together.

Sadly, serious illness in both of our families meant the project had to be put on the backburner at times and it never got finished. But it would never have got off the ground at all but for the efforts of Chris. I will forever be grateful to him for this and he will always be a friend of mine and the Hibbitt family. Chris offered Tim Nash, a former colleague of his at the *E&S*, the chance to carry on the work we had started, and, over the last 18 months, he has worked tirelessly to finally get it over the line. I know Tim has spent many hours of work and my wife Jane and I are very grateful to him for his sterling efforts in writing, re-writing and editing my words and thoughts and we have become firm friends during the process. But the journey could not have been completed without the efforts of many others who have willingly given up their time for free and have helped us along the way.

Just like she has been throughout our 45 years of marriage, Jane has been an absolute rock and my constant support and companion in the writing of this book. She has been with me every inch of the way and has helped in numerous practical ways too. The title of the book, *'Seasons Of My Life'* was Jane's idea and she came up with the photograph which has been used on the front cover, and we think it captures me in my playing days perfectly. My daughter Kelly and husband Eddie, and son Rod and wife Katie, have also been invaluable with their help, love and support, from recalling details and anecdotes which I had long forgotten about to lending us use of their wifi when ours broke down! Thanks to you all.

I am also indebted to Steve Gordos, the retired former *Express & Star* sports editor whose attention to detail has to be seen to be believed, and Wolves fanatic and *E&S* blogger John Lalley for their help proofreading the manuscript and suggesting any changes and/or additions where relevant. I would also like to thank another Wolves supporter, retired headteacher Clive Corbett, whose company *Geoffrey Publications*, published the book. Clive not only advised us every step of the way and formatted the book and laid out all the pictures, but did so without charging for his services, for which we are eternally grateful. Clive also recommended the designer Ruth Bartosik, who has produced superb cover designs. Every effort has been made to contact copyright holders of pictures used. However, if there are any that have not been correctly attributed, then please contact the authors.

A book wouldn't be a book without pictures, and Jane, myself and Tim are indebted to the *Express & Star* for allowing me free use of their photographic library for anything I needed, along with a friendly welcome and generous hospitality. Many of the photos you see are from the *E&S* archives. We thank *Getty Images* for their picture which is the main image on the front cover, and are also grateful to Dave Bagnall, former *Express & Star* chief photographer, for allowing us use of his own personal collection of photographs.

Then there are my team-mates. I owe so much to the lads I played with at Wolves; anything I achieved I could not have done without my colleagues who made playing for the club in the 16 years I was there such an honour, privilege and pleasure. I couldn't possibly continue this section anywhere else but with John Richards. I met John when he joined Wolves in July 1969 and we have been close friends ever since. Not only was he a top-class player and one of the very best I played with, but he is a great guy and will always be a friend. So John was always a natural choice when it came to who was going to write the foreword.

Our respective wives, Jane and Pam, are cousins and whenever we return to the Midlands, we always receive a warm welcome and bed for the night from the Richardses. I never got chance to play with Robert Plant, apart from Dave Woodfield's testimonial in 1974 and a couple of other benefit games in which he featured in, but the musical legend is a huge Wolves fan and interrupted his world tour in Australia recently to take time out and pen a lovely tribute which we have used on the back cover of the book. Thank you so much, Robert – I owe you one, mate! Others who gave up their time to add some flesh to the bones where my memory failed include my close friend Willie Carr, and fellow ex-Wolves team-mates Steve Kindon, Mel Eves and Steve Daley. I was also grateful to Gerry Francis, my old manager at Bristol Rovers, where programme editor Keith Brookman was also a star in recalling details of my time there.

Finally, I would like to thank my mum and dad, and my brother Terry for all the help they gave me to achieve my dreams. My parents encouraged me to play football, and the daily practising with Terry enabled those dreams to become a reality. Seeing Terry go to Leeds United as an apprentice inspired me to become a professional footballer. I'm grateful to Bradford Park Avenue for giving me a chance to start my career, and to Wolverhampton Wanderers for the 16 years I spent there and for giving me somewhere where I can say my heart is. It's been some journey, and I hope you enjoy sharing it with me.

Kenny Hibbitt
May 2018

Foreword

I was in the crowd at Stamford Bridge when Ken Hibbitt scored his first senior goal for Wolves in September 1970. I was just starting my second season at the club and had travelled to London with the first team to gain some experience. Amazingly, it was his full first-team debut and whilst, from what I recall, the goal wasn't a Hibby special, the arms raised, hair flowing celebration was one that would become a regular and familiar sight over the next 14 years. Ken was already at Wolves when I joined in June 1969. He'd been at the club for eight months and had the dubious privilege of being the last signing of Ronnie Allen before he was sacked. We were roughly the same age, Ken was from Yorkshire, I was from Lancashire, and though it may have seemed an unlikely alliance, in the unfamiliar wide new world of Wolverhampton and the West Midlands, our accents and our backgrounds gave us a common bond. A bond that became even stronger when we married cousins Jane and Pam four years later.

Those early days were a succession of new and exciting experiences, from cutting our teeth in the Central League, gaining 'promotion' from the away team changing room to the home team's, travelling on a plane and trips abroad, listening to and learning from players such as Mike Bailey and Derek Dougan, enjoying the sounds and delights of the Wolves Sporting Club and the Lafayette, up to a time when, at the age of 21, we were both regulars in a Wolves line-up that was competing against and beating some of the best teams in England and Europe. On the pitch Ken was a class act, fearless – he could hold his own with all the so called hard men of those days – a beautiful passer of the ball, with a powerful shot that had to be seen to be believed. He played 700-plus first-team games, the majority of which were in a league considered to be the best in the world, and scored well over 100 goals in all competitions. I'm often asked why Ken's international appearances comprised just one England Under-23 cap; a travesty yes, but you have to remember it was at a time when there were 22 teams in Division One and each had one or more English midfielders.

Unlike nowadays, the competition was fierce. His record proves without question that he was one of the best midfielders of his generation. Ken's best game ever, in my opinion, and one that I count myself privileged to have been on the field for, was the home match against Newcastle United at the beginning of the 1974-75 season. To add spice to the occasion, he was up against his very talented brother Terry. Ken was simply unstoppable that day and scored all four goals, including a 'Hibby screamer' which whizzed past my head on the way to the back of the Newcastle net, his fourth goal I believe, at the North Bank end. I still have a singe mark on my right ear as a reminder! More than enough happened at Wolves during the time Ken spent there to fill several books – League Cup wins, FA Cup disasters, relegations, injuries, disagreements with managers, receivership, and the rest. However, those Molineux days are just one part of a much bigger picture.

Ken's whole life has been affected and influenced by football, from his early days at Bradford Park Avenue to working for the Premier League as a referees assessor (and who would have thought that considering all the 'verbal' he used to give referees as a player – poacher turned gamekeeper I believe is the phrase!) In between, he has achieved every young footballer's dream of scoring at Wembley, he's won cup finals, played for his country, played abroad, coached and managed professional clubs, dealt with underhand people and dangerous fans, and even had the time and ability to become a scratch golfer! Ken's been a close friend for a long time and to say he's had a full life is an understatement. As you'd expect of a Yorkshireman and someone with his honest, all-out playing style, he's not afraid to express his opinions. In this book, he doesn't hold back and gives his own forthright views on the good and the not so good of a lifetime spent in football.

It's a frank and compelling read. Enjoy.

John Richards
May 2018

Tribute

The first time I met Kenny was about one month after he had joined the Wolves. He was playing in the reserves at Leeds Road, the home of Huddersfield Town, on December 21, 1968. My late dad, Cyril Wright, took me. He had been a fan of Wolves since his teenage years and was probably one of only a handful, if that, of Wolves supporters in living in Huddersfield. I was nine years old and collected the autographs of the Wolves players, including Kenny, while stood outside the ground before and after the game.

Fast forward just over 12 months, to January 17, 1970, and Wolves reserves were back at Leeds Road. Again, I went along with my dad and collected the autographs of the players before and after the game. This time though, just for reference, Kenny had changed how he signed his name, and he was writing Ken Hibbitt, instead of Kenny Hibbitt. As I was getting his autograph after the match, he recognised my dad from the season before. I thought this was totally amazing. A footballer recognised my dad from last time . . . wow! Kenny asked my dad how he and his mate, John Richards, could get to the railway station as they were going home. Kenny was travelling to Bradford and John to Warrington. Since my dad didn't drive, Kenny and John came with us on the bus to the town centre and my dad showed them where the railway station was and we said our goodbyes.

Eight months on, Kenny had been given his chance in the first team and he made his full debut in the away game at Chelsea on September 12. Wolves drew 2-2 and Kenny scored Wolves' opening goal. The following week the Wolves were at home to Huddersfield Town and my dad had booked us on one of their supporters' travel club coaches. They didn't know we were supporting the Wolves though . . . hee, hee! This was my first visit to Molineux, and I was very excited. Outside Molineux, I was waiting for the Wolves players to arrive. I had my autograph book in my hand, but it was a lot more difficult to get the attention of the players because it was a first-team game so there were quite a few people trying to do the same. The Wolves players used to walk down Waterloo Road from the car park, and as soon as someone saw a player approaching, everyone swarmed on him. I was only ten, so not very tall, and I was really struggling to get anywhere near the Wolves players, let alone get their autographs. But, unbeknown to me at the time, this was about to change. Up walked Kenny Hibbitt, and he again recognised my dad. They chatted for a while, then, as

Kenny knew I wanted to get the Wolves players' autographs, he very kindly took my book and got all the players to sign it and brought it back outside for me. This was quite simply mind-blowing! And because of this, he had suddenly become my hero! Kenny wasn't playing in the game against Huddersfield Town due to a head injury he had received in the midweek game away to Dundee in the Texaco Cup.

The following week Wolves played at Burnley and my dad took me to the game. Again, Kenny and my dad had a good chat afterwards. Kenny even got Bobby Gould to sign a couple of pictures for me. What a great guy this Kenny Hibbitt was turning into! Far better things though were just about to happen as Kenny was once again going home to Bradford. So we all walked in to the town centre. I was carrying Kenny's Wolves bag, and boy was it heavy for me at the time! We all chatted for about 45 minutes in the bus station as the buses weren't too regular. I'm pretty sure my dad and Kenny did most of the talking, and I just said the odd word or two when Kenny said something to me. To be spending time with a footballer from the team you supported – at the time Wolves were one of the top teams in the old First Division – was just too good to be true! I used to tell all my mates at school about how good Kenny Hibbitt was to me. From then on, a friendship developed between my dad, Kenny and myself. At school I was the only Wolves fan and I even had No 8 on the back of my Wolves shirt just like my hero. During PE when we played football the teacher usually made a comment about Wolves. Plus, when I was in the English classes and the teacher said we could write a story about anything we wanted, I always came up with titles (headlines really) like 'Hibbitt Hat-Trick Destroys United' (Manchester United that was) and 'Hibbitt Goal Sinks Leeds'. Then I proceeded to write a report about the game. Looking back I guess my teacher always knew what to expect from me.

When I was growing up my parents never had a lot of money, but my dad was always good at saving it. He had a poor upbringing, so I guess he respected the value of it and I do today. My dad always used to try to save a little bit of money each week so he and I could travel to Wolves games in the north of England, and also visit Wolverhampton for a game occasionally. Over the 14 years that passed from 1970 to Kenny sadly leaving Wolves for Coventry City in 1984, I can't put into words how good he was to my dad and I, always chatting to us before and after games and making us feel very welcome. In addition, he gave us dozens upon dozens of complimentary tickets over the years too. All of this is something I shall never forget, and my dad didn't either when he was alive. He would never hear of a bad word said against Kenny, who was and still is a very kind, friendly, genuine and down-to-earth person. I'd like to think that is probably what he saw in my dad and I and he could relate to it. My dad produced five superb detailed scrapbooks on Kenny over the years. He loved getting cuttings from football magazines, newspapers and programmes and putting them together. The books briefly touched on his early days at Bradford Park Avenue, and, as far as I know, more or less went up to the end of Kenny's playing career at Bristol Rovers. When Bristol Rovers played Huddersfield Town around 1989 or 1990, my dad gave these scrapbooks to then Rovers manager, Gerry Francis, before the game to pass on to Kenny. Sadly for my dad and I, Kenny wasn't there as he was scouting somewhere.

Fast forward again, this time to February 2000, and a West Yorkshire Wolves Supporters Club was formed in Brighouse. During the summer certain ex-players' names were put forward for the position of honorary president. I couldn't state how important it would be for us to have Kenny on board. He had all the necessary credentials – born in Bradford, the club's second-highest appearance player of all time and most importantly of all, Wolves through and through. Kenny got the vote and, luckily, when our then secretary contacted him, he accepted the position. There was even talk of calling our club fanzine, 'The Inhibiter', which I wanted, but it wasn't to be.

A change of name to the Yorkshire Wolves Supporters Club was voted in at our AGM, held at the Ash Tree pub in Wolverhampton on July 13, 2001 as we were in the area for a tour of Molineux. Then, during the summer of 2008, I decided to take on the role of editor of the Supporters Club fanzine as the previous one had emigrated. Having played in bands for over 25 years and done all the PR along the way, as well as making a lot of friends and interviewing a lot of top musicians, I was the ideal candidate to try to contact Kenny for a possible interview, and contact was made through the Wolves Former Players Association. I didn't think he would remember me, although deep down I was hoping he would and we could rekindle a friendship.

When we spoke on the phone it was actually quite funny, because we started talking as if we were the best of buddies! And yes, Kenny remembered my dad and I very fondly, which made me so happy. We both remembered stories from the old days and reminisced for fun. When I mentioned doing an interview for the fanzine covering his entire playing and managerial career, Kenny was more than happy to oblige. Kenny suggested the interview took place at his house and we met on January 23, 2009. On arrival he said 'It's nice to hear someone with a Yorkshire accent!' I asked him well over 100 questions, starting with his schooldays, through his time at BPA, Wolves(every season), Coventry City, Bristol Rovers, his managerial years and right up to working for the Premier League. This was certainly the mother of all interviews for me and definitely the most enjoyable. Part way through it Kenny brought my dad's scrapbooks out. I was lost for words for a few seconds because my entire early teens to early 20s just flashed before my eyes. Wow, did looking through them bring back some wonderful memories! I mentioned a couple of stories behind some of the pictures and cuttings, and we had a good laugh. I know Kenny enjoyed every minute of the interview. He seemed to feel every pass, and every kick, plus he went into great detail at times.

It was a very special day for me as we spent about six hours together. He also showed me his League Cup winning tankards, medals and his England Under-23 cap, which I remember first seeing when Kenny brought it to show his mum and family when Wolves played at Leeds Road in 1970. He also showed me his other trophies, from playing golf. Kenny's friendliness, personality, sense of humour and hospitality was second to none. And this was just how I remembered him from my early teens when I was growing up. Shortly after the interview, as a little thank you from the Supporters Club, I obtained a Bradford Park Avenue polo shirt via a friend and sent it to Kenny for him to wear when he played golf.

When Wolves were in the Premier League it was always nice to see Kenny at Molineux before a game and he has always been very kind and helpful to members of the Supporters Club. Nothing is any trouble to him. Everyday people could learn so much from how Kenny is, not just footballers or pop stars. He is a true gentleman, as well as still being my hero.

Steve Wright
Chairman of the Yorkshire Wolves Supporters Club

For My Family

Contents

Acknowledgements

Foreword – By John Richards

Tribute – By Steve Wright

Dedication

1

A Year To Forget

It was the Queen who brought the phrase 'annus horribilis' to our attention in the modern day, in a speech to the Guildhall in London in November 1992 to mark the 40th anniversary of her accession to the throne. During the year the Royal Family had been rocked by the split between the Queen's son, Prince Andrew, and his wife Sarah Ferguson, the announcement that her daughter Princess Anne and Captain Mark Phillips were to divorce, tapes of Princess Diana telling of Prince Charles's affair with Camilla Parker-Bowles and finally, the great fire that destroyed much of Windsor Castle, the Queen's home. The fire happened just days before her speech.

But if that was our monarch's saddest year, then the Hibbitts have our very own 'annus horribilis' – 1984. Paralleling George Orwell's famous book of fiction with that year as its title, ours was a love story. The bond that myself and wife Jane share was the only way we could have got through it – a brush with our biggest fears and a feeling that we had been left in our own version of hell. In my case, I was worried that my playing career might be over, but Jane's was much worse to contemplate for us both. On top of all that, Wolves were having a truly wretched time and I was concerned that even if I could play again, I didn't know where my next wage packet was going to come from because my contract was up at the end of the season.

My trouble started when Wolves took us to Kuwait for a few days' break in the February in what had become a shocking season that was to end in a humiliating relegation. Rather than the trip having the required rejuvenating effect, it quickly turned into a nightmare – for me anyway. Soon after our arrival we played a friendly game but the crippling stomach pains which I had been suffering for a couple of weeks returned with a vengeance. I felt so bad but somehow managed to stay for the duration of the trip before we made the long journey home. I was never off the toilet. I couldn't wait to get back to England to see a doctor and be with my family. All sorts of horrible thoughts were going through my head.

On our return, the club decided to book me an appointment with Dr Horsley, the club doctor. I really believed in him because about eight years earlier he had diagnosed our daughter Kelly with appendicitis when no one else believed someone so young – she was then just short of her third birthday – could be suffering with that condition. It was a good job he was there because her appendix was ready to burst and we believe he saved her life. He was so caring with children and would never take any chances with anyone. He sent me to see a specialist at the Nuffield Hospital for a thorough examination and arranged an appointment with Roger Grace, later to become Professor Grace. First, I underwent various tests and there was talk of being tested for a tropical disease. I was so worried and frightened and had to spend a full week in hospital being tested for all sorts of things that I could have picked up in Kuwait.

After four days Mr Grace explained why I was in so much pain. I wanted to hear his explanation and yet I didn't – because I thought it was going to be really bad news. When he told me I had ulcerative colitis I asked him what the hell it was. He explained the problem and the way forward but for that few minutes I thought my playing career was over. Then he said there was no reason why I couldn't return to football once the problem was under control. It was the best news I could wish for. After a week I was able to go home but I was still having regular trips to the toilet and passing blood. I had to undergo an intensive course of medication and my wife Jane became very good at administering it, without dwelling too much on that! I had to take that twice a day for some time until the problem was under control. Nobody else knew of my condition. We told everyone it was an acute stomach complaint and I tried to carry on as normal. Jane was brilliant at dealing with my problem and looking after the children, as I wasn't the easiest of patients, especially when I wasn't playing. But this was twice as bad as any injury I'd had, and Jane was my strength. I don't know how she coped. Mind you a bit of bribery did take place; when she had to deliver the medicine, she always asked for a new dress or a pair of shoes before she inserted the dreaded stuff, so it cost me a small fortune!

While I was in the Nuffield Hospital in Tettenhall, Jane had to go into another hospital in Wolverhampton, New Cross, for a routine procedure. The news leaked out that the Hibbitts were both in different hospitals at the same time, which led to a lighter moment. One day a lady in the bed opposite to Jane was reading a copy of the local newspaper, the *Express & Star,* and announced 'Did you know Kenny Hibbitt's wife is in here?' Jane actually played dumb and merely said 'Really?' The paper had approached us to photograph us but Jane said 'No way!' Once I had recovered I continued to have regular check-ups every few months to make sure the condition remained under control. I spent many years under Professor Grace's care, in fact well after we had moved to the West Country in 1986 and the visits continued until after that doctor had retired. I was on medication for 30 years or more. I've always thought charities find you rather than you go looking for them, and through suffering with colitis and learning about it, I became involved in the British Digestive Foundation, one of many charities I have been associated with over the years. On the field, we were struggling desperately, but our relegation fight was soon to pale into insignificance.

Jane returned home from playing in a ladies' golf day complaining about her right knee. I thought she may have tweaked it while swinging the club but she couldn't remember doing anything to it yet struggled to climb the stairs, saying it was sore and felt warm. We couldn't work out what the problem was, and, as she was in terrible pain, I called the club doctor since her discomfort was so bad I had to carry her to the bathroom. As I did so, she caught her foot on the door frame leading to the bathroom and yelled like I had never heard her before. Her knee was now hot and swollen. The doctor arrived and immediately sent her to Wolverhampton's Royal Hospital. Jane's dad Len Clarke came with us and he noticed that the colour of the fluid they drained out of her knee was yellow, indicating it was poisonous. Nevertheless, they bandaged her leg up, put her on crutches and decided to send her home.

But she was still feeling really poorly, and as we left A and E, the sister said to her 'You're not well, are you dear?' Jane replied 'No' and the sister told her to wait. When the sister returned she was accompanied by the registrar, who said within seconds that she had contracted septic arthritis and that it needed to be treated straight away. She asked him whether it was a condition they saw often and he replied worryingly, 'We don't like to see it'. Before we knew it she was admitted and attached to a bloody big drip with antibiotics slamming into her. Len and I went home to see the kids, who had been cared for by Jane's mum Hetty. The next day I dropped the children off at her parents' house and went to see Jane. I was gobsmacked when they told me of her condition. Also known as infectious arthritis, it is usually caused by bacteria, a virus or fungus and results in one large joint in the body being affected, such as the knee or hip. It looked like she had come into contact with poison from a golf course. She had a sore

3

ear from an earring. The only explanation we could come up with was that she must have got something on her finger from playing golf then touched her sore ear, and that was how it got into her system. There was a chance she could lose her leg if things didn't go well. I would have given anything at that moment to make her better and I wanted to swap places with her. It was a shattering blow and we were going through a terrible and frightening ordeal. I was pulled to one side and told that the next 24 hours were going to be critical and I didn't sleep a wink that night thinking about her. All sorts of things go through your mind when something like that happens. I was finding out what many people must endure when they see a loved one suffer that sort of trauma.

She was to undergo an operation the next day. Her knee was opened up and they cleaned out as much of the poison as they could. The following morning I rushed to the hospital to see her and didn't have a clue what the news was going to be. But she came through it and after two weeks, she was finally allowed to come home. That was such a relief after what had been the worst period of our 40-plus years of marriage. We never got to know the name of the sister who stopped her leaving the hospital but we both know if she hadn't seen Jane at that moment, there's every chance my wife wouldn't be here now. If the sister is still alive, I would love to meet her to thank her. We were, and always will be, indebted to the care of the doctors and nurses who saved her life. The young consultant who looked after her – Adrian Joyce – was also magnificent. In fact he was a bit of a hunk, according to some of Jane's friends who went to visit her during her recovery!

On the back of my illness, Jane being so poorly, the horrible inevitability that the team were heading towards relegation and my contract being up at the end of the season, it seemed that life couldn't get much worse. I wondered where I was going to end up. But at least Jane was well again and that was the best thing to have happened.

2

In The Beginning

My early memories are a bit of a mixed bag. I was born in Marsden Street, off Mount Street, in Bradford on January 3, 1951. My grandmother Gertrude, my dad's mum, had a shop on the corner and it was wonderful as she used to spoil us kids by treating us with sweets. She was a lovely lady and I spent many hours watching her slice ham for customers. She was only small but had a right bark on her when she had to raise her voice at my dad Gilbert, and that was quite often as my parents used to argue, particularly on Saturday nights when they came home from the pub. My grandma used to babysit us but when she went home, which was only next door, they would have a row, usually over something and nothing. As they raised their voices, Gran used to bang on the wall and scream at my dad to stop shouting. I was only six or seven, maybe younger than that. My brother Terry and sister Valerie, who were respectively three years older and three years younger than me, couldn't sleep because of the shouting so we hated Saturday nights. My parents only went out together on that evening as money was very tight, but they always found a bit of money to buy us something nice for Christmas.

We lived in a two-up, two-down house in Bradford. Mum and dad had one bedroom and Terry and myself shared the other. Before my sister was born, I would sometimes sleep in mum and dad's room in a single bed but most of the time us brothers slept top to toe. Home comforts were in short supply as we didn't have a bathroom, just an outside toilet, so we kept a bucket in the bedroom in case we needed to go in the night. I wasn't going to light a candle at one o'clock in the morning to go downstairs and into the freezing outside passage! But our parents did the best they could and gave us the best upbringing. It was the same for summer holidays – I have great memories of travelling to Blackpool or Morecambe, always on the train. It was only for a day though – we never stayed any longer. But I loved travelling on trains and that's why steam trains always have a special place in my heart. My dad would never join us on holiday, though, as he was always working. He did different jobs but one I remember was a bookie's runner. He used to wear smart suits and for some reason, black shirts and a black tie. For Christmas, Terry and myself would get new pairs of football boots – well, Terry had new ones and I had to make do with his old ones passed down to me even though they were too big for me. I would stuff the ends with paper to make them fit. That was the trouble with being the younger of two brothers, you always got the short straw and I had to have all or most of my brother's used clothes or shoes. Only once a year would I get a new shirt or jumper or short trousers to go to school in. And being the middle child of three and having a younger sister I thought it was all so unfair because she always had new clothes being a girl and my brother had new clothes as he was the eldest. Poor me!

We had a very hard upbringing, as did many other families back in the 1950s, but we had a great time. Discipline was hard to take at times but it's only when you get older you realise the importance and understand the reasons why we were made to do things. One Christmas when I was about eight or nine and Terry was 12 we couldn't believe it because, as a present, we were given a real white caseball with a lace. We had never seen one of those before – up until then we had only seen brown balls with Dubbin on them but we were promised a white one. We woke up at about five o'clock on Christmas morning to see it all wrapped up on the bed and I remember screaming 'Terry, we've got a ball!' We could feel it through the wrapping paper and we weren't bothered about anything else, not that we got much anyway. Mind you, it must have been a cheap one, because after spending all of Christmas Day battering hell out of it on the shale area in front of our house – bar lunchtime when we went inside to eat – it was brown anyway! The only white bits left were around the stitching. But they were fantastic times and they made you appreciate the good things in life later.

My dad used to come home from the pub with his mates on a Sunday lunchtime and if they saw Terry and myself having a kickabout outside, they would join in with us on the area in front of the house. Several times he and his mates used to fall over and give us all a laugh, but they were all very good footballers. They knew what they were doing and they would trip us up if we went past them. Dad had the chance to play for Port Vale. However, he stayed at home to look after his mum because he was an only child and his dad had died when he was young.

My first football kit was a Port Vale strip, a white V-neck shirt with a black 'V', black shorts and white socks with two black rings round the top. What I couldn't understand at the time was my family kept telling me I was going to play for 'the Posh', who, as we know, are Peterborough United. It was only several years later I found out that part of my family came from there and Nottinghamshire. But far from the Potteries, or indeed, Peterborough being my footballing destination, it was a club much closer to home that became the first port of call on my sporting map.

3

School, Cricket And Pigeons

I didn't enjoy my first day at Bowling Back Lane junior school one little bit. I didn't know anything about school apart from that I didn't like it and would rather have been at home kicking a ball around the field in front of the house where we lived. But I needn't have worried because it proved to be the ideal place to hone my sporting skills. The school had a great reputation for its football team and it produced some top class players over the years. One of them was Barrie Wright, and when he moved to Tyersal, the secondary school we all went to when we left the junior school, he went on to captain the England under-15s schoolboys side, playing six times. He ended up making five appearances for Leeds United and 10 for Brighton at full back before playing football in the United States.

The school wasn't just known for boasting one of the most successful football teams in our part of Bradford but also for an excellent rounders team that won tournaments. When I tell people now I have a rounders medal they just laugh because it was known to be more of a girls game, but I don't care. It was played with what I call half a cricket bat because of the shape of it. The back of it was the same as a cricket bat and I enjoyed hitting it as it helped with my timing when it came to whacking a cricket ball. I just love playing any sport that involves a ball – cricket, tennis, golf and snooker. But I only played squash once and that was it for me and that game. I had agreed to play my Wolves team-mate Andy Gray and he thrashed me. But it wasn't just the pain of losing that hurt. I pulled the muscles in my backside and was furious with myself because I ended up missing a game as a result.

At Tyersal I met someone who was to become my first sporting mentor. Mr Wilkins was a PE teacher who had been a rugby player for Harrogate in his younger days and he ran the school football team. As a rugby man, he was keen for us kids to play with the oval ball but, as a mad keen footballer, I was in love with the round one – and I told him so! I once shouted 'You make me sick you do, sir, always wanting us to play rugby!' He responded 'Well you make me sick, always wanting to play football!' But we got on like a house on fire. His name was Steve and he was a great bloke, a really athletic guy who joined in with everything. We stayed in touch for years afterwards.

The headmaster at Tyersal was called Mr Hogg and he loved his sport. He always made a point of asking how we were getting on and he followed the careers of Terry and myself. We had a good cricket team as well and we were very difficult to beat. As a bunch of lads we grew up together and were very competitive – you had to be to get a game with those boys, at any sport. I used to be a medium pace bowler, loved to open the batting and field in the covers or mid-wicket, that way you found yourself always involved in the game. I did field at fine leg and third man when I was bowling, though, and got frustrated at not having a lot to do in these positions. Batting was my strength and I scored a few runs both for my school and the local cricket club called Laisterdyke, who played in the Bradford League.

After starting with the juniors, I progressed to the first team where a few old county players used to play. There were some excellent players and each team were allowed to have one pro. It might have been two but I'm not sure. In one junior match we played at home, a semi-final in 1965, I was batting against a quick bowler and edged the ball to the wicket-keeper who caught it. I was playing a forward defensive shot, the bowler and wicket-keeper appealed but the umpire gave me not out. I didn't walk and pretended I hadn't touched it and went on to make a good 81. But for the first time in my cricket career, and indeed any sport I played, I did wrong and I still regret it because cricket was a gentleman's game. It was very honest and my dad always said if you play any sport it should be done fairly. To this day I still feel awful about it despite it happening so many years ago, but it taught me a lesson and I have never cheated since, in any sport.

In the same team that day was David Bairstow, who became one of my best friends and we played in the football and cricket teams at Bradford Moor junior school. I used to stay with David most Friday nights before football on Saturday morning as the pitch we played on wasn't far from his house. His father was great and was a wicket-keeper himself in his time, as was David. He had a fantastic career for Yorkshire and England, and I was very proud of him. His achievements were in no small way down to his dad who put in a lot of hard work with him in his youth. I was asked to go to the Yorkshire nets at the same time, but although I loved cricket and still do, deep down I wanted to be a footballer. There seemed to be more money in football but I do regret not continuing my cricket career at the highest level. David played for a team in Bradford called Undercliffe, who were like a feeder team to Yorkshire at the time. It was tragic

9

to hear he committed suicide in 1998 at the age of 46. His son Jonny is a tremendous player for Yorkshire and England. I read recently that a fan had given Jonny his dad's wicket-keeper gloves that he'd had off him 39 years ago. Phil Carrick was another player I played with. He was a left-arm spinner who also went on to play for the Tykes. But my hero was 'Sir' Geoffrey Boycott, one of the world's best batsmen in my opinion. My first real bat was a Boycott-signed Gray Nicholls which I loved and still keep.

Going back to my schooldays at Bradford Moor, I broke a goalscoring record that had been held for some time. I scored 53 goals in 14 games including 14 in one game which we won 22-0. I would get the ball and just dribble past everyone and bang it into the net. Granted the opposition weren't very good, but I think we must have had a very good team. I wonder even now if that record ever got broken as it was so long ago – way back in 1962. I was only 11 at the time. In fact it cost my mum and dad a fortune as they used to pay me sixpence for every goal I scored! When I told them I had scored 14 they said that would be the last time they would pay me for scoring. I didn't mind, though, because I knew how tight money was for them and I didn't take the seven shillings they would have had to pay me. I got a small cup for that record but I don't know where it went. Another time, playing for a team called Moorhill United, I scored ten goals in a game, and that season the club won four trophies, scoring 257 goals and conceding 50. One of my team-mates there was a winger called David Jones, who was a junior player at Wolves when I got there and later played three League games for York City.

At this stage of my youth I used to keep pigeons at the back of our house. We lived in a back-to-back home meaning we had no garden as we lived at the front. But the people who lived at the back let my dad build me a loft out of orange boxes we had collected from all the shops nearby. We put them on our guider, which was a long piece of wood with two wheels at the front and two at the back with a piece of string at the front to pull it along or to guide it if we were going downhill. They are called guiders up north but may be named differently around the country. We would go to rubbish tips and find, say, an old pram that had some wheels on it, then get the chisel and hammer to knock the axle free from the frame. It took us ages as they were welded on but we always managed it somehow. My dad built me a loft and his friend gave me two young pigeons he had bred himself from his own birds. He had some great racing birds and I

10

used to see him every Sunday going across the field to his hen run where he kept them. I would run after him and help him let them out for a fly and while they were out we would clean the loft and put out fresh food and water. He had a big loft and about 30 birds – not like my little loft. He showed me the two birds he was going to let me have; they were not ready to leave the nest as they were only about three weeks old. You could see that one was going to be dark blue check and the other was all white. In six long weeks they were finally mine and I had to leave them in my loft for a while before I could let them out because they had to get used to my loft. It took another six weeks or so keeping them in and by this time they were looking supreme. I was so excited and could not wait to let them out. That day eventually came and I was very nervous because they would fly back to where I had got them from.

Off they went and they flew over the house and all around the area I lived. I ran down the passage to the front and back again to see them flying at the back of the house. I must have run up and down the passageway about 30 times until they landed on the roof of the loft. It was great to see and a wonderful feeling. I had not fed them before I let them out as I was told not to. They would come back if they were hungry. I shook my tin of corn and whistled them to 'Come on, come on' several times and they both dropped down on to the loft and in through the bob hole. It was fantastic and I was so excited I ran and told everyone what had happened. The white one was called Bobby – after my footballing hero Bobby Charlton – and the dark check I named Tommy, though I'm not sure why. Bobby was brilliant and he used to fly through the passage sometimes. I think he saw me do it so often he followed me! I used to race them home from where I let them out about two miles away. I ran home as fast as I could but they were always there ahead of me. They were so enjoyable and I had lots of fun with them and could not wait to get home from school to see them.

One winter was so bad we had snow on the ground for about six weeks and the frost was so severe the telephone lines looked like snow. One morning I opened the loft door to feed my birds, and there they were on the perch, but with their eyes closed and their heads bowed. They were frozen solid. I cried out for mum and dad, ran back to my house crying my eyes out to tell them my pigeons were dead. I was heartbroken and couldn't go back to the loft so dad had to bury them for me. It was awful to see them like that and it was a quite a while before I got some more to replace them. But they could never really be replaced – they were unique and the very first birds I had. I still remember them now so vividly and the fun they gave me. Eventually I extended the loft, got about a dozen more birds and tried to breed them. They were bought in the Bradford market for about a shilling each. I didn't buy them all at once as I had to earn the shilling or save the spending money my grandma used to give us, threepence a day and sixpence on Saturdays, so I had to be patient building my bird numbers.

It's hard to believe but there was a lot of jealousy around and my birds were a lot better than those of some of the other lads. One morning when I went to feed them I found half of them had been slaughtered with their heads bitten off. There was blood everywhere as though they had been fighting to get away from something attacking them. It could have been rats or it could have been a ferret as they were popular around our way in those days but I never did find out what had killed them. It took me ages to clean the loft properly and the lucky birds which did survive just weren't the same again.

When I was about 13 we moved as my mum and dad bought our first house that cost approximately £2,500, which was a lot of money back then. We had our own back garden for the first time so I could build a bigger pigeon loft and keep more birds. The other good thing about moving was that right across the road was a football ground where Bradford Rovers played. It was where Terry and I won a cup final when he scored the winner in 1959 – more about that shortly – and it was where my dad played his amateur football too. I had to sell my other birds to my mates who were just starting out keeping pigeons and I would have to start again. A year later I had built a new loft which housed around 20 birds and I was made up.

After playing my football matches I would spend most of my time taking the birds for a fly. That meant taking them as far as I could in cardboard boxes, but, as I would have to walk everywhere, it was never too far. On Saturday mornings we would play our school games and then after taking the birds out I would go across the road to watch the Rovers play with a few of my friends. At half-time we would go to the far end of the pitch and go into the goalmouth with our ball and a have few shots at goal. It was brilliant because there was a proper net, not like the one we had on the field at my old house. We would play until the groundsman spotted us and shouted at us to get off the pitch but at least we got a few minutes' shooting into the net. We also went on to the pitch at the end of the game as well and we got a little longer before the groundsman spotted us and we had to leave. Some Sunday mornings if the groundsman hadn't taken the nets down after the game, we would creep under the wire netting put there to keep people out. It would be early as we knew he would be back to take the nets down later and we loved it. We played a game called 'Attack' with three or four defending the goal and the other four trying to score, then we would swap around after the attacking team had scored three goals. When the groundsman arrived we did a runner, diving under the wire fencing and running like hell. We had great fun!

4

Jumpers For Goalposts

Like every other kid I had to go to school but I couldn't wait for the bell to go after lessons each day so I could run home and get my trainers on to play football. The only lessons I liked were PE and, strangely, religious education. I'm not sure why I enjoyed the latter but I just took to it. Going back to the trainers, I call them that but back then they were known as 'bumpers'. They didn't last long with the amount of football we played, and playing on the field with shale and stones on it, well you can imagine the state they used to get in. Naturally my parents couldn't afford to keep buying new ones for my brother and me, so when they got too bad we would put rubber bands around the sole and over the top to keep the sole from dropping off. We found they lasted a couple of months longer by doing this.

The field we played on wasn't very good and sometimes our feet would get very sore, so Terry and I came up with a great idea. We put our jumpers down to make a pair of goals – surely something every football-mad kid has done over the years. But we wanted something better, a more realistic set of goals. So we set about finding some wood to build a proper looking goal frame and we also wanted something to stop the ball as it entered the goal. A net would have been fantastic but that was never going to happen so we found some chicken wire on a tip and put it up along with some old lino we came across. It worked a treat but not for long as we battered it, but we kept banging it back together to get a bit more wear out of it. Then we would return to the tip to see if we could find some more lino or something better.

We played a game we called 'Long shots'. There were two sets of goals about 20 yards apart and the idea was to place the ball down and try to score against the other player. We would play it all day long. As we got older – I was about eight and Terry 11 – we decided it would be better if we could dive to stop each other from scoring. We managed to turf a small goalmouth which helped reduce the many cuts on our knees through diving around and it helped develop my goalkeeping skills – something whichcame in handy further down the line. It got quite competitive at times but Terry was always the winner. Well, he was three years older and he had a great left foot even at that age. We used to go to an open field about half a mile away armed with a wheelbarrow and spade we borrowed from my gran next door to cut the pieces up. It took us a month to dig up the turf and cart it back to our pitch and lay it in front of the goals, but when it was finished, all the kids in the area wanted to play on the pit. Of course we always had a ball; people always said 'The Hibbitts will have a ball' if they wanted to play football. They all wanted to go in goal so they could dive around on the grass and all the kids loved it. Terry and I spent all our school holidays playing this game and we could now dive about without cutting our knees and hands. I think playing this game helped us both to develop our shooting and striking of the ball with both feet, and although Terry's right foot wasn't the best, his left was something special. I can still picture him scoring the winner in a cup final with a goal I will never forget. The opposition keeper took a goal kick which landed straight on Terry's left foot and before the keeper could get back into his goal the ball had flashed straight past him like a bullet into the empty net.

I played in that final – but very nearly didn't. We had been practising on the field as usual when I fell and broke my collarbone. I was scared to tell my dad what had happened but Mum took me to hospital where it was confirmed that I had broken it. They wrapped up the injury with bandages in a figure of eight but that wasn't going to stop me from playing in a final. We had a lad named Mickey Roper who was a good player and went on to have a trial at Wolves when he was 15. A big, strong ginger-haired lad, Mickey took no nonsense and he looked after me in that cup final. If he saw a player trying to tackle me too hard he would soon sort them out. Nobody argued with Mickey! We won the cup and I won my first medal at the age of eight. My mum kept it for me up until she died but I have no idea where it went. That final and the season of 1958-59 was the only time Terry and I played in the same team. He was older so when he moved to secondary school at 11 years of age I was left behind. By the time I changed schools and went to Tyersal he was only a year away from leaving his school days behind.

By the time I entered my second year at Tyersal in 1963, my brother had joined Leeds United as an apprentice. That proved to be my final year there as I moved schools to another one nearby called Fairfax. I think Tyersal closed down at the time but I'm not 100 per cent sure. At Fairfax I continued to develop my footballing skills and earned a growing reputation as a goalscorer. Three years later, in 1966, Terry ended up being given a pro contract at Leeds. That was the year I signed for Bradford Park Avenue as

15

an apprentice. So it was a good year for us both and all the hard work we had put in as kids was now paying off because all we ever wanted to do was play football and my dad and mum were so proud of us. With Terry and I taking the first steps to good careers and England winning the World Cup, it wasn't a bad year all round. By this time my mum and dad had installed a black and white TV set so we watched the final. But forget about any nerves before the game or celebrations at full-time, before the match, at half-time and straight after the game, I was Bobby Charlton. Well, I was pretending to be him anyway, smashing balls with my left foot and right foot, practising my technique. Little did I know that I was taking the steps towards sharing the same pitch as one of England's greatest players in just a few years' time.

5

The Apprentice

After representing Bradford Boys as a 13-year-old in their under-15s team and Yorkshire Boys at the age of 15, I was being chased by scouts from several clubs. By this time my brother Terry had joined Leeds United, who went on to become one of the great teams of the late 60s and early 70s, but I decided to join my hometown team Bradford Park Avenue. I turned down most of the big Yorkshire clubs who were all in a higher league because I reckoned if I was going to make the grade I could only go upwards as Bradford were in the Fourth Division. That gave me a better opportunity to make the first team, if I improved enough.

My dad took me to the club to meet the management team of Jock Buchanan and Walter Galbraith, and after a long chat I signed on as an apprentice on £9 a week. That was about £2 a week more than apprentices at other clubs got. Wow! I used to take home £8.15s.6d a week, my mum got £5 and I had the rest to save for a new suit, a grey one which was made by my dad's tailor. I felt so smart in that suit and loved it for years afterwards. I left school on the Friday in 1966 and started work the following Monday.

Within weeks of starting, I got the chance to see a world-class sportsman at first hand. But it wasn't a footballer. We shared our Horton Park Avenue ground with the cricket club, and occasionally Yorkshire played county matches there. One day I was up in the main stand and I could hear clapping so there was obviously a game going on. One of the doors from the football side to the cricket side had been left open, and as I was bored with work and I love cricket, I thought I would take a chance to skive off for abit and watch the game. As it turned out Yorkshire were playing the West Indies who were on tour so I opened one of the kiosks where the boxes of crisps were, I took a box with me and sat down. On centre stage was Yorkshire's best and greatest batsman in my view, Geoffrey Boycott, facing two of the fastest bowlers in world cricket at the time, Wes Hall and Charlie Griffith. 'Boyks', who was still wearing his glasses, was playing both of them with ease. All of a sudden the clock had crept round to 4pm and I had been there for almost four hours thoroughly wrapped up in the game. I thought I had better go back to the football stand and start doing some more painting but as I had

17

scoffed about seven packets of crisps I felt a bit sick. Just as I got back into the football side of the ground, Jack, the groundsman, saw me and gave me the biggest bollocking of my life, threatening to report me to the manager. I said I wasn't feeling too good and was promptly sick in front of him. He said he felt slightly sorry for me but he still told the manager and I got another telling-off and a severe warning not to do it again. This incident followed not long after I'd had a telling-off for trying to get out of cutting the pitch in the close season but on this occasion it was not my fault. I had taken a barrow-load of grass cuttings out of the gate at one end of the ground by the car park where we trained with the amateurs and I witnessed a bloke get knocked off his bike by a car. He just lay there on the road with his legs tucked under him and his arm out straight.

He was in a very bad way and had the biggest gash on his arm I had ever seen. I can't stand the sight of blood and I had to lie down as I could feel a cold sweat coming and I felt faint and dizzy. I must have been lying down on the barrow for some time because Jack came out looking for me. He tapped me on the arm to wake up as he obviously thought I had been sunbathing and was trying to get out of my work. I duly got another sound ticking-off but I eventually convinced him what had actually happened. It all sounds as if I didn't do my work properly or was trying to get out of it but nothing could be further from the truth. I loved my work and always took pride in what I did, whether it was cleaning the boots, the dressing rooms, bathrooms or even the cleaning of the ground and the painting.

Joining Bradford as an apprentice at the age of 15 was my first experience of work and of earning money. I felt so proud and I genuinely thought it was an honour to be playing and training with professional footballers I had only seen from the terraces. There were players such as the star man Kevin Hector, who was sold to Derby County for £40,000 within a few months of me arriving in 1966, and just over two years before I joined Wolves for £5,000. What a player Kevin was! A prolific scorer for Bradford with 113 goals in 176 League games, he still holds the club record for League goals in a season after netting 44 in 1965-66. Then he became a Derby County legend, winning promotion and two League titles on his way to becoming their all-time record appearance maker with 486 League games. He inspired me in the short time I spent with him, as did the goalkeeper John Hardie, who was Scottish and a gentleman who would always find time to chat with me about football. He impressed on me the importance of working hard but above all enjoying the game. We didn't have many big names at Bradford, but one was Mick McGrath. A left half, Mick won 22 caps for the Republic of Ireland and had played for Blackburn Rovers in the 1960 FA Cup final against Wolves, unfortunately for him scoring an own goal in Rovers' 3-0 defeat at Wembley. But with that pedigree, he was a bit of a star. As someone who used to pore over football magazines and see pictures of him in action, to be suddenly in the same changing room as him made me pinch myself. He was a lovely guy with a sweet left foot. Another player who I used to look up to was a left-back called Gerry Lightowler. He made me laugh a lot and one weekend him, the striker Bobby Ham and myself went on a day out in his van. We had a great time and everything went well until we were on our way back home when his van started to belch smoke. By the time we had found somewhere to pull over, the van was now throwing out so much smoke it was choking us. Gerry opened the back door and we had almost forgotten all about his sheepdog in the back. The poor hound's face was a picture – he looked so sad and frightened and just stared at Gerry as if it was his fault. Talk about a laugh – we could not stop and we laughed virtually all the way home even though it was behind the safety of a towing truck.

If I was having a laugh away from football, it was only masking what was happening in my day job. My apprenticeship was very tough. In fact I was the only apprentice and so I had to do the work of 10 lads. Jack, the groundsman, was in charge of all my duties which started at 10am when the first task was to clean about 25 pairs of boots. Then I got the kit out for the pros, hung it out to dry after the morning session and then got it out for the afternoon session. Training would finish around 12.30pm and the afternoon session would start about 2pm. Sometimes I would have to spend the morning session collecting balls from behind the goals when the first team had had shooting practice. I have to say I did a lot of collecting if Hector was not shooting because he did not miss the target very often. He was something else – I used to watch him from behind the goal and he could get the ball on the halfway line and run through before scoring.

Training would finish and I would then go into the dressing room and collect the kit up and take it to the drying room ready for next day, clean the boots with a wire brush and return to the pitch with Jack to put all the divots back. By this time the players had left and I would have to go back into the dressing room and mop the floor and clean the bathroom and baths. That had to be done every night before I went home.

The changing room was the same colour as our first-team kit – green and white. The floor had to be sparkling and I used Vim and a scrubbing brush to clean the white bit. It was very hard to get the scuff marks off caused by the players' studs and sometimes I wouldn't finish work until about 7pm. I had to get to the ground in the morning about 8.30 so the days were long and occasionally I fell asleep on the bus home. In fact once I woke up in the bus terminus I had been so tired. My week would go something like this: Monday and Tuesday after a home game I would spend most of the day sweeping up the whole ground and clearing the rubbish that the fans had left behind. I did not mind this because sometimes I would find a bit of money - a ten-bob note was the mostI found in one go and that was worth quite a bit in those days. There were plenty of coins like halfpenny, penny and sixpences and even a packet of cigarettes that I took home to my dad. He only smoked at the weekends so they would last him a while and save him money because things were still very tight at home.

On Tuesday nights I would stay and train with the amateurs as I was not getting any training during the day and I also did Thursday nights but that was the only training I got for the first nine months. We didn't have a youth team so I had to play in the reserves, mostly on the left or right wing. Wednesdays and Thursdays were much the same but Friday was my best day – not only did I get my wages but the players used to ask me to clean their cars. I charged half a dollar which is 12 and half pence in today's money. I would clean as many as I could, sometimes as many as eight, and that would give me an extra £1 in my pocket. I felt rich!

On Saturdays I would be with the reserves and we played the likes of Sunderland and Middlesbrough who had some top-class players. If I was picked they used to play me on the wing to save me from getting kicked in the air by very experienced players who were trying to get back into their respective first teams, and boy could they kick. In those days the boots came over the ankles with the laces wrapped around to give you more feel, and to protect your own ankles. It wasn't much fun for me and I didn't really want the ball which was completely out of character. But in all honesty, these players scared the living daylights out of me. I was only 15 and not long out of school while these guys had about 10 years' experience under their belts and they were not going to let a kid go past them. My first season had gone by and there was a change of management. The first team had struggled that season and finished in the bottom four so there was a change at the top and in came Jack Rowley.

I didn't know his history as a player until he had been in charge for a few months and eventually I learned he had been a prolific goalscorer for Manchester United and other teams so he clearly knew a bit about the game. Born in Wolverhampton, Jack was on Wolves' books as a youngster but they apparently did not rate him and transferred him to Bournemouth. He did well there and United signed him in 1937. He helped them gain promotion from the Second Division in 1937-38. During the War he made eight guest appearances for Wolves and set a club record when he scored all eight goals as they beat Derby County 8-1 in 1942. Jack also helped United win the FA Cup in 1948 and the First Division title in 1951-52 as well as playing six times for England, scoring six goals. His younger brother Arthur was also a prolific scorer who still holds the overall Football League record with 434 goals, playing for West Bromwich Albion, Fulham, Leicester and Shrewsbury Town. He remains the club record scorer at the two latter teams.

What Jack Rowley did at Bradford changed my belief in football and my confidence came flooding back. One of the first changes was the setting-up of a youth team which meant we took on four new apprentices. That in itself was a godsend because after my first season I honestly felt like packing it all in. It was such hard work being the only apprentice and the only time I could train was with the amateurs on a Tuesday and Thursday night. I had a really long chat with my dad and he persuaded me to give it another six months to see if things improved for me now that there had been changes at the club.

Not only did Jack Rowley alter things on the playing side, but he ordered a radical shake-up off it as well, including a complete change of kit. Whereas we had played in green and white, he decided we would play in hoops – one red hoop and one yellow hoop with the rest of the shirt in white. So that meant more work for me – if not paint the town red then I had to paint the ground red and the new manager wanted every barrier behind the goals and down the sides of the pitch done in the new colours for the following season. It became known as the 'Summer of Love' but the only affection around Bradford Park Avenue in the summer of 1967 was of the tough love variety with a hectic pre-season fitness schedule that included plenty of gruelling cross country running. We would run over a golf course called East Bierley. At the time I thought golf was for the more well-off and I knew nothing about the game. Being a regular golfer now I feel awful about this because we used to pick the balls up and throw them into the bushes as we ran by. If anyone did that now to my ball I would go berserk but we thought it was just a bit of fun at the time. It was a tough run and a big golf course and I was glad when we finished. I would have a shower and then carry on with my duties of putting away the training gear to dry in readiness for the next day's training, clean the bathrooms and changing room. When the pre-season matches finished and the 1967-68 campaign began, it wasn't long before I broke into the first team – more about my debut shortly.

6

Goodbye To Dad – And Bradford

I was doing jobs around the ground one day in summer 1967 when Ken Roberts, who was part of the management team with Don McCalman, who had replaced Jack Rowley, came looking for me and told me he was going to take me home after delivering the worst possible news – my dad had suffered a heart attack. My legs just turned to jelly and the shock was horrendous. I still have that feeling at times when I think about it. When we arrived I could see Mum on top of the steps sobbing her heart out and when I got to her, she just said 'He's gone Kenny'. I rushed into the lounge where the medical people were and saw one of them putting smelling salts under his nose and I could see him take his last breath. I was 16. I just sat with my mum for what seemed forever. Terry was informed and he came home from Leeds where he was in digs and joined me, my sister and my mum. It was the worst feeling I'd ever had and we just didn't know what to do. My dad was only 40 with no history of illness, although he'd been suffering from heartburn and the doctor gave him something for that a couple of weeks before. If he'd been around today it might have been different and the problem might have been picked up with a further test. We'll never know if dad had been told something different at the time by the doctor but our lives had been shattered with his loss.

I was very close to dad, probably closer than Terry or my sister even though he loved us all very dearly. Although I was close to him, he died when I was so young that I feel I didn't get to know him anywhere near as well as I did my brother Terry. He was out at work all day and we were at school, so the only time we would spend together was when we would gather around the dinner table at night. I remember Dad worked as a bookie's runner, putting bets on for people. He also started a fundraising draw locally and I recall at the age of eight or nine him writing out the numbers in his neat handwriting. People in the neighbourhood would pick out a number and the winner would get 10 bob (50p) or something like that. But he got caught and was fined! After he died, my mum was heartbroken for months afterwards but she had to be strong for us kids. You could see how much she missed Dad.

We'd just bought our first house as well and without him we struggled with the mortgage payments. Terry would send money home and I would have to increase my weekly keep from £5 to £6. My sister was still at school as a 13-year-old so she wasn't as aware of what was going on. They were hard and difficult times. As a 17-year-old I needed to talk to someone. My mum was there but I required guidance from my dad but he'd gone, and Terry was living in Leeds so I didn't see too much of him. It was hard to think where I was going to finish up. It was a bad time for us all, but we had to get on with life and my mum did a great job with us. The new season was now just around the corner and after the funeral, things started to settle down a bit. But our lives had been changed so dramatically you wondered what the future would hold for all of us as a family.

Gradually, my mind turned back to football and that season Bradford PA youth team had been drawn at home to Stockport County in the FA Youth Cup. We drew 3-3 and had to replay on their ground a week later. Our goalkeeper, who was an amateur, didn't turn up and so our coach asked if anyone fancied playing in goal. I volunteered to don the gloves and we won 3-0. I made a couple of good saves and used the ball out of my hands very well with pinpoint half-volleys out to our wingers. All the practise Terry and I had put in with the 'long shots' came in handy and I actually quite liked it because you could dive around in the mud. A couple of weeks later I heard Stockport had offered £5,000 to sign me – as a goalkeeper! I was amazed but for various reasons the move didn't come off and it was just as well as I wasn't very keen on goalkeeping as a career.

Thankfully, I was being noticed as an outfield player and I was picked to make my senior debut on March 23, 1968, in a Fourth Division game away to Chesterfield. Although I was just over two months past my 17th birthday, there had been a bit of speculation in the local press about the possibility of me pushing myself into the first team. In the reserves, I was used to playing against experienced senior pros such as Charlie Hurley at Sunderland and Roy Vernon, who had captained Everton and top-scored for them when they won the League title in 1963 and was now at Stoke City. The record books show my debut was a losing one as we went down 2-0 at Saltergate thanks to goals from Ivan Hollett and Kevin Randall (penalty) in front of a crowd of 7,237. But the only memories I have of it were the nerves I felt beforehand – something that stayed with me throughout my career.

I recall absolutely nothing about the game or anything of the build-up. Whatever impact I made on the field didn't seem to have much affect on the results.That defeat at Chesterfield was Bradford's fourth in a row in a run of six straight losses and we were to lose 13 of our final 16 games, drawing the other three in a sequence of 18 matches without a win, stretching back to a 2-1 win at neighbours Bradford City at Valley Parade on February 10. It meant we finished eight points adrift at the bottom of the Fourth Division, 92nd in the Football League, one spot below where we had finished the previous season. In those days there was no relegation from the League, or promotion from non-league. Instead the bottom four clubs had to apply for re-election via a vote of all of the clubs at the Football League AGM. On this occasion, ourselves, York City, Chester and Workington were all re-elected, and in the case of York and us it was for the second year in a row.

After such a gloomy couple of years, I'm not sure the expectations were any higher for the following season and in fact, it proved a bad omen as Bradford finished bottom for the following two years before finally failing to secure re-election in 1969-70 and therefore forced to drop out of the League, ending a 62-year spell as a Football League club. But if the club's progress was uncertain, on a personal front I felt as though things were looking up. The 1968-69 campaign got under way and I was in the first team again. I found out Wolves and a couple of other clubs were showing interest in me. Looking back it scared me because I was now enjoying my football at Bradford and I thought I'd have a long career there. Myself and another first-team newcomer named Garry Hudson, who was a great lad and a good defender, were invited to attend England youth trials at Lilleshall. We had to take our own training kit and we looked so scruffy compared with the other lads from the bigger clubs. I can still see Charlie George with his tracksuit with Arsenal written on the back and Tony Towers, from Manchester City, in his nice matching blue gear. Our kit was made up of anything really and none of it matched so no-one knew where we'd come from. We kept getting asked 'Where have you come from and what league are you in?' It was embarrassing really but we told them and we were proud of playing for our club. Neither of us got into the squad even though we did very well in the practice games, but it was a good experience and we enjoyed it. That trip to Lilleshall gave me an early taste of the big time and I loved it. It was just as well, because I was about to sample it on a regular basis – and not too far away from that Shropshire beauty spot.

7

Thrown to the Wolves

Three months had passed by from when I first heard of any interest in me when I was called into the manager's office. It wasn't a long conversation. Don McCalman said Wolves wanted to buy me and Bradford had accepted their offer of £5,000. The fee was £3,000 to be paid straight away up front, then £1,000 if I made a first-team appearance and another £1,000 if I played for any England representative team. Don said he wanted to keep me but the club were in financial trouble and the money would help them survive. I felt I had to leave after he told me that because I loved BPA. They had done the same a couple of years earlier when they had sold one of their best ever players, Kevin Hector, to Derby County for £40,000. I later read in January 1971 they were chasing Wolves for the final £2,000 after I had played for England Under-23s, by which time they were a non-league side.

I had an inkling something might happen because the Wolves chief scout Joe Gardiner had been following up his spying mission from the previous season when I got into the first team. When the offer came it was still a hell of a shock and I knew it was going to be the most difficult decision because of losing Dad not too long ago. I went home to tell Mum and rang Terry as well. I felt very scared and really wanted to speak to Dad and ask his advice. Terry had a quiet word with the Leeds manager Don Revie, who said I should go, and he reckoned my dad would have said the same. Mum was a bit unsure at first but then said all my dad wanted to see was me and Terry playing in the First Division – the top division in those days. My biggest concern was for my mum and my sister. Terry was living in digs in Leeds, and although it was only 20 miles away he wanted to be with his team-mates at Elland Road, so I had a big decision to make.

Eventually Mum persuaded me to go but I still had to send as much money home as I could to help pay the mortgage. There was a lot to consider when leaving home, not just my football. I was playing cricket in the Bradford League which was a tough and good league to play in. There were professionals in most teams who had played at county level or even internationally and I was enjoying that a lot. And of course there were my racing pigeons. I didn't race them because I couldn't afford to, but I loved them. Although she didn't like them much, Mum agreed to look after them. Wolves said I could go home every six weeks for a weekend and I would be home all summer to play cricket for my club Laisterdyke. I'd now decided to join Wolves and I started to get my gear ready and packed. As I boarded the train south from Bradford to Wolverhampton, I was in a daze. Every time the train pulled in at a station, I wanted to get off. As I looked out of the window and saw cows in a field, without a care in the world, while I was shaking like a leaf, and all I could think of was 'Why am I here?' I didn't know where Wolverhampton was, and as a 17-year-old I was pretty scared because it was the first time I had travelled so far on my own and I didn't have a clue what was ahead. I began thinking about my school days and how my football had developed since those early formative years. Then the nerves started.

Normally, I only felt anxious before a game but this was different – I was alone and I didn't even know where Wolverhampton was on the map! But if my mind was everywhere and my stomach doing cartwheels, my career was on its way. Joe Gardiner arranged to meet me at Wolverhampton station before taking me to Molineux to meet the manager Ronnie Allen to sign a contract and then on to my digs to meet the people I'd be staying with. We hadn't agreed or even discussed money at this point but I knew it had to be more than the £9 a week I was getting at Bradford. However, I wasn't going for the salary – I was going to play in the top flight with the great Wolves who I'd only seen on TV. They were famous for their unique kit of gold shirts and black shorts, and I always felt they looked a tough team in those colours – even though they had briefly switched to all gold at the time when I signed. I was in awe just thinking about players such as the great Derek Dougan and Peter Knowles, and of course, captain Mike Bailey.

After watching the first team in the gym, I was summoned to see Ronnie Allen to talk about my contract. I didn't actually say anything to him, I just listened to him and I was never going to argue with him as I was so nervous and just wanted to sign for Wolves. He could have offered me anything and I would have signed! We sat down and all the time I was thinking 'This isn't going to happen' and that he was going to send me home, but it did happen and I was in a dream for several minutes. He told me I was going to be paid £30 a week for three years with bonuses for winning a reserve game of £4, and £2 for a draw. If I got into the first team my appearance money would double my wages. I simply couldn't believe it. My dad was earning only £14 a week before he died but I did have to pay £5 a week for my digs and I also had to send home £5 a week to help my mum pay the mortgage. So I was left with not much more than £15 after tax but I still felt I was lucky. I also received £250 as my half share of the 10 per cent FA levy of the transfer fee. I couldn't believe my ears. At the end of the conversation, Ronnie Allen shook my hand, wished me the best of luck and said he was looking forward to working with me very soon if I got into the first team.

When all the paperwork had been done Joe Gardiner, the scout who had been watching me for two years, was thrilled he had finally got me to Wolves. He took me to my digs to meet the kindest people who were going to look after me, not far from the training ground at Castlecroft, a suburb of Wolverhampton. We arrived and I was greeted by Vera Screen and her husband Jack who incidentally was a coach who helped youth team. I felt very lucky to have Mr and Mrs Screen look after me. They were close friends of Joe Gardiner and they had a lovely house with an in-and-out driveway, something I had only seen before on television. They had a daughter Wendy, who was going out with a guy called Reginald, and there was also the family dog, a Scottie called Susie, who used to chase after my ankles when I went upstairs to my room. They were a very close family who looked after me as if I was one of their own and they made it so easy for me to settle down. On the first morning for training I caught the bus right outside the house into the centre of Wolverhampton and walked the rest of the way to the ground. I was very nervous as I approached the stadium and when I got there I was shown the dressing room I would be changing in. It was the bottom dressing room, which was for the youth and reserves as the top room was for the first-team squad. You had to earn the right to change up there.

I got into my training kit for the first time and it was all new gear, something I hadn't had at Bradford, where you just grabbed what was available. I walked out of the dressing room when the coach shouted 'Let's go' and to my surprise Derek Dougan came up to me and said: 'Welcome to Wolves, son. My advice to you is work hard and listen, good luck and all the best.' I thought 'Wow' as a household name such as The Doog had taken time out to come and find me. We clambered on to the coach that took us to the training ground where there were about 40 professionals and the apprentices. One of the young pros was David Jones who I knew from Bradford. I'd played cricket with him at Laisterdyke and he helped me a great deal to settle in. He and his mate Michael Kent both played in the reserves or youth team, and, in fact Kent made one first-team appearance in 1969-70. My first week was just a whirl really but I was in for another shock as Ronnie Allen was sacked only four days after I had joined the club. I thought 'Here we go again' because I had played for about five or six managers at Bradford in my two and a half years there and now this happened. A few weeks before I joined Wolves, they were beaten 6-0 at home by Liverpool when their former player Alun Evans, who they had sold to the Reds for £100,000, then a record fee for a teenager, scored two of the goals. But they had followed that up with a 1-0 win at Coventry and I can't remember anyone talking about a change of manager, so this came completely out of the blue and I didn't know what to think. I was his last signing and I remember a former Wolves player Derek Clarke, one of the famous five footballing brothers, saying that Ronnie Allen had told him when I joined that he had just made his best signing, which apparently meant me! I thought if that was true I couldn't believe it.

Ronnie signed several of the players who would become the mainstays of the team over the next few years and give the club great service over the next decade or so, including Mike Bailey, Derek Parkin, Frank Munro, John McAlle, Derek Dougan and myself, while he also promoted Phil Parkes through the ranks. After all the paper talk surrounding the sacking of the manager, it was back to the bread and butter of work. Friday morning came and the teamsheets for the reserves and first team were pinned up in the top dressing room. I was picked for the reserves to play at Manchester United and I thought 'No, this can't be right'. I had only ever seen Old Trafford on the TV and I had expected to be playing for the youth team so soon after joining, not the reserves. This was going to be something special for me. I was used to playing at clubs such as Halifax and Chesterfield with Bradford and I had played at Middlesbrough and Sunderland which were both massive stadiums. But Old Trafford? That was something you can only dream of and to be playing on the same ground as my favourite player Bobby Charlton, as well as George Best and Denis Law, seemed like a fairytale. By then the nerves had started already and I couldn't wait for Saturday morning to come. I didn't sleep very well that night! The next morning Mrs Screen put my breakfast on the table at about 8.30 and although it was a light one of cornflakes and toast I couldn't eat much. She did offer me a full cooked English breakfast but that was out of the question as my tummy was churning with nerves. I arrived at Molineux for the coach at about 10am in my only suit and we then went to a hotel for a pre-match meal of steak and rice pudding. That was something of a change as I was used to tea and toast at Bradford.

29

Again I couldn't eat much but the time seemed to fly as we arrived at Old Trafford about 2pm, and as we got off the coach I was in a daze. I was struck with awe at the sheer size of the place – it was massive, just unbelievable. We went straight down the tunnel to have a look at the pitch to see what studs to put in depending on the condition of the pitch. Not that that worried me too much at the time, what concerned me more was the thought of walking on this magnificent ground that had had some of the best players in the world play on it. As we made our way back to the dressing room there was this distinctive smell of liniment that I hadn't noticed before anywhere. We got a 0-0 draw so I earned a bonus of £2, but it meant much more than that for me. It was the start of my adventure at Wolverhampton Wanderers.

But I was quickly brought back down to earth with a bump – quite literally. A few weeks after I joined Wolves we had a practice match at our training ground at Castlecroft where the first team played the reserves. Playing for the second string, I happened to be wearing the number four shirt – the jersey the captain Mike Bailey wore for the first team. The pitch was frozen rock hard and I got the ball around the centre circle. The next thing I knew, Mike was picking me up off the floor. It was the first time in my life I had seen stars. As he picked me up, he asked how I was and I sheepishly said 'All right' and he replied: 'If you want my shirt, you're going to have to earn it!' Many years later, myself, Mike and John Richards appeared on a football chat show for *Sky Sports* called *'Time Of Our Lives'* and when I reminded him of the incident he seemed quite shocked! But Mike was quite right and it served as a reminder of the battle I was going to have to get into the first team.

When Mike tackled, he didn't tackle with his feet, he tackled with his whole body – and boy, he was a powerful bloke with his barrel chest, as strong as an ox. That was our captain and that taught me a lot in terms of how hard I was going to have to work to get into the first team. As the season unfolded I made a few appearances for the reserves, chipped in with a few goals and we finished around mid-table. I had now turned 18 and was hoping it wouldn't be long before I broke into the first team. It was going to be tough as there were lots of great players in front of me and I knew a lot of graft lay ahead.

Despite the competition for places, I was enjoying myself and one of the highlights of my time at Wolves up to that point was the chance to travel abroad. We went on a youth tour to the International Europa Festival in Altrip on the banks of the Rhine near Ludwigshafen in Germany. I was voted player of the tournament and was awarded a trophy which is still one of my prized awards as the teams involved included Bratislava (Czechoslovakia), Eintracht Frankfurt (Germany) and Bologna (Italy). It was a bit of a shock to have won it as we didn't even make the final. Bratislava, who we drew with in our first game, won the tournament and Bologna were runners-up. As all the teams lined up afterwards, the announcement of the player of the tournament came over the public address system.

It was strange because the announcer couldn't speak much English and I can't remember who nudged me and said 'It's you mate' but as no-one went forward to collect the trophy, all the players were looking around to see who had won it. He said something like 'The best fields player of the tournament is Kennnneee Hibbbeyier' – or something like that. As I stepped forward everybody clapped so I thought he must have said it was me! It felt fantastic and the bronze statuette is my pride and joy. I sometimes wonder if any of the players from those countries ever made it as international players and I was voted ahead of them.

After that we went on to play at Rheinfelden, Baden, for the 15th International Youth Tournament organised by VFR Rheinfelden. We opened with a draw against MSV Duisburg before losing 2-1 to Slavia Prague and drawing 1-1 with Eintracht Frankfurt. I scored the goal and in the final play-off we drew 0-0 with Berne from Switzerland but were eliminated in a spot-kick decider – just like England have done over the years! Dave MacLaren, our youth-team coach and a former Wolves goalkeeper, was great and he did a wonderful job with us. He allowed us to have fun as long as we worked hard in training and on the pitch. These tournaments weren't just fantastic experiences, but acted as a very good learning curve for what to expect in terms of quality if we were ever to make it to first-team level.

Talking of which, in the November we had a new manager in Bill McGarry to replace Ronnie Allen. Several months later it was Bill who gave me my debut, on April 12, 1969 in a Black Country derby at home to West Bromwich Albion. It was the penultimate home game of the season and we didn't have much to play for in terms of League position as we were in mid-table. But local pride was at stake, they were the FA Cup holders and there was 37,920 inside Molineux. I came on as a substitute for

John Farrington after 70 minutes in a 1-0 defeat. The Wolves team that day was Phil Parkes, Gerry Taylor, Derek Parkin, Les Wilson, John Holsgrove, John McAlle, John Farrington, Peter Knowles, Derek Dougan, Frank Munro and Bertie Lutton. Around half of the team would go on to be part of that successful 1970s side.

One of those who sadly didn't carry on into the 70s was the player I was in awe of more than any other. Peter Knowles was one of the best players I had seen wear a Wolves shirt but he never reached his full potential. I thought he could have been a world class player, he was that good from what I saw of him in training. He could make a ball talk. I first saw him when I was in Bradford and Wolves were playing in the area or they were on television. He used to get the ball and then sit on it in the corner of the pitch and beckon opponents to come and get it off him. It was everything about him – his energy, his movement, even his MGB sports car with his initials PK down the side. For me, he was a great loss to Wolves and England as well. He won four Under-23 caps but he would have gone on and played for the full team easily. In today's game he would have been a 'number 10' playing behind a front man. Given that free role he would have been magnificent. He could make goals but he knew where the net was too, as his record of 64 goals in 191 games shows.

The day I joined Wolves and watched the first team train in the gym, Peter stood out so much it was frightening. What he did with a ball and the cheekiness he showed with it was amazing. He would spin the ball by treading on the front of it so hard that it spun away from him. His marker thought he had lost possession and would run after it, but such was the spin Peter put on the ball, it just came back to him as though it was on elastic and he would laugh as he ran away with the ball. It was sheer genius. I would have loved to have played regularly with him, but apart from 20 minutes on my debut, I never got a chance as he retired from football and became a Jehovah's Witness in September 1969.

True, he was a cocky so-so, but he had unbelievable charisma and confidence which I'd never seen before or since. He was special, an entertainer, and the game needs more players like him. Wolves and England lost a great football player who oozed total class. I was shocked at his decision and we all thought he would be back within weeks. Despite the loss of Peter, from 1970 to 1974 was a very successful period for us. I can only think what the team would have been like with someone of his quality because without him, we were a bit of a 'nearly' team. I'm sure he would have helped us get to the FA Cup final in 1972-73 when we lost 1-0 to Leeds in the semi-final at Maine Road and possibly the League Cup final the same season when we lost to Tottenham, also in the semis. We would also probably have beaten Spurs in the UEFA Cup final in 1972 with Peter. He was probably the one player we lacked at the time, even though we had a great side. He would have brought something special and different to the team with his flamboyance, arrogance and cheek. He could score goals and create chances for others, and, even though he wasn't the hardest worker, he would have brought a lot of class to the side. The chances are I might not have got so many games if Peter had stayed on, but I would like to think we could have played together and been a successful partnership in midfield. That really would have been a dream for me.

Nearly 13 years after he retired, we did resume that partnership in gold and black, as Peter rejoined me for one last cameo. In the summer of 1981 he played in my testimonial against Derby and I have the game on video. He was just short of 36 years old at the time but he still had all the skills and he also had that winning passion, as he showed when he was knocked off the ball. He thought he was fouled but the referee didn't award him a free kick and Peter swung his elbow at the culprit with a lot of passion showing. That was the Peter Knowles we had witnessed and admired more than a decade earlier. Before and after the game Peter let photographers take a few snaps of us in the dressing room and I still have them and rate them as some of my prized possessions, along with a photo and autograph of Pele and Eusebio. That's how highly I rated Peter Knowles.

Another player I was quick to admire when I came to Wolves was Frank Munro. He was a great player who cost £55,000 from Aberdeen just a few weeks before I joined Wolves in 1968. His skill on the ball and intelligence about the game was top drawer and he played for Scotland on nine occasions. If we were playing away or on tour we would go for a walk for some fresh air before we got on the coach and he would do his party trick whereby he would toss a coin in the air, catch it on his forehead, open his top pocket and drop it inside and carry on walking as if nothing had happened. If he didn't have a jacket on he would drop the coin on to his foot from his forehead, catch it and then flick it up into his hand with no effort. The younger players – me included – were gobsmacked and admired his skill. When we tried it the coin would come down onto our forehead on its edge and it would bloody hurt. Frank would just laugh at us.

At the end of the 1968-69 season I went home to Bradford to see my mum and sister and try to get together with Terry in Leeds. I was also looking forward to playing cricket again for Laisterdyke. Once again time seemed to fly by and before I knew it, it was time to return to Wolverhampton for pre-season training for the 1969-70 season. I returned to Mr and Mrs Screen and it felt like my second home. They treated me so well and I felt so comfortable there. They really did play a big part in me settling in Wolverhampton. The first day of pre-season arrived and it was never the best of times on the long road to match fitness, but we all knew that hard graft was needed to achieve maximum fitness. Our new manager Bill McGarry was something of a fitness freak who liked his teams to be super fit and liked to run players very hard. He believed fitness was the key to top performances, but his approach didn't go down well with some of the senior players.

The first two weeks were spent on Cannock Chase, an area of outstanding beauty and woodland about 10 miles north east of Wolverhampton. It's an area very popular with ramblers but it was certainly no walk in the park for us and we never saw a football for the first fortnight. Certain players such as Phil Parkes, Dave Wagstaffe and Frank Munro hated the long runs we were sent on but they were all great players and Parkesy was a fine keeper. I don't know if our coach Sammy Chung was aware but those three, among others, used to hide behind bushes and only join in on the last lap.

We did a similar pre-season every summer so we had an idea of what was coming. We used all our energy in training, so much so that when I got home I used to collapse on the settee and get served with drinks because I was too knackered to do anything. We didn't know what was in store next so we couldn't afford to over-eat or touch alcohol because the manager would know. But it was worth it because it was a long, hard season.

Two others who didn't favour McGarry's physical approach were Derek Dougan and Jim McCalliog. 'Jimmy Mac' had signed from Sheffield Wednesday for £80,000, a sizeable fee in those days, and was now sharing my digs with me. It was great because I could get a lift into training with him in his big car. It was a Ford Zephyr with the old column gear change and it ran as smooth as silk. That meant I didn't have to catch the bus until Jim had found a house for him and his family. He wasn't married but he took his whole family wherever he went in his career. Derek and Jim had lots of fall-outs with the manager but they were always in the team because they were such great players. They would put in some good training work but when the manager wanted a bit more they would run within themselves and lag behind at the back. The younger ones wouldn't dare do that and we did what the manager asked.

Then the time came that all footballers dread. An injury. We had been training at Dunstall Park racecourse in Wolverhampton one Friday morning and had finished all the work except for a few short sprints and some turning when I felt my knee lock. I pulled up very quickly, knowing straight away I had a big problem. When we got back to the ground the physio George Palmer examined me and sent me to see a knee specialist. It was just what I had feared – a torn cartilage. My heart dropped and I honestly thought my career was over before it had started. I knew a lot of players had to finish playing from this kind of injury in those days and it was the first serious one I had experienced.

Once I had needed treatment at Bradford PA after I'd kicked the ground and I damaged the top of my foot. I couldn't kick a ball for a few months, but this was different because I didn't know if the surgery would work 100 per cent or not. I had the knee done and thankfully I was back playing again in January 1970. The operation went well but although I wasn't allowed out of bed for 10 days, I was lucky enough to be able to walk out of the hospital unaided.

I was sent straight to a rehabilitation centre at Patshull Hall – adjacent to what later became Patshull Park golf club – to recover during the week and had to spend weekends in my digs. This went on for six weeks, and, while I missed going home to Bradford – I was allowed to go back home every six weeks – this was my career and it was so important to get it right. While I was at Patshull, I was in a dormitory with a lot of other people. Wow, could they snore! I spent most of the night awake, thinking the roof would come off. I hated it and couldn't wait for the weekend so I could get some sleep.

During my time there we did a lot of cycling to strengthen my knee and we would have to pedal up a steep hill in Bridgnorth known as The Hermitage. It was about a one in four climb and only a handful of us could get up it without stopping. It hurt like hell halfway up, but I was adamant it wouldn't beat me and despite the pain, I completed the ride every day. Six weeks on and I was back to the ground for more hard work and I played again after seven weeks out, which was a great feeling. I had to put cold compresses on the knee after a game but I managed to make about 20 appearances in the Central League that season, and it was a great relief to finally be fully fit again.

8

Debut, England calling and silverware

After waiting for what seemed like an age, I finally made my full debut for Wolves in a League game at Chelsea on September 12, 1970. Bill McGarry took a keen interest in the reserves and there were a few lads who were in the mix at the time, such as John McAlle, Dave Galvin, Bertie Lutton, Paul Walker and Jimmy Seal. Fortunately, he picked me. All I remember him saying to me, on the Friday, the day before the game, was this: 'You have warranted your chance and you'll be playing at Chelsea'. Perhaps not surprisingly, I didn't sleep a wink that night. But I was at last getting my opportunity and I was so nervous in the dressing room beforehand. There were no good luck messages or telegrams as I hadn't telephoned my mum to tell her the news and Terry would have been involved himself with Leeds anyway. There was no way of the family being able to get down to London for the game so I had no one close to watch me on my big day.

The manager didn't say anything to me but the senior players such as Dave Wagstaffe and Hughie Curran were great with me. I was frightened to death but they all told me to enjoy the occasion and our captain Mike Bailey said 'Just play it simple, son'. It was strange because I'd been waiting for this chance for so long and yet here I was nearly s****ing myself! After the referee's bell rang to tell us to leave the dressing room we had a final briefing from the manager before walking out and down the tunnel at Stamford Bridge. You could see the pitch right in front but it was raining so hard, the water was bouncing off the track around the pitch. We started to warm up and I'm not kidding, we could have jumped into a bath and not got any wetter. The Wolves team that day was Phil Parkes, Bernard Shaw, Derek Parkin, Mike Bailey, Frank Munro, John McAlle, Jim McCalliog, myself, Derek Dougan, Hugh Curran and Dave Wagstaffe. I was one of two changes from a 1-0 League Cup second-round defeat at Second Division Oxford United three days before. Munro and myself replaced Les Wilson and Bobby Gould, while The Doog had played in the unfamiliar position of centre half at The Manor Ground so moved back up front. As soon as the game kicked off, the nerves disappeared and I told myself 'Just do your best, do what the manager said and I will be alright'. After about 10 minutes we won a corner on the right and Dave Wagstaffe swung the ball in with his famous left peg. The keeper Peter Bonetti punched the ball out and it dropped to me on the edge of the box. I hit it first time, straight into the bottom left-hand corner. I had scored at Stamford Bridge! All the players came to congratulate me and in all honesty I can't remember much of the game after that, I was in a dream. It didn't feel real but it was. Jim McCalliog scored our other goal and we drew 2-2. Ron Harris and Ian Hutchinson netted for Chelsea. I can also remember in the bath after the game Waggy saying to me I should give the goal to Hugh Curran as the ball had clipped him on the heel, then all the other teams would be more fearful of him because of the goals he was scoring. He had already got seven in the first seven League games. But there was absolutely no chance of that happening! The next morning I made the headlines as the Sunday papers had my name in all of them and I went out and bought them all, and Monday morning's as well. Mr and Mrs Screen were so happy for me along with Wendy and Reginald when I got back to my digs and we had a great Saturday evening playing cards with some of their friends. We had snacks and a few drinks during the night. We had a good time. The Swinging Sixties might only have just been over but this was the extent of my 'wild' Saturday night after my full debut!

Four days after the Chelsea game there was a Texaco Cup first round, first leg tie away to Dundee. I hadn't played in Scotland before so it was a new experience for me. I soon found out we were in for a tough game as the Scots didn't let you dwell on the ball for too long before someone came in with a strong tackle. I learned very quickly to pass the ball early. At one point Dundee were in our penalty box when the ball dropped right in front of my head as I was flat out on the ground. I could see a Dundee player running towards the ball to have a shot at goal and the only thing I could do was to try to knock the ball away with my head to stop him. I did that OK, but his studs caught the top of my head and left a gaping six-inch wound.

As I instinctively put my hands to my head they were covered in blood and the next thing I knew was I was in the dressing room having stitches put in. Bill McGarry was holding my hand and asked how I was. I said my head felt OK but it was seeing the blood on my hands that had caused me to faint – just as I had passed out after the cyclist had been knocked off his bike at Bradford a few years earlier. Just then the doctor started to put the first stitch in and as he tried to pull the gash together it felt like my whole head from ear to ear was coming off. I didn't make it back on to the pitch but thankfully we won 2-1 with goals from Jim McCalliog and Derek Dougan. I left the ground with a massive bandage wrapped around my head which gave the lads a great laugh. Two years later we played at Kilmarnock at the same stage of the competition and again I came back with stitches – this time in my knee. I thought 'if this is Scotland you can keep it', but I must stress it was no fault of the Scottish players. They were great.

Being so raw at this time, I was so enthusiastic and sometimes my desire to prove myself got the better of me. In my fourth League start we played Southampton at The Dell. You knew you were in for a hard game against them with tough players such as John McGrath and quality lads like Terry Paine and Mike Channon. The legendary Liverpool manager Bill Shankly had called Southampton 'animals' after a recent clash against them. Anyway our game was every bit as competitive as we thought and it was reported afterwards that there were 47 fouls in the match, 27 of them awarded against Southampton. I ended up having a running battle with McGrath. On one occasion after the ball had gone out, for a goal kick, he swung an arm at me as he ran past, catching me around the face and the blow knocked me to the ground. As it was clearly off the ball, the referee didn't see it, but I was livid.

At full-time – we won 2-1 with goals from the Doog and Waggy – I went to see McGrath and squared up to him. But before anything happened, Ted Bates, the Southampton manager, got between us and cooled things down. I think Ted saved my life because McGrath would have eaten me alive! Years later when I was in charge of Walsall John McGrath succeeded my old Wolves team-mate Jim McCalliog in managing Halifax, who were then fighting to stay in the Football League. Desperate to attract some better players, John sent around a hilarious begging letter to clubs, saying something like 'Even the mice have run away because there's nothing for them to eat'!

Talking of management, I might have been a novice as a player but I got an early taste of what life was like in the dugout – albeit in much lower key circumstances. I had made the Chestnut Tree pub in Finchfield my local, as it was near to my digs in Castlecroft. I soon got to know the regulars, and it wasn't long before I was asked if I would help out with their Sunday League football team. When I say help out, they meant manage them, and I quickly agreed. I enjoyed the lads' company, I was single so it wasn't as if I had to get home and it was a just a lovely social thing to do. It was funny looking back because I could have been playing Arsenal on the Saturday then be standing on some windswept park on a Sunday but the lads treated me as one of them, which is what I wanted and it brought me closer to the Wolves fans. Mind you, the state of some of the lads on a Sunday morning left something to be desired! Often they wouldn't have got home until 5am from their Saturday nights out, then they would roll out of bed and be ready to play for the 10.30am kick-off, trotting out with fags hanging from their mouths and steaming hangovers! I managed them for a couple of years, before I got married, and I was there on the touchline most Sunday mornings before joining them for a couple of pints afterwards in the pub, then back home to watch ITV's *Star Soccer* in the afternoon, because, apart from *Match of the Day*, that was the only regular televised football.

By November I'd got half a dozen League games under my belt and we had won five of them and drew the other. We had also played in the Texaco Cup and I was enjoying every game so much, but I was now starting to get very tense and nervous before matches. I used to sweat a lot but I was fine once we had got on the pitch. But from Thursday onwards I just worried about my performances and whether I was doing well enough and what if I had a bad game and let people down? It was so silly when I look back now but that was how I was. I never got over-excited as I knew there was still a lot of hard work ahead of me, and with the squad we had you just couldn't relax at any time. It was so important to do something on the pitch to give the manager no option but to play me the following week, like scoring or making chances for others, and of course what my dad had always told me to do – work your socks off so when the final whistle went you could hardly walk off the pitch.

He said there would always be someone around to carry you off if needs be. He had actually once carried our Terry off the pitch when my brother was 10 years old. Terry had played in a school match and the weather was so cold with sleet and snow, he was exhausted. Dad ran on to the pitch and carried him to the dressing room and put a blanket round him to warm him up. I will never forget that. I was only seven but that stuck with me, the fact you should always give your maximum in all you do in life. We only ever get one chance and I can't stand sports people who don't give their all. My game was getting better and the team were doing well. I was getting good reports and people were saying things like: 'Is Hibbitt the find of the season?' and 'This kid will play for England.' Reading these reports gave me so much confidence, but I had to keep my feet on the ground and not get carried away with all the headlines. I think our manager Bill McGarry did a great job in this respect as he wouldn't allow any of the young players to get too cocky. I remember once he called me into his office on a Monday morning and he gave me the biggest rollocking ever after I'd told the captain Mike Bailey to 'F*** off' because he shouted at me for not passing the ball to him. I don't know whether someone told him or he heard me, but I don't think for one minute Mike would have grassed on me. The lesson was learned however; he put me in my place and I didn't do it again. He was absolutely right of course and I was so wrong. It must have been frustration on my part as I had nothing but respect for Mike, who taught me a lot about midfield play and I apologised to him.

Soon afterwards England did come calling and it was a shock, but a fantastic surprise when the manager told me I was picked for the Under-23s squad to play Wales at the Racecourse Ground at Wrexham. I had only played half a dozen games so I couldn't believe it and thought the manager was joking when he told me. But when I got the letter with the three lions badge on it I knew he was serious. I thought it was all happening too quickly. I was named as a substitute and my Wolves team-mate Derek Parkin was also picked, but he had to pull out with an injury. I got on the pitch ten minutes before half-time as a replacement for Mick Channon and it was 0-0 when the ball came across to the penalty spot. I hit it towards goal and thought I'd scored but goalkeeper Dai Davies dived to save it on the line and it was cleared. I really thought I had got the winner but it finished goalless and I never got another chance to wear the England shirt.

I often wonder if that had gone in whether I would have gone on and received more international recognition. I will never know of course, but I don't think there's a day gone by when I don't take out that shirt and cap and look at them. It's the only one I won but I treasure that as much as if I had got 100 caps. There were some great players around then and I felt very privileged to have been part of the team. I remember going for a stroll and walking through the town with Colin Todd and looking at the shops early on the day of the game to stretch our legs, while the other newcomers to the squad were Mick Mills, the Ipswich Town full back who would go on to captain England, and the Chelsea striker Ian Hutchinson. The England team that night: Clemence (Liverpool), Mills (Ipswich), Nish (Leicester), Todd (Sunderland), Lloyd

(Liverpool), Bernard (Stoke), Whittle (Everton), Hudson (Chelsea), Hutchinson (Chelsea), Channon (Southampton) (sub Hibbitt (Wolves), 35 mins), Thomas (Burnley).

January 1971 came along and it was FA Cup third round time, a day before my 20th birthday. We were drawn at home to Norwich and I was selected to make my Cup debut. We played in white that day as Norwich played in yellow so it felt a bit odd, especially as it was at Molineux, but it was a great game for us and we won 5-1. To follow up my record of scoring on my full League debut, I also scored my first Cup goal. That had only been done previously at Wolves by former wing favourite Terry Wharton, another who wore the number seven shirt. He netted in the League against Ipswich Town in 1961-62 and followed that with two goals against Carlisle United in the Cup later that season, so I was in good company and I am very proud of it.

It was also a near-post diving header – yes a header! It felt really special as I wasn't known to be the best in the air. There had been a good build-up down the left and Mike Bailey saw me making a near-post run and drilled it onto my head and the ball flashed into the net, giving Norwich keeper Kevin Keelan no chance. It was a brilliant feeling and the fans were just fantastic as I saluted them in the North Bank. The fans were very special to me. Ever since my debut at Chelsea they gave me great support and that provided me with a lot of confidence. To hear them shout my name was just awesome. I never thought in a million years thousands of fans would be shouting my name so loud. The only noise that could compete with them was my mum when I misbehaved!

We were in the top half of the First Division pushing for the top six when we played Chelsea at home in a blizzard on February 13. I scored the only goal and it was said in the paper it was a goal worthy of a title clincher. I didn't know until after the game and reading the sports paper that the England manager Sir Alf Ramsey was watching. The Press reported it wouldn't have done any harm to my chances of getting a call-up. It never happened though, and, while I was disappointed, my first job was to stay in the Wolves team. That paid my living and anything extra was a bonus. Incidentally, that result put us third behind Leeds and Arsenal and we were flying after five wins in six League games from Boxing Day. We had a bonding trip to Malta later that month and beat Marsa Malta 5-1 with four goals in the last 15 minutes. I scored my first senior brace along with Bobby Gould and one from centre-back John Holsgrove. It was a lovely country and one I hadn't visited before – in fact, I hadn't been to many places at that point. My career was going very well and the manager offered me a new contract with a bigger weekly wage and a good bonus structure with appearance money. This enabled me to take driving lessons and look to buy a car instead of relying on the bus. It would also give me the chance to go home to Bradford more often to see my mum. I passed my driving test first time and was on the lookout for a decent car. At the time I had moved digs and was staying with a mate called Dave Richards and his parents who looked after me very well. I was lucky to have stayed with two very good families at an early stage of my career at Wolves. I learned a lot of my driving skills from Dave, who would let me drive his MGB sports car from door to door as he collected insurance payments on Friday nights.

But I really wanted my own car, and the one I craved was a Ford Cortina 1600E, just like my team-mates Bernard Shaw and Mike O'Grady had. Those Cortinas were quick and I was quite taken by the walnut dashboard. There was a garage not far from Molineux and I spotted a gleaming silver 1600E on the forecourt one day and I knew I just had to have it. It cost £650 so I put down £150 and borrowed £500 which I paid off within six months with the bonuses I had earned. I loved driving it as it gave me independence and I was able to fill the petrol tank for a fiver.

Up to this point I had to catch the train back to Bradford, a journey which I did every few weeks. When we played at Huddersfield for example, John Richards and I would walk to the station after the game and he would get the train to Warrington and me to Bradford to see our families. Walking there, we got to know a lad called Steve Wright and his dad Cyril. Steve used to volunteer to carry my bags. They lived in Yorkshire and when I played reserve games at places like Huddersfield, they used to watch me. We've kept in touch over the years and Steve became chairman of the Yorkshire Wolves Supporters Club, while I am president. Sadly, Cyril died but Steve and I are still in regular contact and I write a report in their monthly magazine.

Having my own car meant when I went home to Bradford I could drive around with the windows down playing songs such as my favourite bands Black Sabbath and Led Zeppelin. Robert Plant, the lead singer of Led Zep, was and still is a huge Wolves fan and we got to know each other later on in the 70s when Robert used to attend games at Molineux and we would sometimes see him afterwards in the social club just up from the ground. He even played in a couple of testimonials. He wasn't a bad player either and if he hadn't been a rock star, I reckon he could have played to a decent standard. I picked up my first senior honour that season as we won the Texaco Cup – the first trophy Wolves had won in 11 years since the FA Cup in 1960. After beating Dundee 2-1 on aggregate, we progressed by overcoming Morton 4-2 over two legs and Derry City 5-0 on aggregate before beating Hearts 3-2 over a two-legged final. I didn't play in the semi-final ties nor the away leg at Hearts but I was back for the concluding match at Molineux, where we went down 1-0 in front of 28,462. We also finished joint third in the League (fourth on goal difference, one goal behind Tottenham) below Arsenal and Leeds which was the club's highest finish since they were third in 1960-61 under the great Stan Cullis. We also finished higher than Liverpool, both Manchester clubs, Derby County – who won the title the following year – and deposed champions Everton. I played 39 games in all competitions, scoring three goals and I was happy with my contribution in my first full campaign.

As a regular in the team it felt fantastic to be playing with such wonderful players week in, week out. I enjoyed great support from the senior players and I was now travelling to venues such as Old Trafford, Goodison Park, Anfield, Maine Road, Elland Road and St James' Park – grounds etched in history and places I could only dream of playing at when I was a kid. I had been used to small grounds such as Halifax, Lincoln, Chesterfield and Rochdale, which incidentally is one of my wife's favourite grounds for hospitality. Later in my career as Walsall manager we played at Spotland where they were making a few changes to the ground so the guests and directors were accommodated in temporary cabins. Afterwards Jane said they were the best people she had experienced for hospitality and were very friendly. They couldn't do enough for us and she still thinks the same now. It just goes to show you don't have to be a big club to show the kind of care Rochdale showed that day. It was a very happy club then back in 1990 and I hope it's still the same because manners cost nothing and a smile is worth everything to them.

Finishing fourth in the League these days would mean Wolves had qualified for the Champions League. Back in 1971 it meant we qualified for the inaugural UEFA Cup, the following season, and this brought yet more adventure. The competition had taken over from the Inter Cities Fairs Cup. Three years earlier I followed Manchester United when they won the European Cup, beating Benfica in the final at Wembley when

George Best, Bobby Charlton and Brian Kidd were at their brilliant best. This was a tremendous time for me on a personal note but it all happened so quickly. Barely 18 months earlier I was in a bit of a quandary wondering how my career was going and thinking should I be looking to get away from Wolves as my chances of getting into the team didn't look too good. It just goes to prove how life changes if you work hard enough. Here we were looking forward to the challenge of playing in Europe – most of us for the first time in our careers – and I was about to embark on visiting parts of the world I had only seen on maps. Playing in Europe made me realise being a pro footballer can afford you privileges you may never otherwise earn. Before playing in Europe, though, we had a different continental experience to deal with. Four days after beating Burnley 1-0 in our last game of the season, we played the Israel national team in Tel Aviv, winning 3-1 with goals from Derek Parkin, Paul Walker and Bobby Gould. I came on as a substitute for Mike O'Grady.

But I remember far more about the trip than the game. For a 20-year-old who had barely travelled out of Yorkshire, this felt unreal, as it did for many of the young lads on the tour. This was a place I had only read about at school in history lessons or religious education and in those days there was still a lot of fighting going on following the Six-Day War in 1967 when Israel captured East Jerusalem from Jordan. So we were excited and wary at the same time. The first thing I recall is the heat – it was so hot on the coach to our hotel. The next thing I remember was what the conflict had left behind, with burnt-out trucks by the roadside after being fired at or bombed. In the distance we could hear the crackle of gunfire and bombs going off. Goodness knows what the club were doing taking us there, but I can only imagine they earned well out of it!

During our short stay we had a day trip to Jerusalem, which was about an hour away from Tel Aviv. We visited the famous Wailing Wall, part of the Second Jewish Temple started by Herod the Great, the Roman king of Judea. Jerusalem is recognised as a holy city by many people and I felt a lovely, calm feeling while watching lots of worshippers praying. But that calmness soon turned into torture because of the heat. I had never known an intensity like it, and John McAlle, a couple of other young players and myself took to running from one shop doorway to another just to try to find some shade. Back at our hotel, we thought we had found the answer to counter the brightest of the sun's rays. The hotel was situated on top of a hill and so attracted a welcome breeze, so John McAlle, Derek Parkin and a few of us decided that would be the ideal place to indulge in a spot of sunbathing. After lying there for the rest of the day – without any protection from the sun – we ended up looking like lobsters. Talk about naïve! We thought the breeze would protect us from the sun. Our sunburn was so painful we ended up sleeping on our hands and knees. When we got home after the week-long trip – by which time we had finally invested in sun cream – Jane was peeling the dead skin off my back in sheets! Urgh!

9

Europe Calling

Wolves were in the UEFA Cup for the first time and what a journey it turned out to be for us. With Molineux packed to the rafters, the great Wolves of the 1950s first entranced a nation with those famous floodlit friendlies against the likes of Honved, Spartak Moscow, Moscow Dynamo, Real Madrid and the rest that paved the way for what became the European Cup and now the Champions League. Now, more than a decade later, here we were about to write our own chapter of history.

Although the UEFA Cup wasn't as big as the European Cup, it still gave me and Wolves our first chance to play against some of the top teams on the continent and for us younger players especially, it was tremendously exciting. We started our run in the competition by beating Portuguese team Academica Coimbra 7-1 over two legs in the first round in September 1971. I wasn't involved in those first two games, but when we beat the Dutch team Den Haag over two legs by the same aggregate scoreline in October, I had the privilege of another first – scoring on my competitive European debut in a 3-1 away win when Jim McCalliog, who I replaced as a substitute, and Derek Dougan were also on target. Four days before we played East German team Carl Zeiss Jena in the third round, we had the little matter of Arsenal at home.

It was only six months since the Gunners had become only the second team that century to win the Double so we knew we were in for a tough game. And the omens didn't look good as we trailed 1-0 in a Molineux blizzard at half-time. Rain, sleet and snow all battered us but we turned round and got at them after the break and I don't think they fancied it. Dave Wagstaffe hit one of the best passes I've seen in football – a 60-yard diagonal ball from left to right to put me in on the full back. I took it down went at the defender, turned inside him and smashed it past Bob Wilson with my left foot. That set us on our way and we ended up winning 5-1 with two goals from Derek Dougan, a Jim McCalliog penalty and one from Waggy. That has to rank among the best Wolves performances I was part of, along with the League Cup finals and UEFA Cup final. Thankfully, it was televised too so you can still watch the footage. I felt it was a bit of a turning point and gave us a lot of confidence. That night I had arranged to drive home to Bradford but I had to abandon those plans after getting as far as

Brownhills when the snow was up to the wheel arches on the Cortina. I had to turn around and drive back to Wolverhampton.

We then managed to come away from Carl Zeiss Jena with a 1-0 win – also in the snow – with John Richards's first away strike in Europe, before beating them at home 3-0 in early December with yours truly and the Doog getting the other two. That put us into the quarter-finals where we were paired with Juventus. This was the big one for me and although we didn't play the tie until March, it proved well worth the wait. Here our manager Bill McGarry pulled off a masterstroke by persuading John Charles to be our 'tour guide' for the trip to Turin. A giant of a man, the former Wales international had been able to play as a centre half or centre forward. He was a Juventus legend. Everywhere he took us, people would stare open-mouthed and bowed – not to us but to him! He took us to all the shops so we could buy some Italian clothes and shoes. As we walked in, he was the top man because of his huge success as a player over there and he was able to get a good discount on our shoes, which, being the stereotypical Yorkshireman, came in very handy! John was a giant in every sense of the word and when you shook his hand it was like putting it into a vice. He was a fantastic player who did so well for Leeds United and for his country.

Juventus were packed with household names. They had players like Fabio Capello, who of course went on to manage England many years later, Pietro Anastasi – who had cost Juve a world record fee of £450,000 in 1968 – Roberto Bettega and Helmut Haller, who scored for Germany in the 1966 World Cup final. They were a great team who had reached the final the season before, in the competition's previous guise as the Inter-Cities Fairs Cup only to lose on away goals to Leeds. They were also on their way to winning the league, which they retained the year after. So it was always going to be a tough task, but we were playing well and confident of getting a decent result. It was the biggest game of my career so far, apart from my full debut against Chelsea, and I was very nervous indeed. John Richards, John McAlle and I were the young players in the line-up, and I'm sure they felt the same as me, but they didn't show it. As soon as I got on to the pitch I was fine. What a stadium, though. It was full and loud, the atmosphere was electric with 35,000 there. I thought to myself 'This is the big time and I am part of it' – a kid from Bradford playing against Juventus with World Cup players in their line-up. Despite their big names, we played well and earned a 1-1 draw with Jim McCalliog scoring for us. The draw left everything finely poised for the return leg at

48

Molineux. And on a memorable night in front of 40,421, we didn't disappoint as goals from Danny Hegan and Derek Dougan gave us a 2-1 win to put us into the semi-finals. Danny didn't need any excuse to celebrate and we used to call him 'Champagne Charlie' for his love of bubbly. He liked a drink but champagne was his favourite tipple. He loved the sound of the cork being popped and he used to imitate it when he was joking around in the dressing room. One time I went for a night out with him and met him in a little hotel off West Park in Wolverhampton. We had a few drinks and before long, Danny was on the champers and got absolutely legless. Seeing the state he was in, I said to him, 'Come on, let's get you home. I'll call a taxi. Where do you live?' 'West Bromwich' slurred Danny. 'West Bromwich!' I repeated. Anyway, the taxi arrived and Danny managed to give the driver what I thought was his home address. When we got there, it turned out there were no houses on the street – it was all derelict.

I asked Danny to think again about where he lived and about an hour and a half later, he had sobered up a bit and we ended up back at the hotel at West Park – it turned out Danny was staying there all along so we'd paid for a taxi for nothing! I swore there and then that would be the first and last time I went for a night out with Danny. He was a heavy drinker and would go missing for days on end. The manager Bill McGarry would get Phil Parkes, who was a big mate of Danny's and lived close to him in Fordhouses, to try to find him as 'Lofty' knew all of his haunts. Living on that side of town, those two and Frank Munro used to socialise together. I remember running behind Danny in training on a Monday morning, I'd call out 'Crikey Danny, you smell like a brewery' and he'd say 'I swear I haven't touched a drop in three weeks' and we knew he was lying.

Another occasion out with Danny could have ended in a much worse way as we avoided potentially fatal consequences. We had received an invite to play in a pro-am golf tournament at Effingham Golf Club, near Leatherhead in Surrey. I had just bought a new Cortina, a 2000GT in white, as my mate Phil Brookes had just purchased the same model in yellow. It was 1973 and I think it cost something in the region of £1,358, which was quite a lot of money in those days and I had to borrow some to pay for it. Keen to test out my new wheels, I offered to drive, and Phil Parkes, Danny and I set off. I played with the Welsh golfer, Craig Defoy, who had finished fourth in The Open in 1971. But it was the rest of the day and evening I remember more than the round of golf. After we had finished playing, there was a reception and Phil and Danny were soon drinking. I only had a couple of drinks as I was driving. All of a sudden there was a commotion and we made our way closer to see what it was all about. It turns out Geoff Lewis, who was one of the leading jockeys of the time and won The Derby in 1971, had been taunted by a six-foot guy who had had a few and was winding him up, claiming the horses did all the work. The bloke continued to have a go at Geoff, who took exception to the criticism and warned him a couple of times to stop. When it continued, Geoff punched the guy in the face, breaking his nose and sending him sprawling across a table. Recognising the bloke was a bit of an arsehole, everybody left him to it and carried on with their evening.

We eventually got back in the car, with Lofty in the front because of his longer legs, and Danny in the back, and started the long drive home. The two passengers started play fighting, then they fell asleep, having had a few drinks. Suddenly I heard a heavy bang. We had crashed into the central reservation of the motorway, scraping the entire length of my new car. I had fallen asleep at the wheel and must have drifted into the barrier after dozing off. The noise woke me up, and in the ensuing panic, Lofty hit his head on the gearstick and turned angrily to Danny, thinking he had hit him after their earlier play fighting. I quickly told Phil it was my fault, that I had fallen asleep. I don't even know where the collision happened, but when we finally got back to Jane's mum and dad and I told her what had happened, the shock hit me. Realising we could have easily have been killed, I started shaking. The next morning I inspected the damage and the whole length of my new car was dented and black from where it had hit the barrier. But it could have been much worse.

As for Danny, there was no doubting his ability or his football brain – he was two steps ahead of everyone else and in fact could make himself look bad because he was on a different wavelength. Along with his ability, he was a terrific lad and very funny. I'm sure but for the drink he could have had a better career or at least played for longer than he did. Years later, Danny's son Anthony was an apprentice at Coventry when I was there. Danny and his wife Patsy had split up by then and their son had a different surname. He was a decent player too. With Mike Bailey out injured, Danny's longest run in the team came during our run to the UEFA Cup final in 1971-72. In the semi-finals we were paired with Ferencvaros, who again were a top-class European team who had finished runners-up in the Hungarian league. By now the games were coming thick and fast and we faced a daunting fixture pile-up, but we managed to draw the first leg in Budapest 2-2 with John Richards and Frank Munro scoring, leaving us firm favourites to reach the final. But we were indebted to goalkeeper Phil Parkes, who saved a penalty when we were 2-1 down before big Frank equalised. Lofty also made himself a hero in the second leg, saving another penalty, this time after they had pulled it back to 2-1.

However, before then we had three vital League games and we lost all three, away to Arsenal and then at home to Chelsea and West Brom, just four days before the second leg. It wasn't the best form to take us into the tie but we showed great resilience and patience. Steve Daley gave us an early lead and that helped ease the tension and nerves. We held on to win with Frank Munro scoring again, and went through to face Tottenham in an all-English final. It was back to League duty then just three days later and we had to put all thoughts of the final behind us. The League was, after all, our bread and butter and every match was important. I was rested for the next match against Huddersfield, but Steve Daley got the only goal and we were back to picking up points again.

By now my nerves were becoming a major problem; so bad in fact I actually thought of packing the game in. That's how bad they were. It wasn't just ordinary butterflies – I felt weak and tired because I couldn't sleep, my stomach was turning cartwheels and I would break into sweats. I thought about the forthcoming match too much and then the nerves would take over. It would usually start on the Thursday before a match and last until I actually crossed the white line on a Saturday. I knew the anxiety wasn't doing my game any good and I could feel my strength just draining away as I was becoming weak with worry. At first I tried going to bed early but that only made things worse as I would still be awake at midnight and through to the small hours. Then our manager Bill McGarry advised me to try staying up late the night before a match. So every Friday evening I would settle down to watch television at about 10.30pm before switching on the late-night film, which would finish at about 1am when I would go to bed. Amazingly that did the trick and I started to get some quality sleep and felt much better the next day. We had a good result at Everton late in March and I scored both goals in a 2-2 draw. I loved playing at Goodison Park; it's one of the old grounds that hasn't changed too much and I always seemed to do well against them. It was a good warm-up for the UEFA Cup final, the first leg of which was on May 3 at Molineux. We expected a full house and 38,632 turned up to watch us lose 2-1 when a late goal by Martin Chivers knocked the stuffing out of us, after his header had been cancelled out by Jim McCalliog's equaliser. A draw would have been about right on the night but now we had a lot to do in the return leg at White Hart Lane on May 17.

There were 14 days between the two legs of the UEFA Cup final, but five days after the first leg, on May 8, we had our final League game of the season, at home to Leeds. I have gone into more depth about this game in another chapter. After finishing our League programme, we had to get ready for the second leg of the final at White Hart Lane and we knew we had to get an early goal. But Spurs were tight in defence and we found it hard to break them down. Alan Mullery headed them in front and at 3-1 on aggregate it looked as though the tie was all over before Waggy scored a great goal to put us right back in it just before half-time. He struck the ball with great power from long range and it went in off a post – just what we needed. We gave it our best shot in the second half, but we couldn't force another goal and the game ended 1-1. Spurs lifted the cup and we were all gutted. I could have cried because this was the biggest game I had played in, but fair play to them, they were just that bit better than us over two legs.

10

Around The World In 40 Days

Despite playing 57 games in all competitions that season, just four days after losing to Tottenham in the UEFA Cup final, we were back in action, on tour to the United States and Canada, then on to New Zealand and Australia, playing 12 matches in six weeks. We faced Aberdeen on four occasions, in San Francisco, Seattle, Vancouver and Los Angeles, losing the first two and winning the last two. Then it was a case of packing our bags for Down Under and on to Auckland, Wellington, Christchurch, Melbourne, Sydney, Brisbane, Adelaide and Perth. Such an exhausting schedule would have been dismissed as ridiculous these days, but back then players were regarded more as commodities and it would have been looked upon as good business practice to spread the club's name to promote the game in less well-known footballing places, as well as no doubt bringing in extra revenue for the club.

The first meeting with Aberdeen saw us heavy-legged through jet lag, and, coming four days after losing against Spurs in the second leg of the final, it was little surprise that we were beaten 3-1 in San Francisco after Jim McCalliog had put us ahead. Three days later we lost again, this time 3-0. But two nights later at Empire Stadium, Vancouver, pride was restored when myself, John Richards and Hugh Curran scored for us to win 3-0. We went one better in Los Angeles when former Aberdeen player Frank Munro added to a Richards hat-trick to give us a 4-0 win. That night all the Wolves and Aberdeen players got together in the bar and things were going well until some players went over the top with the booze and a fight broke out. Myself and another young player, Paul Walker, ran for the lift to get to our room as quickly as possible. We hadn't been drinking and neither of us fancied getting caught up in a scuffle.

There may have been some red faces that night after the fight broke out, but on one evening it was a case of 'red nose day' – and there was no shortage of comic relief for the lads, if you'll pardon the pun. I was sharing a room with our striker Hugh Curran, a great lad who wasn't the tallest but had the best leap and spring of any player I have come across, which made him a formidable force in the air. Earlier in the day Hughie and some of the younger lads had been play fighting and Alan Sunderland got him in a headlock and starting rubbing his nose so hard that when he had finished, Hughie's nose looked like Rudolph the red-nosed reindeer. Our manager Bill McGarry always insisted we wore a collar and tie when we came down for dinner in the evenings, and, after getting dressed, Hughie took one look in the mirror and said 'Look at my bloody nose – I can't go down to eat looking like this!' I somehow convinced him that he looked fine and he eventually agreed, even though his nose was still a shiny scarlet! Well, as soon as the lads saw the state of his hooter, they burst out laughing – it was like a bright red beak. Hughie was not best pleased and went berserk, chasing me around the tables!

We were due to fly all the way to New Zealand for the next leg of our tour, but we had to wait for Derek Dougan and Danny Hegan to join us as they had played for Northern Ireland in the Home Internationals and had beaten England 1-0 at Wembley a few days earlier. The goal came from a corner taken by Danny which was flicked on by the Doog for the player-manager Terry Neill to score. It was a big win for them and the two Wolves lads celebrated all the way to the other side of the world – and yes, they were both in a state! As we waited for them, we saw Danny carrying the Irish flag and both of them were singing at the top of their voices. They were stopped and had their bags searched which annoyed Derek who jokingly said: 'Yeah, we've got drugs and everything!' But he had barely finished speaking when police drew their guns and that was the signal for them to sober up very quickly. They were detained for ages and we had to wait until they were released. But we managed to make it in time for the flight. It had scared the living daylights out of both of them and they slept most of the journey.

Once there the schedule was hectic as we played eight games in eight cities in 17 days, starting with a 3-2 win against Auckland followed by victories over Wellington (6-0) and South Island (2-0) in Christchurch. We then flew to Australia for a further five matches, the first two of which were against the national side. The first of those ended in a 1-0 defeat in Melbourne and I didn't feature for some reason – but had an experience afterwards which was to have pleasant repercussions many years later. As I hadn't played, an Australian supporter asked me for my shirt, a request which I was happy to oblige. Fast forward to about 1990, by which time we were living in the West Country, and that fan's son, Ray Johnson, had moved to the area and happened to be a member at the same golf club as Jane and myself, Cotswold Edge. Ray told me his dad still had my shirt from all those years ago. Ray and his now wife Estelle have since become firm friends and we have had many happy times playing golf together. I came off the bench for the next game against Australia in a 2-2 draw in Sydney and got myself on the scoresheet in the next two friendlies, a 6-2 win against a Queensland XI in Brisbane when Peter Eastoe scored a hat-trick and a 3-2 victory against South Australia in Adelaide, before we rounded the tour off with a 3-0 win over Western Australia in Perth. We had a great time and the games came thick and fast; you got one out of the way and then another came along so we did not have much time to see parts of the countries we visited. It had been a long season with successes and disappointments along the way and to end it with such a long tour was tiring. I was looking for a good rest before the following season began. But before that, I had the biggest match of my life ahead.

11

Love Is In The Air

With things all starting to happen to me on the field, they also got pretty exciting off the park too. After a game on a Saturday, a lot of the lads used to go to a nightclub in Wolverhampton called The Lafayette, which was the 'in' place at the time. In 1971 I met a girl there called Jane Clarke from Wednesfield. It wasn't a case of me being a hellraiser or regularly going out drinking – I didn't enter a pub until I was 19 so I was just following the boys who said it was a good night out, and it was. The owners and the staff who worked there were all Wolves fans and they would let us in for free, although the senior players used to get them tickets for the games. Whenever we got there, usually about nine-ish, there would be long queues, but the doormen used to call us to the front and let us in without having to queue up. On reflection I wouldn't have been too happy if I was in the queue and that happened to me, so I am apologising now to all the people who watched us go ahead of them and had to wait longer to get in!

One such occasion led to a 'sticky' situation – quite literally in my case. John Richards, who broke into the first team not long after me, had become a good friend and he and his then girlfriend Pam, who soon became his wife, would often go out together with Jane and myself. Pam and Jane were cousins. One time after a midweek away match around this time, John and I fancied getting a bite to eat so we went to The Lafayette with Phil Parkes, Jim McCalliog and Danny Hegan, arranging to see the girls downstairs in the bar afterwards. I was wearing a cream suit that I had recently bought – I was the original 'Spice Boy', long before the Liverpool team wore similar suits for the 1996 FA Cup final at Wembley, though theirs were white so mine was classier! We sat down and placed our orders. I think John and myself ordered steak and chips, and when his meal arrived, he liberally sprinkled it with tomato ketchup before proceeding to tuck in. I prepared to do the same, but as I picked up the bottle and shook it, I didn't realise the lid was loose and ended up with sauce all down my new suit! The girls couldn't believe it when they saw me walking downstairs with sauce all down the front.

Meeting Jane was a bit scary because I hadn't experienced this feeling about anyone else before. I had gone out with some girls but the way I felt about Jane was so different. I couldn't get her out of my mind and was thinking of her all the time. In fact

I thought of nothing else and it frightened me as I wondered what effect it would it have on my career. I wasn't looking for a long-term relationship at the time as my football was too important and my whole focus had to be on my job to stay in the Wolves team. But there was just something about Jane that got to me. Before we met I thought my career was more important to me than anything else, but after meeting Jane and seeing each other for some time, our love blossomed. It wasn't long before we got engaged. My proposal went like this: 'Do you want a ring?' She looked at me and said 'What do you mean?' I said: 'Do you want a ring, an engagement ring?' I didn't know what the answer was going to be but she said 'Yes' and we gave each other a hug and made arrangements to go to a jewellers in Wolverhampton. She selected a really nice ring, but being a Yorkshireman, I was wondering how I was going to afford it! However, I continued to show my 'romantic' side and decided we would go somewhere special for lunch – the chippie, Snelling's on Snow Hill. I hadn't got a lot of money so we took fish and chips back to the car and ate them out of the paper before I drove her back to work. Very romantic, eh?

First, though we had an enforced break as the club took us on a six-week tour from May 1972, as I've described in the previous chapter. It was an incredible trip and one I will never forget, but not for anything that broadened my horizons culturally. All my thoughts were firmly focused on home, on the girl I was in love with who I was missing so much and had to leave behind. We wrote to each other every other day, but we had to gauge where I would be at the time she wrote, so I would receive her letter in a certain state, country or province. I'm sure some of the letters got lost or I had moved on before they arrived, and it was really tough knowing I would not see her for six weeks. The days went by very slowly, and, while I should have enjoyed the experience of being in some wonderful places, I missed her so much, it hurt. I was homesick – or maybe it should be lovesick – and had Jane on my mind most, if not all, of the time. This had never happened to me before. I was always so focused on my game, but I couldn't wait to get back home, and when the day came to leave, I was so glad. I knew she was the girl I wanted to share my life with. I only hoped she thought the same, and, luckily for me, she did.

Our very own Match of the Day came on June 2, 1973 at St Thomas's Church in Wednesfield – the same church where Jane had been christened. But before we could get hitched, first we had to buy a house. Eventually we found a new one being built in

Penn, just outside Wolverhampton, not far from my digs in Castlecroft. It was a three-bedroom detached costing £11,000. We put down a £1,000 deposit and had £10,000 on mortgage so we had to save like mad. We would put every penny into a savings account, and we would go out once a week. We couldn't wait to get married and start a family. Thankfully it was lovely and warm on our big day. Arriving early at the church, my best man Kenny Wright and I popped into a pub opposite, and had a couple of pints and chasers to settle the nerves. However, I needn't have worried, it was the best day of my life.

We had our reception at The Mount Hotel in Tettenhall, Wolverhampton, but before the celebrations could get under way, I nearly had the shock of my life. Just as we were about to enter the dining room, the receptionist called me over to take a telephone call. I thought it was someone wishing me all the best but I nearly dropped the phone when the caller said I had to report to the England training camp. There had been speculation in the press at the time that I might be included in the Under-23s squad again but it never materialised. I said 'I've just got married and we're about to enter the reception'. My heart was beating so fast and I just didn't know what to say. All sorts of things went through my mind. It all went quiet for a minute, no one said anything, then I heard someone laughing and I knew it was a wind-up. Martin Brough, a friend of my father-in law who was always joking and a really nice guy, was the prankster, and he had me a treat as I fell for it hook, line and sinker. After my surprise 'England call-up', the reception went brilliantly. The cake fell into the lap of Jane's sister Lynn as we cut it and we had a right laugh.

The next day we left for our honeymoon on the Lleyn peninsular in north Wales. It was an area where we had spent time with Jane's family and I loved it. We spent two weeks there, and in the the second we were joined by our great friends Phil and Janet Brookes. Jane went to school with Jan and they have known each other for 50 years and that is how I met her husband Phil, who is an ardent Wolves fan. The weather was fantastic – temperatures ranged between 80 and 85 degrees the whole time so we felt we could have been anywhere in the world. It was hard to believe we were in North Wales! Phil and Jan eventually emigrated to West Palm Beach in the United States and have lived there for 35 years now but we still get to visit each other a lot. We loved our friends but we loved our time together – and still do. Jane was and still is my rock and my best friend. A superb cook, she was also my nutritionist when I was playing. We had a ritual. On Thursday nights we'd have steak and Fridays it was spaghetti bolognaise. She came to all our home matches and provided great support but it was hard work for her putting up with my moods when we lost or I had a bad game. It was then she would console me and make me feel better on the drive home. But she knew if we lost on a Saturday we wouldn't go out on the evening. When I look back now I must have been a nightmare to live with – a real pain in the backside, but without her I don't know what I'd have done. We couldn't have been happier when our first child, daughter Kelly-Jane, was born. We spent a lot of time together and it was lovely coming home from a hard training session and playing with her. By the time the 1974-75 season was in full flow she was nearly two years old and was toddling around. But the one thing she wasn't good at was sleeping through the night. She wasn't naughty, she just thought sleeping was a waste of time. I remember taking her out in the car loads of times to try to get her off to sleep. Once I settled her down, I would carry her upstairs to her bed. Then just as I was about to lay her down she opened her big eyes and wanted to get up again!

But if Kelly was difficult to get off to sleep in 1974-75, then it was me who was proving to be a pain in the backside to my family the following season. It's never nice to be fighting against relegation but we found ourselves in that miserable situation and I must confess I took my problems home with me, especially if we had lost or I had played poorly. This was the first time I had experienced a battle like this. At Bradford we were always looking to be re-elected back into the Football League but I was so young and played only 16 games for them. This was totally different. I was a senior player and a father. Kelly was only two and so wouldn't have known anything about it or picked up on my sullen moods. Our second child was due in August 1976. We were so excited and it helped to take away the relegation blues as we battled the drop at Wolves. Jane was coping terrifically well with the combination of expecting again and my moods. She wanted me to believe in myself more and be more optimistic. Later, once our son Rod was born, she would take the kids to her mum's on Thursday and Friday afternoons so I could get some rest and go to bed for a couple of hours before the weekend games.

12

Leeds And Leeds

Wolves had numerous classic and memorable encounters in the heady days of the early 1970s, but few as notable – or crucial – as those against Leeds United. Leeds were a super team and one I'd followed because of our Terry playing for them. They were full of internationals with bags of experience and were a great side. But they weren't exactly the most popular in the country at that time. As a squad they could look after themselves and each other. My brother played over 60 games for them but he had the great Eddie Gray ahead of him in his position – left midfield – so he didn't get as many chances to play as he would have liked. Terry told me their winning mentality was second to none and he was right; from number one to 11 and all the fringe players they had a great squad, all desperate to succeed.

On May 8, 1972, Leeds had just beaten Arsenal to win the FA Cup and only needed a draw to clinch the double, which the Gunners had done the previous season. Wolves stood in the way of Leeds becoming only the third team in the 20th century to win both League and FA Cup in the same season. Leeds were ordered by the FA to play us two days after the Cup final, which I thought that was a bit tough on them, but the decision was out of our hands and the game went ahead.

Before the game there had been a lot of whispering that some form of bribery was going on. There were rumours flying around that several of our players had been offered substantial sums of money to 'go easy' on Leeds. I think one of our players must have told our manager Bill McGarry that they had been approached because he gathered us all together on the morning of the game. There were stories saying that McGarry had the meeting on the pitch because he was so concerned about anyone reporting back what he said, or that a bug had been planted. Who would have thought that was possible in 1972? But that wasn't true, we had the meeting inside. He told us if any Wolves player were caught accepting bribes, he would never play for the club again. He went on to say we had to win the game because if we had have lost it, fingers would have been pointed at us. The younger players such as John Richards and myself knew nothing of the alleged bribes being offered at the time, to the extent that when we were called together for the meeting, I thought he had called it to talk about the game, as we did that on a regular basis. But if certain players were looking to 'nobble' anyone, it wasn't me. I honestly don't know 100 per cent if players were approached, but the allegations didn't go away.

Later that year *The Sunday People* first suggested Wolves players had been offered £1,000 each to let Leeds win. Investigations by both the FA and the police revealed little substance in the allegations. Five years later, when the former Leeds manager Don Revie left the England job to head for Dubai, the allegations were raised again and my team-mates Frank Munro and Danny Hegan claimed they had been offered money to give away penalties during the match. I don't think the matter should have gone any further, but maybe Danny, who was out of the game by then, had his own reasons for bringing it to court. But it was very difficult to prove, unless you had people filmed on video making the alleged offers. In 1982, the former Leeds captain Billy Bremner was also accused by Hegan of trying to 'tap him up' from his hotel room before the game. The case went to the High Court where it was reported that Munro claimed he was offered a £5,000 bribe to concede a penalty.

Munro claimed the offer was made twice by Bremner, once on the Sunday before the game and again during the match. Bremner sued the owners of the *Sunday People* and Hegan, and was awarded £100,000 in damages. In Peter Lansley's book *'Running with Wolves'*, Munro claims four Wolves players were approached in an attempt to 'throw' the game – goalkeeper Phil Parkes, the right back Bernard Shaw, himself and winger Dave Wagstaffe. Yet 'Lofty' made some great saves and Waggy and Bernard were involved in our opening goal scored by Frank. If Frank was being offered money to throw the game, why did he end up smacking one in the net? When big Frank scored he was called a 'f*****g Scottish b*****d' – by Billy Bremner of all people! The ball did catch Shaw twice on the hand in the penalty area, only for the referee to wave play on. But I would never say he did it on purpose and it must have been on the blind side of the referee on both occasions.

I can honestly say I didn't come across any talk of bribes. If there were – and I honestly don't know because I wasn't involved in anything – then myself and John Richards wouldn't have been high on the list to have been approached because we were so young. Danny never said anything to me about it and I would have been surprised if Bernard had either because he was such a quiet lad. We used to share lifts to training, and he hardly ever said a word. Talk of bribes was never mentioned again after McGarry's meeting and Bernard left for Sheffield Wednesday within a year. As for me, I just wanted to play to try to beat a great team. The press had built this game up so much, and, with the talk of bribes, the interest in a game that had no bearing on us if we won was huge. But because of all the speculation we had to perform well or there would have been a lot of questions asked. Molineux was packed to capacity. The official attendance was 53,379 – but there were about 10,000 fans locked out and they were climbing pylons and trees, hanging on to anything they could to get a glimpse of the match.

Any game against Leeds at that time was incredibly competitive. Our midfielder Jim McCalliog used to set up the defensive wall at free kicks and Allan Clarke used to stand in front of it. Jim shouted at the rest of us to pull Clarke into the wall because he was blocking our view standing where he was. The next thing I knew, Jim went around the wall, marched up to Clarke and kicked him. Another incident I remember was going into a very strong tackle on Johnny Giles, who turned to me as he got up and said: 'Do you know we're on 15 grand a man to win the Double, you little b*****d?' I said: 'I'm on forty quid mate!' which was true. That was my win bonus. As a young player all I wanted to do was win, the money was secondary and we were really determined to win that game. As it happened we turned them over 2-1 with Derek Dougan scoring our second. John Richards would have made it 3-0 before they pulled one back but his effort was ruled out for offside. Derby, whose players were already holidaying in Majorca by that time after finishing their season, instead won the League and Leeds finished runners-up for the third successive season. Derby boss Brian Clough was on holiday with his family in the Scilly Isles when he heard about our win over Leeds and Liverpool's 0-0 draw at Arsenal the same night which gave the Rams the title. The Leeds game was really big anyway but with all the talk of bribes, it was huge and us winning it shut a lot of people up.

Our next really big encounter with Don Revie's side came the following year, almost 12 months after that defeat took the League title away from them. This time it was in the FA Cup semi-final at Maine Road. Despite their reputation, status and quality in their team, we fancied our chances. We had beaten Manchester United, Bristol City and Millwall – all at Molineux by a 1-0 scoreline – then met Coventry in the quarter-finals in front of 50,106, the last recorded 50,000-plus attendance at the ground. Facing our future midfielder Willie Carr, we sensed we were in for a tough game, as they were on a 16-match unbeaten run at the time. Things didn't get off to the best start for us after Steve Kindon mistakenly knocked out Derek Dougan with a wayward shot in the warm-up! The Doog had turned to acknowledge the North Bank who had been chanting his name when he was caught smack on the head by a rocket from Kindo, who was our substitute and was warming up Phil Parkes by firing shots and crosses at him. Bill McGarry was sitting in the directors' box at the time and within seconds raced on to the pitch, screaming at Kindo 'That's it! You're on your way back to Burnley!' This was Kindo's first season with us and it's fair to say he didn't set the world alight during those first few months. The previous summer Wolves broke their transfer record by signing him from Burnley for £100,000. I remember hearing about it when I was back home in Bradford during the close season. 'Kindo' was a great lad but his career at Molineux didn't get off to the best of starts.

My first memory of him was in a pre-season friendly against Notts County. Mike Bailey hit a ball out to Steve on the left wing and poor 'Kindo' was still trying to control it as he was running up the terracing behind the goal! 'Kindo' had raced down the wing and I was getting into the box from the opposite side anticipating the cross. But the next thing we knew he was halfway up the terracing having over-run the ball. Being so fast, he continued sprinting beyond the pitch, the perimeter track and up into the stand. Mike turned to the dugout and called to McGarry: 'What the hell have you signed here?' Welcome, Steve! Knocking out our centre forward before an FA Cup quarter-final tested McGarry's patience to its limits. Sammy Chung, our trainer, thankfully brought the Doog round by putting smelling salts under his nose and he recovered to start the match. And the Doog proved there was nothing wrong with his head by flicking the ball on for John Richards to outpace Sky Blues defender Bobby Parker to score the opener in a classic Dougan-Richards goal. We never looked back after that. I sealed victory with a 49th-minute penalty after Parker had fouled JR for us to win 2-0.

By the time we met Leeds in the semis, we were a team coming together; a fine blend of youth and experience. Alongside the senior players such as Derek Parkin, Mike Bailey, Frank Munro, Derek Dougan and Dave Wagstaffe, there were younger lads such as John McAlle, myself, Alan Sunderland, John Richards, Barry Powell and Steve Daley. But on this occasion we weren't helped by the fact one of our most experienced

63

players, Bailey, was only fit enough to be named on the bench. Both Mike and Frank Munro were carrying hamstring injuries and in the end the manager took the decision to name one of them, Frank, in the team and the other as the substitute. You could only name one in those days. In the end, Mike came on for me. The only goal came after a ball was played to the far post, and as it dropped down over my head I tried an overhead kick to clear it. Big Frank, our centre half, said he shouted at me to leave it. I didn't hear him because of the noise of the crowd and I didn't get the best connection on the ball, which dropped at the feet of Leeds captain Billy Bremner, who promptly smashed it into the net. We played really well and tried in vain to get back on level terms, John Richards seeing a shot bounce agonisingly off the inside of the post and along the goalline after he had beaten David Harvey. Yet they hung on to win 1-0 and we were out of the Cup. Years later, whenever we met up, Frank always mentioned my mistake and he blamed me for that defeat. There was a lot of banter between us but sadly Frank passed away in August 2011 and is missed by so many.

Leeds went on to play Sunderland, who were in the Second Division at the time, and lost 1-0 in one of the biggest FA Cup final shocks of all time. Jim Montgomery, the Sunderland keeper, pulled off one of the best saves ever. I thought it was equal to the amazing one Gordon Banks made against Pele in the 1970 World Cup. When I look back, I reckon if we had beaten Leeds, the Cup might well have been ours because we would have fancied our chances against Sunderland. But it was not to be, and, to be fair, Sunderland showed great courage and worked very hard to beat Leeds. It was a great win for them but I feel a great chance lost for us.

13

Oh Brother!

My first competitive game against my brother Terry, who now played for Newcastle, came on New Year's Day 1972 at Molineux, two days before my 21st birthday. I knew it would be very strange playing against him. Being three years older and having played in a very successful Leeds team before he moved to Newcastle, he had far more experience than me, but I thought at the time brotherly love wouldn't come in to it. We both desperately wanted to win and at the same time hoped neither of us would get hurt. I had a lot to thank Terry for – he was there for me after our dad died as I had no one else to go to for advice. When Wolves came in for me, Terry had a word with his manager at Leeds, Don Revie, to see what I should do and Don had advised Terry to tell me to say yes to the move. Now we were about to face each other on opposing teams for the first time.

There was no contact between us during the week building up to the game until the day of the match. There was a bit of banter and I remember him saying to me 'If you're there to be kicked, I will kick you'. I replied, 'Yeah, and if you're there to be kicked, I'll kick you as well!' But if either of us went down injured, we'd always be the first one over to the other, concerned. We both agreed our dad would have loved to have been there to see us play against each other because that's what he would have wanted and he'd have been so proud. It felt strange because in all the years we'd spent growing up, we'd never been on opposite sides and here we were, me playing on the right for Wolves and him playing on the left for Newcastle, so as I was chasing him, then he was chasing me. We managed to win 2-0 with goals from Derek Parkin and Derek Dougan, but for me it was great to be on the same pitch as my brother, especially as that hadn't happened since I was 12 or 13 years old. Our dad would have hoped for a draw, I'm sure of that. My mother always hoped we drew our games when we played against each other.

The following Saturday I had just about recovered from my 21st birthday party before we were due to play at Manchester United, who won the European Cup in 1968, the year I joined Wolves. We made it four league wins in a row with a 3-1 victory against the likes of Bobby Charlton (who I loved watching play and who I used to try to copy with his shooting with either foot) Denis Law, Brian Kidd and Willie Morgan. George Best would have played but their manager Frank O'Farrell punished him with a ban after 'extra-curricular activities'. It was reported he was holed up in a London flat with the actress Sinead Cusack. The headlines said we had mauled a great team that day and to do so at Old Trafford against the league leaders was indeed something very special as it doesn't happen too often.

The next time Terry and I faced each other, on February 17, 1973, the circumstances were joyous for a different reason, even overshadowing us brothers scoring for our respective teams. We were delighted to see our full back Derek Parkin playing again. 'Squeak', as he was always known for his high-pitched voice when he shouted, had been out for over five months while being checked over for a heart problem. It was strange how it happened – we had been playing 'keep ball' in a circle in training when all of a sudden, Derek collapsed face down in a heap on the floor. We naturally panicked, but he got straight back up on to his feet and when we asked if he was OK, he said: 'What are you on about?' He hadn't realised anything had happened, but we immediately summoned our coach Sammy Chung who referred him to the doctor. He was eventually sent to see a specialist in London. But what had worried us was he had been one of the fittest players at the club. It was a long and worrying process for Derek and his family. A Geordie, 'Squeak' eventually returned to first-team action against his hometown team Newcastle at Molineux in a 1-1 draw in which our kid equalised with a deflected effort in the second half after I had volleyed us in front after 22 minutes. But for all the pride myself and Terry shared in facing each other again, it was great to see Derek back in the first team after what he had been through and the worry and time he had spent out.

This was the second full season of the prolific partnership between another Derek – Dougan – and John Richards and John was to benefit particularly this campaign as he finished as the country's top scorer with 36 goals in all competitions, the highest by a Wolves player since Dennis Westcott scored 39 in 1946-47. The Doog set up so many of those goals for John, but on this occasion Derek was slightly off key when he had the chance to get on the scoresheet. After rounding goalkeeper Willie McFaul, he ended up mis-kicking right in front of an open goal at the South Bank end. It was so funny, the whole crowd laughed and even the Doog couldn't help but grin. It was also captured on TV as it was one of the few featured games to be shown. In those days the

66

only televised domestic games were two from the First Division and one from the lower divisions on BBC's *Match of the Day*, while in the Midlands there was a regional programme, ITV's *Star Soccer* shown on a Sunday afternoon. But the Doog's miss ended up being broadcast time after time and it became a regular feature on *Star Soccer*. Mind you, it didn't seem to do him any harm as he scored five goals in his next three League games as his partnership with JR blossomed.

The most memorable of all my matches against Terry and Newcastle came on August 24, 1974. It was the third match of the new season and I had one of those games where nearly everything went right. I hadn't scored in the 13 competitive games since the League Cup final in the previous March, so I was looking to hit the goal trail again. We beat them 4-2 and I managed to score all four of our goals. One was a penalty but the fourth was my favourite. We were leading 3-2 with about two or three minutes left when I cut inside from the right about 25 yards out and smashed the ball with my left foot into the top left-hand corner of Willie McFaul's goal. Wow, that felt good! I hadn't managed to score more than two in a game since I was at junior school back in Bradford in the early sixties. Terry was gutted at losing but so thrilled for me.

As we walked off the pitch at the end, he said 'If we had to lose, I'm so glad you scored the goals, our kid'. I thought they were really kind comments from our Terry, who I had learned so much from with all the shooting practice into our home-made goals all those years ago. I was also the first Wolves player to score four goals in a match for 12 years, since Ted Farmer did the same in an 8-1 win against Manchester City in August 1962, and the first recognised midfield player to achieve the feat for the club. I felt so proud, I just wish the match had have been televised so I could watch it again. I still have the match ball but it's not in great shape after spending most of the time in my attic and surviving several house moves over the years. I was named man of the match but JR had a magnificent game and made two of my goals. He looked back to his best after a few months' lay-off with the pelvic injury he'd had when we won the League Cup back in March.

Terry moved from Newcastle to Birmingham City in 1975 for £100,000 and in the September of that year we were at home to Blues. We would never have believed it when we were two young kids playing in the streets that either of us would be worth that kind of money. Our manager Bill McGarry had told me a couple of years before that a club had offered the same amount for me but I never knew who it was. I had an idea it was Birmingham but wasn't sure and the manager never told me. Terry and myself had played against each other a few times when he was at Newcastle and I always seemed to come out on top, while the Magpies were a lucky team for me as I scored several times against them when he was there. I was hoping Terry would bring me the same luck against Brum, who boasted a strong forward line of Trevor Francis and two former Wolves strikers in Peter Withe and Bob Hatton. On this occasion I didn't enjoy the same fortune in front of goal as I'd had before against Terry, but at least we got the right result with a 2-0 win, and in front of the live TV cameras as well. When we got a penalty I was confident of scoring from the spot again. But for some reason when I put the ball down I thought Terry had had a word with the Blues keeper Dave Latchford and told him where I put my kicks. It was the first time I'd had such negative feelings, and anyway the keeper would have known which side of the goal I was likely to shoot because he must have done his homework on me. But I just wasn't positive and as I ran up I changed my mind. Instead of putting to the side I normally did, I put it to the keeper's left, only for the ball to fly wide and into the South Bank. I couldn't believe it and was livid with myself. Fortunately for us Willie Carr scored two terrific goals from long range in the second half to spare my blushes.

My final encounter against Terry on the pitch came in the FA Cup. In 1978-79, we were drawn to face Newcastle at St James' Park in the fourth round of the FA Cup on January 27 and by that time, Terry had rejoined them for his second spell in the North East. They were a Second Division side at the time, but it was going to be a very tough tie for us. St James' Park was and still is one of the best grounds to play at. The atmosphere is superb. People used to talk about the 'Roker Roar ' at Sunderland but it was just the same at Newcastle. I was looking forward to facing Terry again but also to pit our wits against our old manager Bill McGarry for the first time since he left Molineux two and a half years earlier. But I also knew deep down Terry owed me one as I'd been on the winning side more times than him in our previous meetings. I was also way up on goals scored against him as well so I wasn't as confident about meeting him this time as before.

We travelled to the North East the day before the game, and in the hotel over dinner, someone mentioned the time when McGarry was our manager in the early 1970s and blew his top in a restaurant. McGarry was very strict on what players could eat the night before a game. We really didn't have a choice of menu, it was always soup to start and then something simple like a roast dinner followed by rice pudding or fruit salad. But one particular night McGarry wasn't around when the waiter took our orders. As a young lad I was expecting the lads to order the usual but experienced players such as the skipper Mike Bailey, Derek Dougan and Dave Wagstaffe thought it was a chance to have what they wanted and all ordered prawn cocktail for starters and fillet steak for their main meals. But just as the waiter carried in the starters above his head, McGarry walked in. Realising they were for us, he shouted to the waiter at the top of his voice 'Take them away now and bring them some f*****g soup!' The room was packed and everyone looked up as we all bowed our heads. It was embarrassing and completely out of order. McGarry had changed our pre-match menu from fillet steak and rice pudding to eggs on toast or boiled chicken and toast when he first came to the club. It got to the stage where we all tried to avoid sitting on his table because he'd watch everything you put on your plate. He once even told me off for having four boiled potatoes instead of three! I had to take one off my plate and Jane, sitting next to me, glared at me, but before she said anything I motioned her to 'Shhh!' He sometimes treated us like kids, which the senior players resented and quite a few of them fell out with him over that.

When match day came it was very frosty and the pitch was rock hard, so we were lucky the game went ahead. Terry and I captained our teams. It wasn't the first time we'd shook hands and tossed the coin, but it always felt special. When you look back from being kids all those years ago we never thought we'd be captains together playing in an FA Cup tie. I can't remember who won the toss on this occasion, but we kicked off and our former striker Peter Withe – who McGarry re-signed after he had won the League title with Nottingham Forest the previous year – put Newcastle ahead in the 71st minute with a header from a cross. He got between George Berry and Geoff Palmer to nod past Paul Bradshaw. They were well on top and playing quite well while we struggled for long periods.

As the game went on it looked like we were going out of the Cup and our kid was going to put one over me. Then with five minutes left, our Terry conceded a throw-in on our right. From it, Peter Daniel's diagonal pass from Geoff Palmer's throw-in was touched back by Norman Bell to Willie Carr on the edge of their penalty area. I saw a space behind the Newcastle defence and Willie chipped it over the defence into my path and I volleyed it into the roof of the net. I struck it as sweet as a nut and gave their keeper Steve Hardwick no chance. It was around this time that people spoke of me being the best volleyer in the First Division and I always prided myself on my shooting in either foot. The match was televised and after I scored, the commentator Martin Tyler said I was one of the 'best volleyers in the business'. I was proud of that comment because volleying was a technique I was comfortable doing. But I also practised it in training with drills Sammy Chung used to have us doing. So it was somewhat ironic that I scored against my brother again having honed that particular skill with Terry all those years ago on our makeshift pitch in front of our house. When the final whistle went, our kid looked at me and said 'You little s***, that's the first f******g kick you've had!' Terry was right as he'd kept me quiet all game, but if it was the only touch of the ball I'd had, I made the most of it. Walking down the tunnel I was confronted by McGarry, who shouted 'Damn you, you little b*****d!' I just laughed as it was a light-hearted gesture – it wasn't malicious, he was just very upset to concede late on, but it felt fantastic for me. Sadly my mum didn't make it to the match as she didn't drive, and neither did our wives because they were looking after the kids, who were very young at the time, so no other family members were there to see us play against each other. The equaliser knocked the stuffing out of them and we were happy to take them back to Molineux. I got another one over our kid in the replay as we won 1-0 with Norman Bell scoring the only goal. I loved playing against Terry and I usually came out on top against him, plus I had a habit of scoring against his team as well!

14

Wembley Winners

Our manager Bill McGarry was known as a fitness fanatic and he worked us really hard. The first two weeks of pre-season training were spent on Cannock Chase. It's an area very popular with ramblers but it was certainly no walk in the park for us. We never saw a football for the first fortnight. As I've mentioned before, certain players such as Phil Parkes, Dave Wagstaffe and Frank Munro hated the long runs and actually avoided them if they could. On one occasion, Waggy drank a bottle of Vimto which turned his mouth red, and claimed he had developed a bug, even managing to get out of the session and get sent home.

We did a similar pre-season every summer so we had an idea of what was coming. We used all our energy in training, so much so that when I got home I used to collapse on the settee and get served with drinks because I was too knackered to do anything. We didn't know what was in store next so we couldn't afford to over-eat or touch alcohol because the manager would know. But it was worth it because it was a long, hard season. We had played a total of 59 games in 1972-73, many of them on heavy, muddy pitches, and it was only our superior fitness levels that got us through such a tough schedule.

After all the near misses over the previous two seasons – the UEFA Cup final defeat in 1971-72 and falling at the semi-final stages of both the FA Cup and the League Cup in 1972-73 – we knew we needed to win some silverware if this exciting Wolves team was to fulfil their potential and avoid the tag of being labelled 'nearly men' in years to come. Six months after beating us in the UEFA final, Spurs accounted for us in the semi-final of the League Cup. They were fast becoming our nemesis. At home we had 28,357 backing us but lost 2-1 – I scored from the penalty spot – and there was 41,716 at White Hart Lane for the second leg. We went 1-0 up through a Terry Naylor own goal to make us level on aggregate, but Martin Peters put them back in front. John Richards equalised to take us into extra-time, but once again fate conspired against us and Martin Chivers got the decider to deny us the chance to play at Wembley.Thankfully in 1973-74 it finally came together for us. We were hit and miss in the League, winning our first two games before losing five in a row in a run of just

71

one victory in our next 14 then getting our act together to lose one in 11 to finish 12th. That was still above both Manchester clubs – United were relegated – and the likes of Chelsea, Newcastle and West Ham. But if our form in the League was milky at times, then we were the cream that rose to the top in the League Cup.

We started our cup campaign on October 8 with a 3-0 win away to Halifax in the second round thanks to goals from the Dougan-Richards combination and Alan Sunderland. The game saw the debut of Geoff Palmer, and the young right back was an ever-present in our run to Wembley. Another Third Division side, Tranmere Rovers, were next to be despatched, 2-1 in a replay at Molineux when the Doog and Barry Powell were on target after Alan Sunderland earned a 1-1 draw at Prenton Park. In the fourth round we were paired at home with Fourth Division Exeter City but what was unusual was the match had to be played on a Tuesday afternoon. The introduction of the three-day week to save power during the coal miners' strike meant floodlights weren't allowed to be used. With most supporters at work, Molineux hosted just 7,623 and the missing thousands weren't missing much to start with as it remained a boring 0-0 stalemate until just before half-time. That was when I gave us the lead and we went on to win 5-1, with another from myself, two from John Richards and one from The Doog. After the game Bill McGarry turned to me and said: 'Well played son'. That was the first time he had said a word of praise to me so I was truly honoured.

That put us through to the fifth round, and, after overcoming three lower division opponents, we were drawn against the mighty Liverpool. I honestly thought that was going to be end of our cup run because they were the League champions and a fantastic team who would go on to lift the FA Cup that season. They had also beaten us 1-0 at Anfield in the league just over a month earlier. But somehow we managed to pull off an unlikely 1-0 win courtesy of a fantastic goal from John Richards in front of another three-day week affected midweek afternoon crowd of 15,242 to earn a two-legged semi-final against Norwich City. The Canaries were struggling at the wrong end of the First Division and would be relegated that season in bottom spot. Now, I wondered, was my dream of playing in a cup final at Wembley finally about to become a reality? Richards scored again as we drew 1-1 away in the first leg but we still knew it would be a tough second leg at Molineux. Unusually for the League Cup, we were able to play the home leg on a Saturday afternoon because both of us were out of the FA Cup. In front of a healthier crowd too we scraped a 1-0 win on a real mudbath of a pitch to send the vast majority of the 32,605 gate home delighted. I was ecstatic to think I was heading for Wembley, which I had only ever seen on television when England played, or the FA Cup final.

It was one of the best moments I ever experienced as a player so the date of the final, March 2, 1974, will always hold a special place in my heart. But I knew I had to continue playing well and steer clear of injuries if I was to be picked for the game. It was a great achievement for Wolves because the club hadn't won a major trophy for 14 years, since beating Blackburn Rovers 3-0 in the FA Cup final in 1960. We were up against a star-studded Manchester City boasting a forward line of household names – Mike Summerbee, Colin Bell, Denis Law, Francis Lee and Rodney Marsh. By contrast we had a younger side with Geoff Palmer and Barry Powell in their first full seasons and John McAlle, Alan Sunderland, myself and John Richards all still very young and relatively inexperienced. As the final approached I had a thigh strain which kept me out for a couple of games and I was concerned whether I would regain full fitness in time. In addition, my replacement Barry Powell did so well I was very worried he would keep his place. I didn't find out I was playing until the morning of the game when we went into the dressing room and my boots were next to the number seven shirt. That told me I was in – the manager didn't. I couldn't help but feel a sense of disappointment for Barry but this was my chance and I had to take it. Before the game all the squad walked on to the pitch and it was a wonderful feeling just to feel the grass, let alone play on it. I had always wanted to play on it as a kid.

The build-up to the game was fantastic as Bill McGarry had taken us all away for a week to prepare, away from the attention in the Midlands in the quiet south coast resort of Worthing in Sussex. There we were able to relax with some golf in between training and preparing for the final. But come the day of the final, the tension was high in the dressing room and the nerves really started to take over, certainly for me anyway. I was as nervous as a kitten and I remember the bell going and all the players wished each other all the best. We were stopped halfway down the tunnel and had to wait to be called forward to walk on to the pitch. As we were waiting, I looked across at the City team, who were full of big names and internationals. They were laughing, smiling and juggling the ball as if it was a run-of-the-mill game. After all I suppose Wembley was like a second home to many of them who had played there for England or, in Denis Law's case, Scotland. My thoughts at seeing that were unprintable as they seemed to be so full of confidence, while our young side were stood in a straight line, all tense and nervous but concentrating hard. Then we were waved down and as we approached the mouth of the tunnel, the sight of gold and black from thousands of Wolves fans opposite was amazing and one I'll never forget. I immediately felt the nerves disappear and couldn't wait to get out there and do battle to win it for the 50,000 Wolves supporters in the ground and all those at home. They really did inspire us and played a massive part in winning that day.

The game started well for us and I was fortunate to put us ahead. I say fortunate as I screwed a side-foot shot past their goalkeeper Keith MacRae into the bottom corner. I have to hold my hand up and say I mis-hit it. Geoff Palmer crossed it and I lost track of the ball for a second so it came off the outside of my right boot. So I was relieved to see the ball fly into the net. To see my name up in those Wembley lights for the first time ever was an incredible feeling and I knew my mum sitting in the stand would have felt incredibly proud. It was something we never thought would happen to the Hibbitt family. All those years watching cup finals hoping, wishing, praying that one day your name would be up in lights and it happened. My one regret is my father wasn't there to see it happen, but I'm certain he was looking down on us that day.

We had a bit of luck during the 90 minutes because with quality players such as Mike Summerbee, Colin Bell, Francis Lee, Denis Law and Rodney Marsh they pounded our goal. But our goalkeeper Gary Pierce was outstanding – he produced the best goalkeeping performance I had ever witnessed. It was very sad our first-choice keeper Phil 'Lofty' Parkes missed the final with a broken ankle, but Gary seized his chance with aplomb and the back four of Palmer, Munro, McAlle and Parkin were all magnificent and well led by our captain Mike Bailey, who was the best skipper I played for.

John McAlle – or 'Scouse' as he was known, and still is – played 508 games for us and yet was one of the most under-rated players we had at Wolves in that era. A left-sided centre back who played alongside Munro at the time, he was a great lad who I got on really well with. A fine family man, he was one of those players who got on with the job and didn't seek the limelight or headlines. A 'steady Eddie' type who would be among the first three or four names you would have on the teamsheet every week, Scouse was without doubt one of the hardest tacklers I played with. Geoff Palmer could really put his foot in, but playing full back, he was able to challenge players side on, whereas Scouse had to make head-on tackles from the centre-back position. Frank Munro read the game better than anyone and he swept up a lot of the loose balls, but John was really brave and never shied out of a tackle. Their partnership worked well. Thankfully Scouse toned down his fierce tackling in training because he was aware he was up against his mates so would never go full throttle and didn't want to hurt anyone. But come match day, he was a different beast and I think he was one of the most honest players I ever played with.

For all the saves Gary made in the final, probably our biggest slice of luck was John Richards being able to play. John suffered a serious pelvic injury before the final and had missed the two previous League games, but he wanted to play so much and you don't leave your top goalscorer out unless you have to. He was in so much discomfort that he was about to be taken off when Dave Wagstaffe suffered a recurrence of a pulled hamstring and had to go off. So JR had no choice but to stay on for the last seven minutes. In those days teams were only allowed one substitute and, having missed out on a starting place, it was lovely to see Barry Powell come on and play his part. Despite his obvious discomfort, we were soon grateful John did remain on the field as he hit the winner with six minutes to go. It was a great passing move down the right between Mike Bailey and Alan Sunderland that set it up. As 'Sundy' crossed it, the ball clipped the heel of Rodney Marsh and dropped perfectly for JR to lash it low to the keeper's right. The fans went wild and JR had written himself into Wolves folklore. The cup was ours!

As the final whistle went JR collapsed on the floor and I went up to him. I'm sure he didn't feel the injury as the ball hit the net but he was obviously in a lot of pain. But he managed to drag himself up and join the celebrations. The time came to walk up those famous 39 steps, and the sight of Mike Bailey lifting the cup will live with me to the day I die. We began running round the pitch with the cup and I recalled the many times I had watched teams do that on TV. Now it was my turn. Somebody gave me a bobble hat and scarf which I put on but I remember my socks were around my ankles like Nobby Stiles's were in 1966 when he danced his jig of joy after winning the World Cup. The euphoria I felt was difficult to put into words. It was just amazing. Afterwards we celebrated at the Hilton Hotel in London. As my wife and I went into our room we both felt a bit peckish so I rang room service and ordered two chicken sandwiches. I've still got the bill for those sandwiches. A Yorkshireman doesn't forget paying so well over the odds! But it was a wonderful celebration, one of the happiest periods of my Wolves career.

The next day we came back up the motorway and it was a wonderful sight to be greeted by thousands of Wolves fans leaning out of the pubs and houses. All the fans who had been at Wembley turned out in their thousands to welcome us back to Wolverhampton. One player who wasn't in such celebratory mood however was Waggy. Having been in the game for so long waiting for his first major honour – which came against his hometown club and former team – he found it all difficult to take in and went and sat on the back seat. Waggy was to play just three of our last 11 games, while The Doog failed to start the final eight, but JR's season ended there and then.

Years later I learned I had an extra reason to celebrate winning the League Cup because of an incredible statistic – I was the first Bradford-born player to score in a Wembley cup final. The Bradford connection didn't stop there either as a few weeks later my brother Terry played in the FA Cup final for Newcastle against Liverpool. Two brothers playing in cup finals within two months of each other – it's difficult to take in because as kids this was something we'd dreamed of and here we were now, playing it out for real. Unfortunately though, Newcastle were soundly beaten 3-0 but nevertheless it was still a season to savour and my dad would have been so proud of us.

Talk about being brought straight back down to earth, in the days after our final I was busy wallpapering the hall at home. In those days we all had mortgages and footballers thought nothing of getting stuck into domestic jobs. I have always done as much as I can around the house and will only call on tradespeople if I need them. One day two Swedish journalists knocked on my door asking to interview me and I opened it, in my paint-spattered jeans with the hall covered in dust sheets and ladders. They looked at me in horror, and said 'What are you doing?' I replied 'What does it look like? I'm decorating.' They said I shouldn't be doing that as a professional footballer but I asked them who else was going to do it, and carried on. In those days reporters got to know where you lived and knew your home telephone number, and no one batted an eyelid. But to 'doorstep' a top-flight footballer's house these days would no doubt cause an outrage and be a story in itself. Maybe those journalists had a point though, because training under Bill McGarry was bloody hard and we needed all the rest we could get.

Grim and bear it – I don't look too happy here for some reason, pictured with Terry (right), mum and dad and my grandma.

All smiles – I look a lot happier here! Looking smart in my dotted tie, I must have just beaten our brother Terry at 'long shots'.

A rare picture of my dad Gilbert, seen here second from the left (kneeling), with his football team. My father could have played for Port Vale, but had to stay at home to look after his mum when his dad died at a young age. Dad was a tough centre-forward and a good player.

Up for the cup – me with a trophy playing for Bradford Moor School. Bottom right is David Bairstow, later the England wicketkeeper, father of Jonny, who plays for Yorkshire and England. David also played football for Bradford City. Tragically he took his own life in January 1998 at the age of 46.

Up for the cup again – me, bottom row, second from the left, at Bowling Back Lane School, the only time Terry and myself played in the same team at Bradford Rovers' ground, which was opposite our house in Lower Lane. I was only eight – and the youngest in the Under-11s team.

From vertical stripes to horizontal ones – me, second from the right, bottom row, lining up for Bradford Boys Under-11s at Bradford Park Avenue. Who's cut my hair? Look at my dodgy fringe! I must have the poorest fitting shirt too!

Say cheese – my first team photo at Bradford Park Avenue, and there's me all smiles for the camera, centre of the middle row. *(Kevin Haley)*

Here's pointing at you – Steve Wright, (left), the chairman of Yorkshire Wolves, with his late dad Cyril. They were a great support to me in the early days at Molineux and Steve has kept in touch to this day.

Eyes down – my face is a picture of concentration as I focus on the ball in a lunging pose for some reason. Looks like Park Avenue's old ground has seen better days.

What a scary, hairy bunch! From left, John McAlle, Mike O'Grady, Dave Woodfield and I look like we're having a competition as to who can grow the bushiest sideburns as we prepare to set off for a pre-season training session at Dunstall Park in July 1971. *(Express & Star)*

Preparing to pounce . . . waiting to see if Juventus goalkeeper Massimo Piloni drops the ball. A goal from Jim McCalliog earned us a 1-1 draw in Turin in March 1972 before we beat them 2-1 at Molineux to reach the UEFA Cup semi-finals. Bill McGarry's masterstroke was persuading John Charles to be our guide. He was idolised there and was happy to take us around the shops for clothes and shoes. *(Express & Star)*

Suits you sir! Don't we look smart? That was the idea anyway. To be honest, the outfits weren't the best fit on everyone. The Wolves party pictured before going on tour to Australia, New Zealand, the United States and Canada in May 1972. Derek Dougan and Danny Hegan joined us later on the trip, in some state or other! *(Express & Star)*

Ready for take-off . . . preparing to fly to then East Germany behind the Iron Curtain to face Lokomotiv Leipzig in the UEFA Cup in October 1973. I look as if the emotion has got too much for me. It's either that or I've got something in my eye! Sadly there was no repeat of 1971-72 as we lost 3-0 away before winning 4-1 at home to exit on away goals. *(Express & Star)*

Don't drop me! That seems to be Jane's concern as I carry her out on her last day at work before we got married.

Suits me, sir. A very smart and proud husband, leading Jane down the aisle after we were married on June 2, 1973.

Pick that one out – me turning to see my mis-hit shot fly high into the net past Keith MacRae to give us the lead in the 1974 League Cup final against Manchester City. I always fancied a pop at goal.

Look at those ties and lapels! Me and fellow goalscorer John Richards with the League Cup on the balcony at Wolverhampton Town Hall in 1974. The fans' support both at Wembley and when we got back to Wolverhampton was incredible. *(Express & Star)*

In the book . . . booking myself to save referee Tommy Reynolds the trouble against Manchester City at Maine Road in March 1974. I was tempted to write 'Terry' instead of 'Kenny' Hibbitt but honesty got the better of me in the end! I had my fair share of brushes with officials down the years, before switching to their side of the fence as a referees' assessor. *(Express & Star)*

Pick that one out, Jimmy . . . scoring from the spot against Jimmy Rimmer to give us a 1-0 win against Arsenal at Molineux in February 1975. It was welcome as it was our first victory of the year. I was happy to take penalties and this was one of nine I scored that season – a club record. *(Express & Star)*

Hibbitt 4 Newcastle 2. Sadly there is no video of one of the most memorable games of my career, but here are the last two of the four goals I scored against my brother Terry's team on August 24, 1974. I always seemed to fare well against Newcastle. Poor Terry (top photo, bottom right) must have been cursing me when this went in!

That's how I did it, Kelly . . . my daughter and
me with the match ball that I scored four goals
against Newcastle United in August 1974.

A golfer to a tee . . . me and son Rod – who became a professional
golfer – showing promise at a young age as he prepares to take a
tee shot in our back garden. Now it's him doing the teaching!

It's ours! Willie Carr, Gary Pierce, John McAlle, Mike Bailey, Sammy Chung (coach), myself and Alan Sunderland don't look as if we want to let go of the silverware after winning the *Daily Express* national five-a-side tournament at the Empire Pool, Wembley in 1975. *(Express & Star)*

Ours again! Making history as the first team to retain the silverware. From left: Willie Carr, Gary Pierce, Steve Daley, me, Alan Sunderland and Martin Patching. *(Express & Star)*

Alright, our kid . . . Terry and myself captaining our respective clubs, Newcastle and Wolves, before the FA Cup fourth round tie at St James' Park in January 1979. My late equaliser earned us a 1-1 draw – an occasion when Bill McGarry, then in charge of the Magpies, was not happy with me netting for a change. We won the replay 1-0.

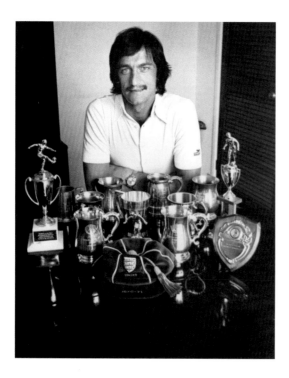

Me and my silverware . . . pictured with my treasured cups and my only England Under-23s cap. I also have my white England Under-23s shirt with the number 14 on the back, which is in surprisingly good nick. I was proud to have played for my country and wished I could have represented the full side but injuries at the wrong time counted against me.

Two pictures of my team . . . Kelly, Jane and Rod in our house in Wolverhampton. White and blue must have been the 'in' colours of the season, while Jane appears to be modelling an outfit to join an airline cabin crew! Just look at that settee! *(Express & Star)*

Eyes on the ball at cricket in action for a Wolves team . . . and at golf. Look at those collars – I'm surprised I didn't take off! I've always loved any sport involving a ball, even rounders, which I'm proud to say I've won a trophy for.

We're there . . . being chaired off the Molineux pitch by jubilant Wolves fans after beating Swindon Town, in February 1980, to reach the League Cup final at Wembley.

And the celebrations were in full flow afterwards when we had a rather special visitor to the dressing room – the great Eusebio, seen here with George Berry and Geoff Palmer (right). Our manager, John Barnwell, loved big-name players and invited the Portuguese great to the game.

Meet our new signing – Robert Plant. A pre-Wembley shot as the legendary Led Zeppelin frontman joins us. I love Robert, and the fact he's a big Wolves fan makes it even better. We got to know each other quite well in the 1970s, when he played in a few testimonials at Molineux. Robert has paid me a lovely tribute on the back of this book. *(Dave Bagnall)*

Ee-aye-adio we've won the cup! Me with my close mates Andy Gray, Willie Carr and John Richards after winning the League Cup in March 1980. Andy scored the only goal as we beat the holders Nottingham Forest. We should have built on that success, but sadly just like after the 1974 final, we ended up being relegated two years later.

Just four weeks after beating Manchester City in the final, we had to travel to Maine Road to face them in the League, so we knew they would be out for revenge. Unlike the final, which was an open, entertaining game of plenty of chances, this game – which saw the return of Phil Parkes in goal after recovering from his broken ankle – was tight and we drew 1-1 with Steve Kindon scoring for us. But something happened to me in this game that I hadn't encountered before – I ended up booking myself! The referee Tom Reynolds warned me for tackling too hard. Now that was a first. He then said if I committed any more fouls he would book me.

Ten minutes later I caught somebody late and he blew for a free kick. He then said 'OK, I have warned you, so you're going in the book. I know your name but I don't know how to spell it'. With that I took his notepad from him and wrote my own name into his book. For one moment as I started to write I thought about putting my brother's name instead but changed my mind. I would be in trouble with my manager anyway and I didn't want to be in any more hot water. We both had a laugh about that. I remember Paul Gascoigne doing something similar when he was at Rangers more than 20 years later – he got booked for his troubles after booking himself when the referee had dropped his notebook and cards and Gazza picked them up for him.

Buoyed by winning a major trophy at last, we ended the 1973-74 season in mean if unspectacular form, losing just two of our final 11 League games, winning four and drawing five. But we were without our main goalscorer John Richards and, for the most part, his strike partner Derek Dougan, who failed to start the last eight matches. Bill McGarry largely opted for a youthful strikeforce of Alan Sunderland and Steve Kindon, but initially gave Peter Withe his chance and he made a scoring debut in a 3-1 win against Ipswich a week after the Wembley final. Peter had arrived from a spell in South Africa on the Doog's recommendation to the manager after failing to make the breakthrough in the League, but struggled to get regular action for us.

He ended up being transferred to Birmingham City in the summer of 1975 for just £50,000. In hindsight of course with the type of player he became and the excellent career he had, Peter would have seemed to be the ideal replacement for The Doog, which was what I think Derek had in mind when he recommended him. But Peter's touch wasn't the best during his time with us and I couldn't see him breaking through, even though he was a thoroughbred in the cross country runs McGarry had us doing –

he was always out in front, leading the way. In truth he was a real late developer and he only really blossomed after leaving us, winning the League title with both Nottingham Forest and Aston Villa, where he also won the European Cup, scoring the winner, and was capped by England. But McGarry clearly saw something in him as he signed him for Newcastle sandwiching his spells at Forest and Villa. Withe's departure was one of several as the Doog retired at the end of that season while Waggy was soon on his way out, to Blackburn. It was Bob Dylan who sung 'The Times They Are a-Changin" in 1964 about the way culture and society was altering but he may well have been referring to Wolves a decade later. Sadly, things didn't work out as well as we hoped.

15

Penalty, Ref!

If Wolves fans are asked for an image of how they remember me, I think they will invariably say the sweat-soaked shirt and long hair plastered to my forehead and hopefully my workrate. I don't mind that; my dad always said to me you should give everything in what you do and I always tried to take that out on to the pitch with me. But along with all-out effort, I wanted to give the fans something else to remember me by. Ever since our kid Terry and myself had played 'long shots' on the field opposite our house in Bradford, I had continued to practise my technique by hitting balls with either foot. I loved the way Bobby Charlton could strike a ball and over the years I tried to emulate him by mastering how to manipulate it.

I was lucky to be able to strike a ball very cleanly but I could also bend it, dip it, ping it, drive it, volley it or put backspin on it. It was this ability I believe that convinced each manager I played under to ask me to be responsible for dead-ball situations. So at Wolves I was more often than not the one taking corners and free kicks. At corners I could drop the ball on to the head of Derek Dougan or later Andy Gray at the near post so they could flick it on to John Richards or a midfielder running in. It was the same at free kicks. It was a tactic which proved quite successful and it's still used today because it is hard to defend against. I also possessed a long throw-in and always fancied myself to reach the near post from anywhere from level with the 18-yard box to the goalline.

But it was another set-piece that I became known for which earned both myself and Wolves many goals down the years. When I first got into the team Jim McCalliog was our penalty taker and I recall Derek Parkin taking the odd one around that time. A 4-2 televised win at home to Southampton in 1971-72 springs to mind, when he scored after having to re-take it. I assumed penalty-taking duties the following season and it wasn't long before I was finding the net from 12 yards. But while I never reached the levels of Francis Lee's 13 penalties in a season, I enjoyed a lot of success from the spot, and none more so than in the 1974-75 season. Beating Newcastle 4-2 in August 1974 when I scored all four, including a penalty – more about that game elsewhere – continued our unbeaten start with two wins and a draw after defeating Burnley 2-1 then drawing 0-0 at home to Liverpool. But we couldn't maintain it as we went six games without a win before we managed three victories in 10. Two of those were against clubs who ended up being relegated in Chelsea and Carlisle – when Peter Withe scored only his second for us and Derek Dougan grabbed his last, in a 2-1 defeat at Jack Charlton's Middlesbrough. Both had come on as sub. During that miserable spell we also lost our defence of the League Cup at the first hurdle, against lower division Fulham 3-1. Things were changing at the club at the time, with our record signing Steve Kindon now finally enjoying a regular run up front alongside John Richards, with Derek Dougan mainly exiled to the reserves.

We started to turn things around with a 2-2 draw at home to Stoke in November. Stoke were riding high in the League at the time and all the talk was about their new signing from Leicester three days earlier, Peter Shilton, who cost £340,000, a world record transfer fee for a goalkeeper at the time and supposedly the last piece in the jigsaw for them to win the title. He was magnificent throughout, some of the saves he made were unbelievable. I felt his brilliance most as he must have made three superb saves to deny my best efforts. One was from a glancing header from point-blank range in the 68th minute and I remember thinking 'What do you have to do to beat this guy?' I reckoned I was never going to score but John Richards was pulled down for a penalty, and with barely seconds left on the clock, I had my chance.

I was very nervous as Shilton had been brilliant and we were losing 2-1. I picked up the ball and slowly put it on the spot, which you couldn't see too much of because of the mud. The referee blew his whistle and I placed the ball and turned away to run up. The crowd went pretty quiet as I stepped back my usual six paces, and the goal suddenly appeared very small with Shilton looking as though he could touch both goalposts. But I needed to keep calm and I decided to place it where I always put them and drilled it low to his right. I caught the ball just right with the inside of my right boot. It was heading into the corner of the net but Shilton guessed right and his right hand spread like a giant fan. My heart sank for a moment, but just as he thought he'd got to the ball, it hit a piece of mud and bounced over his outstretched fingers and into the net. Phew! To score against the keeper who cost a world-record fee gave me an enormous sense of satisfaction and the fans went wild. It was the most nervous I'd felt before taking a penalty so you can understand my relief, and the fact it earned us a much-needed point. Stoke went top of the table a week later and they were in contention for the title until the last few weeks of the season when their challenge fell away. The spot kick that beat Shilton was part of another record I achieved that season. Not only did I out-score John Richards for the only time with 17 League goals (a feat I matched in 1976-77 when I was Wolves' top scorer in the League), but the nine penalties I scored was a club record. For the record – if you'll pardon the pun – they came against Newcastle, QPR, Stoke City, Everton, Arsenal, Stoke again (in another 2-2 draw, this time after we'd been 2-0 up) Manchester City, Luton Town and Middlesbrough.

I listen to a lot of commentators, pundits and reporters talking about how you should take penalties, but unless you have actually taken one in the pressure-cooker environment of a game with a big crowd watching, only the taker will know what it feels like. If you haven't been in that situation, I don't think you should comment on it. Practising free kicks and corners is one thing, but with penalties, there is someone actually standing 12 yards from you trying to stop it. When you look up from the spot with everybody in the ground looking at you as you step back to take it and the goalkeeper is standing in the middle with his arms outstretched, the goal always looks smaller. I took many penalties in my career and whatever the scoreline was, they were always so important. That may sound silly, but if you score, it gives you the confidence to take another. Whenever I missed from the spot, it put doubt in my mind for the next one. Some players decline to take them because they don't want the responsibility and I don't blame them. You have to be really confident.

Take the World Cup or the European Championships where England have gone out in a penalty shootout. The players who missed got a lot of stick from the press and pundits alike but I always put myself in their shoes. When they stepped up to take their spot kicks, I got nervous for them because I know what might be going through their mind. Taking penalties is one of the most difficult things in football, so whenever England have lost shootouts at big tournaments, I never complain because I know how they are and how difficult it is to take them.

The penalties I scored helped significantly swell my goal tally, and 1974-75 was to prove the most prolific season of my career. But if things were going well for me on and off the field, it wasn't going too well collectively, and when we lost 1-0 at home to Birmingham on March 1, we were firmly entrenched in mid-table, in 14th place. The fans were having a pop at the manager Bill McGarry but the players should have taken more responsibility. I felt we had a good team, after all, only the previous year we'd won a major trophy. We needed a lift – and quickly. We soon got it, with an inspired signing from McGarry.

16

Carr Revs In, Doog Out

By the time manager Bill McGarry bought Willie Carr from Coventry City in March 1975 for a vastly reduced fee of £100,000, we were badly in need of a pick-up. We had previously tried to get him for around £230,000, but he failed a medical because of a bad knee. But for me, he was one of his best signings we made in all my time at the club. Willie was one of the best players I played with. He had a great football brain with a superb touch and passing skills. A Scotland international, he was a terrific midfield player who I learnt a lot from and we became big friends on and off the field.

We roomed together and considered ourselves good professionals who looked after ourselves. But our way of ensuring a good night's kip the night before a game wouldn't find its way into any modern-day coaching manual. Willie and myself were well known by the rest of the lads for drinking a couple of tins of Banks's bitter in our room the night before an away game. Some of the lads used to listen at the bedroom door to hear the sound of the beer cans being cracked open. We only had two and we also used to share turns to bring snacks such as chocolate, salted nuts and wine gums. My favourites were – and still are – Lion Midget Gems, although they make your jaws hurt after chomping half a pound between two of us! This was always our Friday night ritual for away games. It helped us relax and enabled us to have a good night's sleep. We'd watch the late film on TV while talking about the forthcoming game, who we'd be facing in midfield and what we would do on free kicks, or anything we thought would help us win the game. We'd sit up talking until past midnight but we only had one beer each the night before a game. For me it was vital because of the nerves I suffered from before games and I'd sleep much better for it. We roomed together for all of Willie's seven years at Wolves and our socialising extended away from the club.

On the pitch, Willie and myself were known for being creative players, so it may come as a surprise to some to be told that I believe we saved a lot of goals scored against us. It was our job to stand on the posts when we were defending corners, myself on the right post so I could use my left foot to clear the ball and Willie on the other so he could use his stronger right foot. It was amazing how many times we stopped the ball going into our net and it saved us so many points and goals against. I watch a lot of games where teams leave both posts unguarded and then they complain about conceding goals from set-pieces. But no one ever mentions that no one was covering the posts. I find it extremely annoying these so-called top coaches don't have a player at least on the back post, because it's where a lot of goals are scored. Even Barcelona under a world-class manager in Pep Guardiola lost a game or two with no one covering the back post and they had one of the best teams on the planet. That remains one of my biggest pet hates in football. You don't have to be too clever to know the only place a goalkeeper can get beat is in the corners of the goal, and yet it is remarkable to see no one guarding the post.

Before Willie's arrival we had lost to Birmingham City and Sheffield United without scoring and been defeated in six of the previous nine games – seven in 10 if you include the FA Cup, where we fell at the first hurdle to a 2-1 defeat by Ipswich Town. But Willie's debut, at home to Chelsea on March 15, couldn't have been much sweeter. We won 7-1 and Willie scored a beauty from just inside the box, rifling past their goalkeeper John Phillips, who must have had a bad back from picking the ball out of the net so many times. I felt a little sorry for him as our strikeforce of John Richards and his mate Steve Kindon were just electric and so powerful that day. John scored twice and 'Kindo' once as they battered the Chelsea defence of John Dempsey and Ron Harris. Myself, Mike Bailey and Dave Wagstaffe – with their final goals for the club – were the other scorers. I had never seen a Chelsea team so wide open at the back. This result gave everyone a massive lift and we hoped it would be the turning point for us.

But we were sadly mistaken as we lost the next two games, 3-2 at Leicester and then on Good Friday, March 28, 3-0 at struggling Tottenham, who were fighting against the drop. After a long period out of the team, Derek Dougan came on as substitute at White Hart Lane, but the Doog was looking tired in what proved to be his final season as a player. Thankfully we bounced back with successive wins over Easter. The first was against Manchester City when I scored the only goal with another penalty against Joe Corrigan, a top-class goalkeeper who was capped by England. Their manager Tony Book wasn't too happy with the decision when Dave Wagstaffe went to ground under the challenge of Colin Barrett but we needed that bit of luck and welcomed the points. We followed that up with a really good performance in a 5-2 win against Luton Town, when I was lucky enough to score my second and last competitive hat-trick at Wolves. Derby striker Roger Davies – who I went on to play with at Seattle Sounders in the

United States – had scored all five against them a couple of days earlier in another heavy defeat as the Hatters were on their way to being relegated. One of my goals was a penalty, my eighth in a row without missing. I still have the match ball, although it's not in the best shape.

But rather than push on, we only won one of our final five games, 2-0 at home to Middlesbrough. I scored my ninth consecutive penalty which followed our opener when I rattled in a 25-yard shot after a one-two with Willie Carr from a free kick. We were always making eye contact with each other at set-pieces. On this occasion I put the ball down, looked up and Willie was ready to take the quick pass. So I played the ball into his feet and followed the pass and Willie waited until I was near him before touching the ball to the side and I rifled it into the top corner. I recall saluting the fans before thanking Willie.

That season we finished 12th for the second time in a row. It proved to be the closing chapter for two players who became regarded as Wolves greats in Derek Dougan and Dave Wagstaffe. The Doog featured just six times in 1974-75 and three of those were as substitute, while Waggy made just 13 appearances then three the following season before joining Blackburn Rovers. We had Steve Kindon and John Farley to come in for them, but how can you replace players of the quality of the Doog and Waggy? It was going to be very difficult for both younger lads and it wasn't their fault they were put in that position. I don't think anyone could have replaced them but things had to change and Bill McGarry had the tough task. Only time would tell if he would get it right.

17

Relegation

The 1975-76 season proved to be very difficult for us. We hadn't had the best of times since winning the League Cup in 1974, and with our senior players either leaving or getting older, changes were needed. A 2-0 home win against Birmingham City on September 13 was our first victory of the season after six games and it took some of the pressure off manager Bill McGarry. But that winning feeling wasn't one which came along too often that season as we struggled to recapture the form we had showed earlier in the 70s. The team were in transition, which saw the departure or gradual exit of several senior players who rightly became regarded as legends of the club in Derek Dougan, Dave Wagstaffe and Mike Bailey. It also allowed the emergence of several bright talents who would serve us well as the decade progressed.

After making his debut in 1971-72, Steve Daley was now having a major impact. It was a great chance for the lad who had all the ingredients to be a top Wolves player. He could pass the ball with either foot, he wasn't bad in the tackle, he had good vision and he could score goals. McGarry was trying to change things and give young players a chance to blend in with more experienced players like our summer signing from Arsenal, full back Bob McNab, plus Phil Parkes, Mike Bailey, Frank Munro and Derek Parkin, and younger players such as Geoff Palmer, John McAlle, Alan Sunderland, Willie Carr, myself and John Richards, with the likes of Martin Patching and Norman Bell coming through. They were all very good players but we weren't getting the right results, and, when we lost 4-0 at home to Manchester City on November 29, the fans turned on the manager, with plenty of booing and chants for his dismissal.

I think this may have been the game where Geoff escaped serious injury. Geoff being Geoff – let's face it, he loved a tackle – he had been having a bit of a running battle with Dennis Tueart and he caught the City winger late two or three times. Perhaps not surprisingly, Dennis took a dislike to this and threatened Geoff in no uncertain terms, saying he 'would break his f*****g leg' in their next challenge. A while later Geoff got the ball under the clock on the old Molineux Street Stand side and I suddenly became aware of Tueart hurtling past me, steam coming out of his ears as he made a beeline for Geoff. I remember thinking 'Get rid Geoff, just get rid'. Well Geoff did get rid as he chipped the ball up the line, but sadly for him, not quite quickly enough as Tueart laid him out with a high tackle. Thankfully for Geoff, he was able to continue as Tueart's challenge hadn't broken his leg.

Things went from bad to worse, with the City defeat being the first of five in a row up to and including Boxing Day during which we scored just once, my penalty in a 2-1 home defeat to Middlesbrough. When results turn sour and you go on a bad run, the dressing room is rarely a happy place. Often players will look to others to blame rather than themselves, while team-mates frustrated with poor results and maybe their own form can be uptight and miserable and arguments are sometimes not far from the surface. Very occasionally that boils over as tempers become frayed and grievances are aired. One day in training at Castlecroft we witnessed one such incident, which left us all open-mouthed. Alan Sunderland was a really skilful player who had very quick feet and could play several positions from right back to anywhere in midfield and up front, as he proved with us and later Arsenal.

At the time, Sundy was 'on one' as we used to say. It seemed like everything he touched turned to gold, or goals, and when he was in that mood, it was almost impossible to get the ball off him. He was also a great lad too, not short on confidence with a ready wit, which made him very popular with the other players. We had a full scale practice match, first team against the reserves. This sort of game was always an open invitation for the second string to kick those in the senior side, because the reserves wanted the first-team's places. Sundy was playing for the first team and Derek Jefferson, a strong centre half who wasn't the quickest but was powerful in the air and in the tackle, was playing for the reserves. Sundy decided to take the mickey out of Jeffo by nutmegging him. As a pro on the receiving end, this is one of the most humiliating things that can happen to you, and, not surprisingly, Jeffo wasn't too happy after Sundy stuck the ball through his legs. For a nutmeg to 'count', you had to say 'nuts' as you performed it, which must have only increased Jeffo's frustration. 'Sundy, stop taking the piss, I'm warning you!' shouted Jeffo afterwards. No doubt spurred on by getting away with it, Sundy did it again. This time, Jeffo wasn't as accommodating and after reminding Sundy that he'd been warned, promptly clobbered him with a right hook to the face, leaving him spark out on the ground! Everybody's jaws just dropped as we stood open-mouthed, barely believing what we had just witnessed. Eventually some of the lads helped Sundy to his feet and Sammy Chung, who was refereeing with Bill McGarry sitting in the stand, blew the final whistle, the game being almost over anyway. I think Sundy got away with some bruising to his face for a few days, along with some dented pride.

Sundy wasn't short of confidence but his self belief backfired on him again one day. Three or four of us younger players – Sundy, Steve Daley, Peter Eastoe and myself I think it was – decided we were going to ask for a wage rise. It was decided that Sundy – with all the swagger of Del Boy from *Only Fools and Horses* – would go first, so we all crept down the passageway to Bill McGarry's office to listen in as he knocked on the door. 'Come in' barked McGarry. Sundy went in and duly asked for a rise and McGarry said no, adding 'I'll tell you what – you pretend you are me, and I'll pretend I am you'. Sundy went along with it, and when McGarry played the role of the player, saying he wanted a rise, Sundy replied 'Yes gaffer, how much were you thinking of?' McGarry, who was like a sergeant major, then lost it, screaming 'Get out of my office!' and we all fled, giving up any chance of negotiating a better deal after the frosty reaction Sundy got.

Going back to training ground scuffles, the only other time I recall anything resembling a punch-up at Wolves was the pre-season after this campaign, the very hot summer of 1976. We had been cross country running on Cannock Chase and were on the coach on the way back to Molineux when Steve Kindon had a row with Bob Hazell. Apparently Kindo had agreed to sell his wife's car to Bob for £750 cash after initially wanting £850 for it, but Bob only paid him £350 and agreed to pay the rest at £50 a week but hadn't coughed up the remainder. Kindo kept on at Bob, who was quite calm at first, saying 'Just cool it, Kindo'. But Kindo wouldn't, and by the time the bus pulled into the players' entrance on Waterloo Road where we all got off, all hell was preparing to break loose. As soon as they were in the away team dressing room, they went at it. And remember, these were two of the biggest blokes at the club who you wouldn't want to get into a fight with. Within seconds, you could actually feel the walls of the dressing room rocking as the pair of them literally bounced off the walls. The only two who were big enough and brave enough to get between them were Lofty (Phil Parkes) and big Frank Munro, who shouted 'Stop, for f***'s sake, you'll have the gaffer down here!' Success was proving hard to come by but we salvaged some pride by winning the *Daily Express* five-a-side championship at Wembley Arena with a team of Gary Pierce, Mike Bailey, yours truly, Alan Sunderland and Willie Carr, with John McAlle as substitute. We met a familiar foe in the final in the shape of Tottenham but for once things went our way against our bogey team and we won 3-1 in front of a full house with goals from myself, Mike and Willie. By now we had re-signed Bobby Gould from West Ham, five years after he had left us for West Brom in 1971. Bobby was a very experienced striker who was a prolific goalscorer. He could play alongside John Richards and he helped plug the gap left by Derek Dougan. The Dougan-Richards combination had been one of the best strike partnerships in football; they proved it in Europe and in what I felt was the strongest league in the world, the First Division. It was going to be very difficult for the manager to find that lethal partnership again with little money to spend.

Despite our relegation battle, we were enjoying another good cup run, this time the FA Cup. After beating Arsenal 3-0 at home in the third round, we were drawn against Ipswich Town away. Back then they were one of the hardest teams to beat on their own ground and to draw them at Portman Road was a tie no one wanted. It was also the former club of our manager Bill McGarry and coach Sammy Chung, who left them to join us in November 1968. For that reason, the build-up to a game against them was always different because getting the right result was so important for those two. A very tough tie saw us gain a well-earned 0-0 draw which pleased our manager but not me after I sustained a back injury in the last minute following a collision with Brian Talbot in midfield. I was very worried I wouldn't be available for the replay, but I managed to declare myself fit and Bobby Gould scored the only goal from out on the left wing when his attempted cross sliced over the head of Ipswich keeper Paul Cooper. Gouldy wouldn't admit that though!

From there we beat Second Division Charlton 3-0 at Molineux with a hat-trick from John Richards, who had been relegated to the substitute's bench to accommodate the return of Dave Wagstaffe from his month's loan at Blackburn. John achieved a bit of history as he was the first substitute to score a hat-trick in the FA Cup. In the sixth round we were drawn away to Tommy Docherty's Manchester United. Fantastic, I thought, Old Trafford is a great place to play and this was one of the biggest games of the season. We lost 1-0 there just before Christmas but after a good run of results and having not conceded a goal in four Cup ties we really fancied our chances. A 1-1 draw in front of 59,433 with John Richards scoring for us was about the right result and it gave us the chance to bring them back to Wolverhampton. There was 44,373 at

Molineux on March 9 for the replay, creating a brilliant atmosphere and both teams really went for it. Kindon and Richards scored for us and Stuart Pearson and Brian Greenhoff netted for United to leave it all square at 2-2 after 90 minutes so we went into extra-time. Unfortunately we were finally beaten by Sammy McIlroy's winner. That left us bloody shattered and gutted, as we had played well enough to go through. United beat Derby 2-0 in the semi-final at Hillsborough before succumbing to Second Division Southampton in the final. Saints featured our former midfielder Jim McCalliog, who had joined them from United, and he set up Bobby Stokes for the only goal of the game in the final. We had given it our best shot and now we had to pick ourselves up for the fight to stay up.

We had some strange results towards the end of the season, some good but mostly bad. Four days after our Cup exit we beat Sheffield United 4-1 away but three days later lost 1-0 at home to Spurs, then got beat 3-2 at Manchester City. We were unlucky not to get something at City but played better when we drew 2-2 at home to Leicester to complete March. We followed that with a 0-0 draw at West Ham and then walloped Newcastle 5-0 at home to make it three games unbeaten and give us a good chance of survival. Again I was on the scoresheet against my 'lucky' team. It was the right time to be scoring goals but we still had a lot to do. Successive trips earned us nothing at Arsenal then Coventry. Two days later we beat Norwich 1-0 at home but we were still in deep trouble as May approached – and it wasn't about to get any easier.

We had to beat Liverpool at home to stay up and they needed a win to overhaul the leaders Queens Park Rangers and be crowned champions. It was going to be a mammoth task for us but it was a double-edged sword for the Hibbitt family as my brother Terry was in a similar position at Birmingham City. They only needed a draw at already-relegated Sheffield United to be safe, whereas we had to win, so one of us was going to join the Blades in the Second Division that night. My mum was sat at home wearing a blue and white scarf over one shoulder and a gold and black scarf on the other. She did not know what to do as she knew one of her sons was going down. We were dealt a blow before the game as we were without both regular centre halves for the first time that season as we lost Frank Munro and John McAlle, forcing Mike Bailey and Derek Parkin to play in unfamiliar roles. Despite this we took an early lead with a super goal from Steve Kindon who outpaced the Liverpool defence before he smashed it past Ray Clemence and we went in at half-time 1-0 up. The official attendance was 48,918 but there were stories that many more had managed to get inside the ground and the atmosphere was incredible. The second half was going to be the toughest 45 minutes of the season and it was going to be difficult to hold on as Liverpool were determined to win back the crown they last won in 1973, were packed with quality players and were a bloody great side. Kevin Keegan equalised and we didn't get many chances after that as they took a grip of the game and won 3-1 with goals from two more fantastic players in John Toshack and Ray Kennedy.

So we were down – the first time Wolves had been in the Second Division for nine years and it was my first relegation as a player. Birmingham drew at Sheffield United 1-1 so even if we had won, the outcome would have been the same. Not surprisingly, it was a very sombre dressing room afterwards and I don't think anyone spoke a word for some time. That room was choked full of tears and huge disappointment. Boots were thrown down and our gold shirts and socks were spread all over the floor as one by one we trooped into the showers. Hearing the celebrations from the Liverpool players in the away dressing room just made it worse.

Ours was like a morgue, you could hear a pin drop as we just sat there for ages, stunned. I looked around the room and thought 'How the hell have we allowed this to happen with these players?' But with Birmingham drawing we could have had the best players in the world that night and it wouldn't have made any difference. It was what we deserved over the nine months. We just weren't consistent enough and hadn't played well enough so we could offer no excuses. It left a horrible feeling. These days players get accused of not caring enough but I didn't sleep a wink that night and in fact I never got over it until we started the first game the following season. By the way, guess who scored Birmingham's goal? That's right, the other footballing member of the Hibbitt family! Winning the League Cup just two years before seemed a million miles away at that moment. It just goes to show how quickly things can change in football. There is no time to dwell on the success as it can soon kick you in the teeth, so you must enjoy all the good times because the bad times can be just round the corner. Our manager Bill McGarry had been under a lot of pressure for some time and it looked like he might pay the price with his job. The inevitable happened and Bill McGarry was sacked soon after the end of the season after relegation proved to be the final straw for the board. I was very sad about this as he did so much for my career in the near eight years he was at Wolves. He gave me my debut and made me a regular along with several other young players who went on to have good careers, such as John Richards, Alan Sunderland, Steve Daley, Geoff Palmer, John McAlle, Barry Powell and Norman Bell. He made Steve Kindon the club's record signing at £100,000 from Burnley and got Gary Pierce for a snip, but one of his best buys was Willie Carr from Coventry City for a similar fee to Kindon. We still had our great skipper Mike Bailey, Frank Munro and Derek Parkin, one of the best full backs the club ever had who went on to become Wolves' record appearance maker, and the experienced Bobby Gould. So the squad looked strong and well equipped to challenge to get straight back into the First Division. It is the only league to be in as a footballer but we knew it wasn't going to be an easy task. Most teams in the division were wanting and waiting to put one over us so every game was going to be tough. We were all determined to get back to the top flight with an immediate return and I can't remember any player wanting to leave. It would probably have been a different story these days as the best players would have been lured to stay in the top flight. But in those days there weren't the same riches in the game and players felt it was their duty to help the club back up and not think too much about themselves. After all, the players had as much to do with the relegation as the manager did. That was another worry for the lads – who was going to be the new manager and would we fit in with his plans?

There was some speculation that Derek Dougan, who had retired as a player a year earlier, might return as manager. But the club didn't waste much time in their search for a McGarry's replacement as they promoted our coach Sammy Chung instead. McGarry left a good, young team behind and we were all happy with Sammy's promotion. He was familiar with all the players and didn't have to change much. It was a little surprising though as it was his first managerial post but the lads seemed happy enough with the board's decision and he was a great coach. So I could understand why he was the directors' choice. But this was going to test him as he was a bit of a mate to the lads. He and McGarry were a typical 'good cop, bad cop' team to us. We used to moan about McGarry to him, whereas Sammy would explain things in a more positive and understanding way than the manager, whose approach was more or less 'If you don't like it, tough'. You couldn't really have a sensible conversation with McGarry, but Sam had to change because he was going to upset people by having to drop players or change tactics, and I was one of them – but more of that later.

18

Promotion

Nowadays they say the Championship is a really difficult league with so many big clubs in it trying to reach the Promised Land of the Premier League. Let me tell you something – nothing has changed. The Second Division, as the Championship was called then, was always known to be a tough one to get out of with so many good clubs. Burnley and Sheffield United, who were relegated with us, were going to be looking to get straight back up and there were others such as Nottingham Forest, Bolton Wanderers and Chelsea boasting strong squads. Forest were resurgent under Brian Clough who was determined to prove himself again after his bitter and brief experience at Leeds and would make his team champions of England within two years and champions of Europe in three. Bolton had a strong team with players such as Sam Allardyce, Peter Reid, Paul Jones, Neil Whatmore and Alan Gowling, who combined the brawn with guile to be a challenge for anyone. Chelsea had rebuilt after relegation two years before and were reaping the benefits of some exciting young talent in the shape of captain Ray Wilkins, Garry Stanley and Kenny Swain. And what of Fulham? They certainly had the most glamorous and talked-about line-up in the division with Bobby Moore and Rodney Marsh already at Craven Cottage soon to be joined by George Best. But we had a bloody good squad of players to make sure we went straight back up and we were determined to do so. We felt we had a good blend of youth and experience for any new manager and Sammy Chung knew that. I felt all he needed to do was keep a happy ship and not change too many faces. A new guy may have rung the changes and done it too quickly and it could have backfired, but Sammy kept us all together.

Off the field, I had plenty to keep me occupied in the blistering summer of 1976, the hottest I have experienced. Jane was expecting our second child in August. I can remember having to sit in the garden at 2am and 3am to cool down because it was too hot for us to sleep. Being heavily pregnant, Jane found it particularly uncomfortable. Thankfully she didn't have to wait too long and our son was born on August 2. It took us a while to name him but eventually we settled on Roderick Kenneth. Now our lovely family was complete. We'd been away on pre-season tour and got back on the Sunday and I drove Jane into hospital the next day. I'd come back with tonsillitis and so was unable to stay with her in case I was contagious and passed on the virus, so it was a few long days before I got to see my son. The new season kicked off and I wasn't getting much sleep as Jane had to go back into hospital for a short time. But I was helped by Jane's mum, who looked after the kids to let me rest before games as she knew how important that was until Jane came home. With my wife in hospital, I was a great mum as well as dad to Roderick! I was more than happy to make bottles up and change nappies. The children were good most of the time and Roderick slept very well and never gave us any problems at night, unlike his sister! He could fall asleep on a clothes line and not wake up.

Back at Wolves we soon got used to life in the Second Division and got off to a good start with a six-match unbeaten run. After that we lost 2-1 at home to Luton when I scored, but we bounced back with a vengeance at Hereford United on October 2, thrashing them 6-1. It was a great performance and we could have scored more. But remarkably, we were brought back down to earth with a bump the following Tuesday when we lost 6-2 at home to Southampton. It was the strangest match I have ever been involved in. We must have had 70 per cent of the game and they seemed to have had only six shots on goal but they all went into our net. What a difference three days makes, 15 goals in two games. I wonder if that has happened before? But against Saints it was nice to catch up with one of my favourite ex-Wolves players, Jim McCalliog, who had arrived at The Dell after helping Manchester United to the Second Division title in 1974-75. I'd shared digs with Jimmy Mac a few years earlier and I learned a lot from him on how to play midfield. But that night he taught me and his old club a lesson, scoring one of the goals as well.

A 2-0 loss at Hull City made it three defeats in four games. That proved to be a wake-up call and the penny dropped – we realised how hard it was going to be. We got to grips with our play and had some good wins that put us in the top six. By February 1977 we were playing really well and scoring plenty of goals. On the 19th we played at home to Fulham. They were full of good players but whose best days were behind them. The 1966 World Cup-winning captain, the great Bobby Moore, plus George Best and Rodney Marsh were playing for them. It was always an honour to be on the same pitch as Bobby, and Bestie was the greatest player I played against. Earlier that season, in the October, I had the honour of playing in the same team as them both for the only time in my career when they guested in gold and black in Mike Bailey's testimonial and Bestie netted twice in a 3-0 win against West Brom after Willie Carr had opened the scoring. Fulham also had John Lacy, a truly great guy who is now a friend I play golf with. But that didn't count for much as we hammered them 5-1. Steve Daley and myself both scored twice and John Richards got the other. It rounded off a great February for us with three wins and a draw.

With results going well in the League, the FA Cup came around very quickly and we progressed to the fifth round having knocked out Rotherham United and Ipswich Town 1-0 after a replay. Now we were drawn at home against Third Division Chester City, whose general manager was Ken Roberts, one of my old assistant managers when I was at Bradford Park Avenue in 1966-67. Ken had a lot to do with me becoming a professional footballer. He brought in a couple more apprentices when I was the only one and he helped to set up a youth policy so we could play regular football in our own age group. I hadn't seen Ken since I left Bradford so this was a good opportunity to thank him. Ken was also the guy who told me about my dad's heart attack and drove me home so I could see him take his last breath before he left us. I will always remember Ken, not for just that day but for his advice he gave me on my decision to join Wolves. He was a truly wonderful man, so I was looking forward to seeing him and thanking him once again.

In the build-up our manager Sammy Chung took us to Southport for some training and a good break. Our preparation couldn't have gone much better as we had gone 14 matches unbeaten in all competitions. But on our way to the ground I remember telling Willie Carr I'd got a funny feeling about this game, something didn't feel right. We ended up producing our worst performance of the season so far but we got through 1-0 with me getting the winner with a volley nine minutes from time. When I went to see Ken Roberts afterwards he was so disappointed but pleased with my progress and we had a really good chat about our time at Bradford. We were so lucky to win but we got away with it as Chester deserved at least a replay. They would have had a full house at Sealand Road and it would have made them more money. From past experience of being at smaller clubs, cup runs are vital. When you're drawn away to a bigger club, one of the best results is a draw so you get a replay and have a good gate for the club and an extra bonus for the players. I'm not a fan of penalty shootouts, and I believe if you draw away you should have the chance to beat them on your own ground. I don't see the current format changing back to a system where you could have multiple replays, however. Another rule I would look at is deciding when a European game is drawn on aggregate. What a load of tosh that is! How can one goal scored count as two? I don't believe that rule has improved the game as an attacking spectacle one bit.

A few days later we enjoyed a great game with Blackpool, who were also in the top six. It was a very muddy pitch at Molineux and heavy going on the legs after a tough Cup tie but we produced a very good performance to beat them 2-1. Steve Daley scored the first early on but Blackpool equalised and then with only five minutes left, I rifled the ball into the Blackpool net from 25 yards. That wasn't the end of the action, however. As the final whistle drew close, Blackpool pushed hard for another goal. I was in the right place at the right time on the goalline to kick a shot away with our keeper Gary Pierce beaten. My goal was our 65th of the season but more importantly, it secured our ninth home win on the trot and extended our unbeaten run to 16 games, no doubt giving Wolverhampton-born Don Howe, who was sitting in the stand, plenty to think about. Don was assistant at the time to Jimmy Armfield, manager of our FA Cup sixth-round opponents Leeds United. The two points gained also meant we were now just a point behind leaders Chelsea but with two games in hand. They were under a bit of pressure and we were flying. Pride they say comes before a fall and we lost our next game, as Luton completed the double, winning 2-0 at Kenilworth Road. But we were still very confident about promotion with only a couple of months to go because our team was full of goals. Five of our players finished with double figures in the League – John Richards (15, despite only playing 27 League games), Bobby Gould with 10 (from just 11 starts), Alan Sunderland 16, Steve Daley with 13 and myself with 17. Between us we scored 71 goals, while in addition, Willie Carr and Steve Kindon netted four each. The midfield of myself, Willie and Steve Daley was one of the best I had played in. We could all pass the ball, we all had good shots on us and we just seemed to gel so well. When two of us broke forward, the other stayed back and we all shared our responsibilities. It was great to play with those guys.

We had now reached a vital period of the season, facing a massive Cup tie at home to Leeds. But first we had to play Hereford at home. It looked like an easy one on paper as we had battered them on their own ground 6-1 in October. But it turned out to be one of our hardest-fought games and, luckily, we scraped home 2-1 with a goal from youngster Kenny Todd and myself, much to our relief. The Cup game finally came around and there were 49,770 at Molineux on Saturday, March 19 to see us take on

Leeds. Our fans were rocking with the hope of a visit to Wembley in sight but it was not to be as we lost to a lone first-half goal by Eddie Gray. We gave it our best shot but the players Leeds had – including Eddie's younger brother Frank, Paul Madeley, Paul Reaney, Gordon McQueen, Tony Currie, Allan Clarke and Joe Jordan – were superb and we just weren't good enough on the day.

Our Cup run might have ended and but, if anything, the tight battle with Leeds had only whetted our appetite for an immediate return to the First Division. At the end of March we beat Hull City – they fielded another Leeds great, Billy Bremner – 2-1 with goals from myself and John Richards, who unbelievably had gone six games without scoring. That was almost unheard of for a player of John's prowess in front of goal but the win put us right in there with a chance of winning the title. We followed the victory over Hull by kicking off April with a 1-0 success at Bristol Rovers to make it four straight League wins. The good results continued through April, although we lost 2-1 at Carlisle before bouncing back with wins against Orient and Cardiff City to leave us with the chance of securing promotion at Plymouth Argyle with four games still left. With us needing a win to guarantee our return to the top flight, thousands of Wolves fans travelled down the M5 to be part of the promotion party.

A 0-0 draw meant we were up, but we still needed a point to be certain of the title as Chelsea, who had two games left, were only two points behind us, and Bolton, who were then in fifth place, still had four matches to play. After a 1-0 defeat at Southampton, it was all set for a bumper clash at Molineux between us and Chelsea, first and second respectively. What a game for both sets of fans and there were 34,205 to see the best two teams in the division battle it out. Chelsea took the lead through future Wolves striker Tommy Langley and went in ahead at half-time. Our dressing room was a bit quiet but manager Sammy Chung picked us up by getting us wound up for the second half. He told us if we scored they might panic and that's exactly what happened. John Richards equalised and they got nervy and put all their players behind the ball. A 1-1 draw is how it ended up – neither team needed to go chasing the winner because with the scoreline as it was, we had won the title and they were all but sure of promotion so both teams sat back and played the game out and we all congratulated each other. The fans went wild and the celebrations went on all night after we secured our return to the big time in what was also the club's centenary year. It was a great time to be part of the club and I think what helped us that season was the continuity. It was a very settled team, with numbers one to four – Gary Pierce, Geoff Palmer, Derek Parkin and Steve Daley – ever present, while Alan Sunderland and myself only missed one League game and John McAlle the last three. I missed my only game away at Bristol Rovers on April 5 after cracking my ribs, but despite a lot of discomfort I managed to return as substitute for our next game four days later at Cardiff, when I scored in a 2-2 draw. I remember telling my team-mates not to hug me because of the pain.

After Chelsea, we still had a one game left and it was a big one too, away to Bolton on May 14. They needed to win to pip Nottingham Forest, who had completed their fixtures, into third – then the final automatic promotion spot with no play-offs in those days. We might not have needed a result but we weren't going there just for the ride – 8,000 fans travelled to watch us at Burnden Park in a crowd of 36,954. We didn't want to let down the travelling faithful and we went there to win. They could join us in the First Division with a draw against us and a win against Bristol Rovers the following Tuesday. But we had to go for the win for the sake of other teams around them and for our travelling fans. The game started well for Bolton, and, with a huge home support cheering them on, they threw everything at us. In fact, they battered us, kicking us and tackling as if their lives depended on it. They launched corner after corner and free kick after free kick into our penalty box for big Sam Allardyce, Paul Jones, Neil Whatmore and Alan Gowling, with Peter Reid pulling the strings in midfield.

But somehow we managed to keep the game scoreless until we broke away and got a free kick about 30 yards out. Willie Carr and myself stood over the ball and we decided to work a free kick routine we had talked about for some time. I ran over the ball and ran behind Bolton's defensive wall, Willie dummied to take it, delaying a split second while I carried on my run until I was close to the wall, then he chipped it over their heads and I caught it sweetly on the volley. It worked a treat, and although Bolton keeper Jim McDonagh got a piece of the ball, he couldn't hold on and the force of the shot took it into the net. Bolton's players complained I was offside but the television highlights proved I was onside. From then on, however, Ian Greaves's side hit us with everything but the kitchen sink. It was also getting a bit naughty with some really hefty challenges inflicted on us. Half-time came and in the dressing room more than half of the team had knocks of some sort. Our goalkeeper Gary Pierce injured his leg but he carried on. Suddenly someone shouted 'No f*****g way are they going to beat us lads, so come on – let's keep them down, and if that's how they want to play it, let them do it because we are the champions!' We held all the aces as we were in front, so we stood together. The second half was like the Alamo. They threw the lot at us. Gary Pierce got another heavy blow, this time on his other leg and had to go off which left us down to 10 men as our substitute Bobby Gould had already come on for the injured Frank Munro. 'Gouldy' took the gloves and green jersey and I heard the Bolton bench and players saying 'Put the ball under the crossbar and get it in the box at every opportunity'. We were parked in our own penalty area for long periods but we hung on to win 1-0. Bolton were left having to face another season in the Second Division and Nottingham Forest went up instead. It was the second time in five years we had 'helped' Brian Clough after his team's season was over by beating Leeds 2-1 in May 1972 when his Derby side were sunning themselves in Majorca and Clough was doing the same in the Scilly Isles. I never did get that bottle of champagne from Cloughie! But he responded by telling his players their promotion had nothing to do with us beating Bolton. He said it was his players earning the right to be promoted with their results. He was right but I still think we did them a big favour.

19

England Call-up Dashed By An Enforced Break

We were now preparing for battle back in the First Division, and, as usual, we had a difficult and hard pre-season to ready us for the rigours ahead. We were always a fit team anyway from the way Bill McGarry worked us, and Sammy Chung kept that tradition going. Not many teams were fitter than us, though Aston Villa always looked a fit outfit under Ron Saunders, who was in the same disciplinarian mould as McGarry. A pre-season tour took us to Sweden, where we had been the previous two years and where I enjoyed eight summer trips during my time with Wolves. It is a lovely country and we were well looked after by great people. Given how regularly we toured there in the 1970s, it's no surprise there is a Wolves supporters club there. I've met them many times and they're a great bunch of fans.

The weather was hot when we arrived and we had to take a boat to reach an island to play one particular friendly. It wasn't long since we'd touched down at the airport so we hadn't had much time to rest. We played the game in scorching temperatures and won comfortably. Normally in the dressing room afterwards there is plenty to drink, whether it be water, squash or juice, but on this occasion there was nothing, which was wrong and certainly would never happen today. I always used to sweat a lot during games and I would lose something like seven or eight pounds in weight. As you can imagine, I was rather thirsty and needed to re-hydrate, but we had to board the coach in a hurry to catch the boat back to where we were staying.

I had become big mates with Willie Carr since he joined us over two years previously and we remain close to this day. We would sit together on the coach or wherever we travelled to and chat away. I said to Willie, 'I need something to drink, mate'. Anyway with nothing else to hand, Willie suggested we have a nip out of our duty free we'd bought earlier that day at the airport, which happened to be a bottle of Scotch! We opened it, filled the bottle top with whisky and had a sip, screwed the top back on an put it back in the bag. But it wasn't long before we had another, then another, until we were drinking it from the bottle. Pretty soon we both got legless. At some point we stopped off for a bite to eat, by which time we were the worse for wear. Having staggered off the bus for some fresh air, I was slumped against a lamp post and Willie was trying to hide a few bottles under his jumper that he claimed no one else was having. Back on the coach and now fortified with Dutch courage, I lurched down the aisle at one point and went up to the manager Sammy Chung and demanded a wage rise, even threatening him that a mate of mine who represented England at karate would come after him if he refused to meet my demands. Isn't it strange what the demon drink does to you? None of the other lads challenged me, but it wasn't the brightest thing to do in hindsight and when we woke up the next morning, we were so battered we didn't know where we were.

We slept in bunk beds but I couldn't remember which one of us was on the top one – and we had to get up for a morning training session too. The following day Sammy called all the lads together and we got the biggest b*****king ever. He threatened to send us both home on the next plane, saying we would have been if he had got another two players available. We should have been sent home too, but Sam knew he needed us both for the new season. Had it have been an end-of-season tour we would have definitely been on the first flight home. We apologised to the manager and the boys but I still think they should have had soft drinks for us after the game.

Another time on the tour a few of us were standing in a nightclub enjoying a few drinks minding our own business facing the dance floor when all of a sudden a half pint glass rolled towards us on the floor. Willie Carr looked behind him from where it had come, and, spotting three lads sitting nearby, placed the glass on their table. A few minutes later the same thing happened again, the glass rolling past our feet and Willie picked it up again, and put it on the table. When it happened a third time, Willie picked up the glass and pretended to throw it at the trio. All hell broke loose and Phil Parkes and big Frank Munro waded into the three lads, while Willie and myself pretended to be bringing up the rear! Lofty and Frank were our minders who looked after us when there was any trouble afoot.

We returned from Sweden following a successful tour of three wins and a draw from six friendlies, but my fortunes were about to take another turn for the worse. We played at Brighton in another pre-season game and I broke three ribs going into a tackle. My right elbow was tucked under my body and went into my rib cage. The pain was terrible and I couldn't get my breath. It took me back many years to when I was kid and my mum and dad were play fighting on the carpet and my mum put her knee into my dad's ribs and she broke a couple of them. My dad was in agony and told my mum to get off him, shouting 'You have broke my bleeding ribs' but she didn't believe him and carried on until he pushed her off and lay there in deep pain. He went to the doctors and then had an X-ray which showed he had broken two ribs. They strapped him up by putting a sticky bandage around his rib cage. Nowadays they let them heal on their own. It is not the bones that takes the time to heal, it is the flesh between the ribs, and when you have an injury like that, the last thing you need is a cold because when you cough or sneeze, it's agony.

I made my comeback in my native Yorkshire, in a reserve game at Huddersfield. It always felt good to return to my home county and have a nice pint of Tetley's bitter – one of my favourite northern beers – after the match before we left. Despite the absence of any summer signings for the challenge of the top flight, we had the appetite for the top flight and got off to a good start with back-to-back wins against Bristol City (3-2) and QPR (1-0). Many senior players such as Mike Bailey, Dave Wagstaffe and Bobby Gould had departed while Frank Munro, who had captained us in our promotion-winning season, was in dispute with Sammy Chung and not playing and was soon to join the growing exodus with a transfer to Celtic.

Having reached the FA Youth Cup final in 1976 where the Wolves youngsters were beaten by West Bromwich Albion, Sammy replaced the experienced heads with homegrown talent. Several of these lads had impressed in the reserves such as central defenders Colin Brazier, Bob Hazell and George Berry, left back Maurice Daly (whose introduction initially saw Derek Parkin switch to centre half), midfielders Martin Patching, Jimmy Kelly and John Black, and strikers Norman Bell and Mel Eves, while winger John Farley, who had been bought from Watford for £50,000 in summer 1974 to replace Waggy, was still around. Maurice didn't hang around for long, though. After a breakthrough season which saw him make all of his 32 appearances for the club in 1977-78, he went back to Sweden never to return, having fallen in love with a girl there during our pre-season tour. He was such a calm, composed lad so it wasn't what we thought he would do. I remember we waited for him at the airport to go home, but he stayed on with his new love before returning there later to join IFK Vasteras. I believe he eventually went into coaching there and has built a successful life for himself.

Changes had to be made and the youngsters needed to be given their chance, but it was a bit unfair on those players having to come into a team who were soon struggling after that bright start. We had a few players who weren't getting any younger and as a club we probably should have made changes earlier. The early 70s team was now breaking up and we needed some experienced First Division players. After missing the first five games of the season with broken ribs, I returned for the short trip to The Hawthorns against West Bromwich Albion for our first Black Country derby in four-and-a-half years, as one of three changes with Colin Brazier, myself and Norman Bell replacing the injured trio Derek Parkin, Steve Kindon and John Richards. Big Norm and Steve Daley earned a point for us in a 2-2 draw in the second of five successive Midlands derbies. Those were the days, my friend!

More changes were afoot, though, as Alan Sunderland left at the end of October, joining Arsenal for a club record sale of £240,000, while Steve Kindon rejoined Burnley after asking to be transfer-listed when he was unhappy about having to play in the reserves after being injured, rather than be recalled to the first team. Phil Parkes, our long-serving goalkeeper, played the penultimate game of his Wolves career on September 23, 1977. He eventually joined Vancouver Whitecaps in the North American Soccer League the following March after rescuing a goalkeeping crisis for us at West Ham. Frank Munro returned to Scotland in the December after falling out with Sammy. Big Frank had always wanted to play for Celtic. Paul Bradshaw, a hugely talented goalkeeper from Blackburn Rovers who had been capped by England at Under-21 level, arrived to replace big 'Lofty' in goal, his £150,000 fee smashing our incoming transfer record in the process. Two hundred and forty grand was a lot of money back then, but I don't think 'Sundy' was in any particular hurry to leave. I think the club thought they would use the cash to buy three or four new players, which they did with 'Braddy', striker Billy Rafferty, who arrived for £125,000 from Carlisle in the March followed by Peter Daniel, who became our new record buy at £180,000 the following summer when he signed from Hull City.

Pete was a lovely lad and I got on well with him. His biggest success during his six years at Wolves was the role he played in the 1980 League Cup final, supplying the pass from which Andy Gray scored the only goal but also for the tactical role he played to nullify the threat of John Robertson, the brilliant Nottingham Forest winger, which saw me switched to central midfield. Pete was as fit as a fiddle, quick and sharp and he

103

was one of the best in the club at closing players down. But before he went into a tackle, he would look and see who he was up against and the brakes would go on. I just felt he could have been even better if he had sometimes gone in a little harder. He was a bit of a moaner and used to complain if he got kicked. That counted against him on one occasion where he was genuinely hurt. We played Aston Villa at Molineux in February 1981 when they were going for the League title and he was caught by a challenge from Tony Morley. Pete was helped off but Richie Barker, our assistant manager, ordered him back on to the field, thinking he was crying wolf a bit when he had actually broken his leg and I think had torn his cartilage as well. If someone such as John McAlle or Derek Parkin went down, you knew they were hurt. I always remember 'Scouse' getting seriously injured after coming on as a substitute against Watford in the fifth round of the FA Cup in February 1980. After a purely accidental challenge in midfield, he simply sat up in the centre circle and said 'I've broken my leg' and he had. But Pete was important to us and he did well. He could play in two positions, and after coming to us as a right back, he was soon switched to central midfield, which he made his own. I felt it was too congested for him in middle of the park whereas at right back he could see the whole picture, but his way there was blocked by Geoff Palmer.

With several long-term team-mates on the move, it seemed I might be the next to leave Molineux. Just before Christmas 1977 I read a story in *The Sun* saying the Ipswich Town manager Bobby Robson was looking to strengthen his midfield and I was mentioned, along with Graeme Souness, who was then in his final season at Middlesbrough before a big-money move to Liverpool, and Gerry Daly, who had not long been re-united with his old Manchester United boss Tommy Docherty at Derby.

Being linked with an established high-flying team was flattering. Ipswich went on to win the FA Cup that season and from 1972-82 only finished outside the top six once, finishing runners-up twice. Yet at no time was I looking to leave Wolves. I had been told after we played them by one or two of their players that they wanted to sign me. But the Ipswich link reminded me of a time a few years earlier when Bill McGarry was our manager. He called me into his changing room one Friday after training to tell me he had accepted a £100,000 offer from an un-named club for me and asked me if I wanted to go. It stunned me at first so I asked him who this club was, but he wouldn't tell me. Coming right out of the blue and particularly on a Friday – before we set off for a game at Ipswich – it left me in a daze. I left his room with no idea who the bidders were, but I wasn't happy thinking he wanted to sell me. We travelled that afternoon to Ipswich and it played on my mind all that night, so I didn't sleep a wink thinking about it. McGarry had told me not say anything to anybody and concentrate on the game, but I thought 'You must be joking – concentrate? You have put so much on my mind I can't think about the game'. The next day my mind was full of anything but the match and I was so annoyed with the manager for telling me when he did. We walked out for the warm-up I and couldn't help but to look up at the directors' box to see who was there. I spotted the Birmingham City manager Freddie Goodwin with his chairman and there was no one else I knew, so I wondered if it was Birmingham who were interested. I had a nightmare of a performance and never heard anything more about it. Whoever it was, I don't blame them for not following up their interest as I wouldn't have bought me after that performance. I blamed McGarry for it – or was he being cute and knowing that by telling me the day before the game, it would put me off as he knew I was such a worrier before games? Or was the chairman behind selling me? It was a big fee at the time but I never found out if the interest was from Blues. I knew Ipswich were interested because of what their players had told me. In fact they were looking for a house for me so it must have been close to happening, but the first concrete evidence of their interest was when I saw it in the paper.

Off the field, my preparation was disrupted by an outbreak of mumps in the family. Kelly and Rod both caught it and ended up passing it on to Jane. The illness can affect adults much more than children and Jane was left feeling really rough. Any thoughts that I could share the domestic load were swiftly put out of our heads after I was ordered by the club to stay in a hotel to avoid catching it as it was feared I may then have passed it on to my team-mates. So not for the first time, Jane's mum came to the rescue and I was holed up in a hotel for a few days. Jane remembers me picking up Kelly at the front door when I wasn't allowed in to my own home!

Our bright start had faded alarmingly, and by the time we had lost 4-0 at Bill McGarry's Newcastle on December 17 for our third straight defeat, we had won only three times in our last 18 League games. One day Sammy Chung took us to Wolverhampton races for a change of scenery to 'gee' – if you'll pardon the pun – the lads up. Some of us weren't too interested in the horses, but JR liked a flutter – nothing big but he enjoyed that. As for me, it was the first time I had been to a race meeting, and although I enjoyed the day out, it wasn't for me. At one point I looked up at one of the jockeys and a guy shouted to him to 'come on' and he put his thumbs up. I thought 'Hey up, he is going to win this race' and I nearly backed him, but being a Yorkshireman I thought the money was better staying in my pocket than the bookies' – but the bugger won and I lost out! The trip to the races had the desired effect, though, as our form picked up, with four wins and two draws in eight in all competitions. I scored what turned out to be my only brace of the season in an emphatic 3-1 win at home to second-placed Everton on January 21 when Steve Daley put me through twice at a snow-covered Molineux and scored the other himself.

We had made early progress in the FA Cup with a 3-1 win at home to Exeter City, when I also got on the scoresheet, in a replay. Our reward was a fourth round trip to Arsenal. It was a bloody tough draw but Highbury was always a good place to play with its proud history and it felt great playing at the home of a big London club. But before we could face them in the Cup we had to play them in the League two weeks before. We lost 3-1 so we thought the Cup tie was time for us to get our own back. We didn't manage that but it was memorable to me for scoring one of my all-time favourite goals for Wolves. We were losing 1-0 when I called for the ball. Seeing the great Pat Jennings off his line, I transferred the ball on to my left foot about 25 yards out and chipped it over his head to equalise. Now to do that against one of the finest keepers ever gave me as much satisfaction, if not more, than all the goals I scored for Wolves, apart from the one in the League Cup final.

We were playing well enough to earn a replay but a crazy incident sparked the end of our Cup run. Arsenal won a last-minute corner and our defender Bob Hazell held on to the ball as Derek Parkin was off the pitch injured. In the ensuring melee, Bob threw a punch at their midfielder Graham Rix and the referee Clive Thomas sent him off. From the resulting corner and with five seconds left, Arsenal striker Malcolm Macdonald headed home and we were out of the Cup. It was a really sickening blow. When the final whistle went just after the restart Willie Carr and myself were cautioned for dissent as Thomas was surrounded by all of the Wolves players. It was no consolation that our old mate Alan Sunderland was on the winning side that day and the Gunners went all the way to the final, where they lost 1-0 to Ipswich. But if I thought our luck was out that day at Highbury, then much worse was to come from a personal point of view on March 4 at Molineux. We were losing 3-2 to Norwich in a game that featured the debut of our new striker Billy Rafferty when the ball was pulled back to me inside the six-yard box. As I fired home the equaliser, their left back Colin Sullivan tried to block the shot and caught me on the ankle. Going down in pain, I just managed to see the ball enter the Norwich net but I couldn't celebrate as I was lying on the ground. Steve Daley, who had scored our other two goals that day, came running up to congratulate me – or so I thought – but he shouted 'Get up – you're only milking your goal'. I told him to piss off, saying 'My ankle is done' before he again told me to get up. The trainer came on and I limped off behind the goal for some treatment before attempting to go back on just to shut Daley up, but I collapsed and had to go off.

We drew 3-3 and that night I was told I had been picked for the England B squad for a tour in May. So when an X-ray the following Monday morning showed a clear crack across the bottom of the ankle and I would miss the chance to pull on the Three Lions shirt, I felt sick. That call-up was the closest I got to playing for the full England team, and my chance had gone. In the event, my team-mates Steve Daley, John Richards and Mel Eves went on the five-match tour to the Far East with games against the full national teams of Malaysia, New Zealand and Singapore. I was delighted for them, but devastated I couldn't join them. I ended up missing the final 13 games of the season and finished the campaign with six goals from 23 League appearances, my lowest total of games since becoming a regular in the team in 1970. In fact it equalled the lowest appearance total I made in a season at Wolves since establishing myself in the side, although in 1983-84 four of my appearances were as a substitute.

Being injured, and initially with my right foot in plaster, I couldn't even drive to start with and I was stuck at home for long periods. If I did go out, I had to be chauffeured by Jane or cadge a lift from someone. So apart from seeing the physio, I stayed away from the club on a match day for about the first month. I don't mind admitting I was a bit of an arsehole to be around. I tried not to let the kids see it but for someone who felt he was cheating by having a day off from training, it was the most frustrating time of my career, not being able to do what I was being paid for. I couldn't wait to get fit and start playing again, but there was a long road and plenty of hard work before that happened.

20

Sammy Out, Barney In

In May 1978 there was a lot of speculation in the press that Manchester City were interested in me. I knew Newcastle were also interested because their manager was our old gaffer Bill McGarry. He wanted to pair me up with our kid Terry, who had returned to Tyneside for a second spell after leaving Birmingham that summer following a three-year stint at St. Andrew's. So if Wolves were going to make changes and I was one they were looking to move on, I hoped clubs would be interested. Let me say straight away I had no desire to leave Wolves. I loved the club and the fans, who were very supportive of me during the bad times as well as the good. Fans have their favourites and others they don't like much and I was no different, but I wanted to stay, and, as it turned out, the manager Sammy Chung wanted me in his plans. I was very happy with that as Jane was a local girl and my children Roddy and Kelly were settled in the area.

After the disappointment of breaking my ankle and missing out on the England B tour it was a hard summer for me. Instead of being able to relax like most close seasons, the plaster came off after about six weeks then it was down to hard work to build up my stamina with long runs three times a week and lifting weights to strengthen my upper body. My golf suffered a bit but the priority was to be ready for the start of pre-season training in July.

I achieved my aim and got back into the team for the start of the season. But despite my best efforts, we got off to a poor start, losing our first three games without scoring, against Aston Villa, Chelsea and Leeds. In fact we lost six of our first seven, with only a 2-0 win at home to Bristol City, when I scored, to interrupt the run of defeats. But after the next match, a 3-2 defeat at Southampton on September 9, the manager Sammy Chung axed me from the team. I wasn't the only player out of form and I wasn't very happy about it, and told Sammy so. This wasn't the first spat I had with him. He gave me a b******g for not reporting for training one morning after my daughter Kelly, who was two years and nine months old at the time, was rushed into hospital with severe appendix problems and had to be operated on immediately. My wife and I were really worried because it was quite rare in a child so young and we shed a few tears as they wheeled her down to the theatre. Fortunately the surgeon said he had just caught it in time before the appendix perforated which could have been disastrous in someone so young. I let rip at Sammy because he inferred training was more important than my child. Later when we had calmed down and Kelly was out of trouble the next day, we had a chat and Sammy apologised profusely. Being left out of the team really hurt me and I went to ask if I was still in his plans because if not, it would be best for both parties if I moved on. He said he still wanted me but he had to do something as the results were poor. I said 'I understand that Sam, but we as a team are playing poorly. I'm your captain and I want to be out there trying to put it right, not sat on my backside in the stand'. I accepted what he had done but it still hurt me badly as this was the first time I'd been dropped. I'd been rested when I was younger under Bill McGarry but being axed acted as a kick up the backside.

By the start of November we had lost nine out of our first 12 League games and been dumped out of the League Cup by Fourth Division Reading. After dropping me, it was now Sammy who was under threat of the axe. The inevitable happened just eight days into the new month when he was sacked after yet another defeat, 4-1 at Derby. Sammy's dismissal came 18 months after he'd taken us back to Division One at the first time of asking with the same group of players. I really felt for Sam, who worked very hard to bring in new blood. But I don't think he was helped much financially to bring in the players we needed to go forward. It seemed the club had come to a halt. Just four and a half years on from winning the League Cup in 1974 and playing in Europe, here we were struggling at the wrong end of the table and playing very poorly. Results are all important in football, and any manager losing more games than he's winning will be in trouble and Sammy paid the price. It was sad to see him lose his job, though, because he was a great guy and the players loved his training methods. We enjoyed some great ball work in the afternoons, which followed on from when the players used to ask him to come back and do similar stuff all the time when he was coach to Bill McGarry.

Now we were looking for a new manager, but in the meantime Brian Garvey took over on a temporary basis. Brian had previously run the successful youth team when players such as Geoff Palmer, Steve Daley and Alan Sunderland were coming through the ranks. He had his own way of working but the players tried to help him as much as they could. He decided to do something new – a 10-minute warm-up before the game, but it didn't work as we got battered 4-0 at home to Villa in his first match in charge. Heads were down and we started to wonder where our next win was coming from. I was still settled though. The disappointment of Sammy leaving me out just spurred me on and I wanted to be part of the team that helped us stay up. We then got a good 1-1 draw at home to Leeds on November 18 when Peter Daniel scored to become our three-goal top scorer – from 15 games, which tells its own story.

John Barnwell was watching from the stands that day and within a couple of days he was unveiled as our new manager. I knew he'd been a good midfield player with Arsenal and Nottingham Forest and liked to pass the ball around. He'd carved out a good reputation at Peterborough, where as assistant to Noel Cantwell he had helped Posh to promotion to the Third Division, then in sole charge had narrowly missed out on promotion to the Second in his only season in charge in 1977-78. I thought it was a great appointment. He could help me and the other midfield players to improve. But first we had to win him over. It's always the same when a new manager comes in, you always think 'Will he like me?' or 'Will he want to get rid of me?' So it was a case of knuckling down and just hoping I was in his plans.

As soon as he came in, the dressing room felt different. He spelt out what he expected and told us if anyone didn't fancy the challenge ahead they could leave. He was very firm and assertive and everyone knew he meant business. The club needed a kick up the backside and he was here to do it. A big shake-up was coming and quickly. 'Barney' brought a spark back to the club. His enthusiasm was second to none and I had a feeling I might like this guy. He was straight and honest and we all knew he meant every word he said.

His first game in charge was away to Bristol City; not an easy one as they were sitting comfortably in mid-table and we were second from bottom. But the new manager worked with us the day before the game on how to close the opposition down together as a unit – not one at a time. He reasoned that would improve results and bring back the confidence a lot of players had lost. We won 1-0 with a goal from Steve Daley. It was the hardest-working 90 minutes we'd put in all season; a great team effort and it helped restore our belief. We had a great trip back from Bristol and we got to know our new boss a bit better. Well, Willie Carr and myself did. Barney plonked himself in front of us on the coach and all the way back he never stopped telling us stories. We couldn't get a word in and you sensed he was very much relishing managing our great club. He got off to a great start and we were all now looking forward to games again. Four days later we were at Tottenham and this was going to be a bigger test as they were eighth in the table. But we were confident of getting something from the game and the new manager named an unchanged team. He'd transformed the feeling so much around the club in such a short time and the atmosphere was building. Unfortunately we didn't get the result we deserved at White Hart Lane, losing 1-0. But we were unlucky as we lost goalkeeper Paul Bradshaw with a broken finger sustained saving a penalty after 35 minutes.

With only one substitute, we didn't have a keeper to replace 'Bradders', so yours truly went in goal. It was the first time I'd been between the sticks since I played for Bradford Park Avenue against Stockport County in that FA Youth Cup tie. But I always fancied playing in goal; all that shooting, diving and catching in front of my house with our kid was about to pay off. The previous occasion we lost our keeper – when Gary Pierce was injured at Bolton in 1976-77 – substitute Bobby Gould went in goal. This time I just put the green jersey on, grabbed the gloves and off we went. In those remaining 55 minutes I made one fisted clearance, dealt with a back pass and contended with the usual goal kicks. But the defence protected me very well and we had a lot of the ball, which helped. I do remember Spurs winger Peter Taylor racing through from halfway with only me to beat. As he came towards me I ran out knowing that was just what he wanted me to do so he could chip me. But just as he went to lift the ball over my head, I back-pedalled and managed to collect the ball quite comfortably. I looked at him and pointed to the side of my head as if to say 'Read you like a book, son!' We had a laugh about that after the game, but we weren't happy as we didn't deserve to lose. That was the last time I played in goal but I kept a second clean sheet, so I have a 100 per cent record of never conceding!

With the FA Cup sadly out of reach after we lost 2-0 to Arsenal in the semi-finals – more about that in the next chapter – we had to put that bitter blow behind us quickly as we faced nine games in April to climb away from the drop zone. It was all hands on deck and our concentration had to be spot on because the games after the semi-final were some of the most important since we were relegated three years earlier. Our heads were down slightly after Arsenal but the manager picked us up and we were ready for the fight. It was just as well too as we returned to action just three days later at home to

Tottenham. It was a really big game and a good test of our character. It turned out to be a very tight and tough encounter, and it was delicately poised at 2-2 as we approached the final minutes on another heavy muddy pitch. John Richards and Steve Daley had scored our goals and a point looked the most likely outcome.

We were tiring, but with seconds to go the ball broke to me on the right of the penalty area and I only had to beat Mark Kendall. Having played in 19 of their previous 20 games, he was having an extended run in the Spurs side almost a decade before he starred regularly for Wolves. I can see him now like it was yesterday, coming out to close the angle down. I rolled the ball just wide of him towards the far post and there was just enough pace on it to take it into the corner of the net. It was a fantastic feeling and I ran round behind the goal to celebrate with the North Bank. The fans were ecstatic and we closed the game out to win 3-2. It was a great win, especially so soon after the semi-final defeat. Those two points – three points for a win didn't arrive until 1981-82 – gave us all a boost for the rest of the season. But four days later we lost 3-1 at Manchester City. I found the net again but it wasn't enough and another defeat, this time 1-0 at home to champions-elect Liverpool three days later on April 18, left us feeling like we were back to square one again, deep in trouble.

Worse was to follow but this time football was put firmly into perspective. On April 23, 1979, the day before our home game against Derby, John Barnwell suffered a horrific car crash which nearly cost him his life. He suffered a fractured skull and it was touch and go for a while whether he would survive. We missed him being around but his assistant Richie Barker held the fort admirably in his absence and was instrumental in our successful fight against relegation.

By the end of the month, we'd been on a six-match unbeaten run and won four and drawn three of those nine games in April, which were all played on heavy grounds. I don't think such a schedule would be allowed now but we got on with it and we were on our way to staying up. Boosted by what turned out to be Steve Daley's final goal at Molineux, we won the Derby game, which was televised, 4-0 before beating the reigning champions Nottingham Forest 1-0 as they closed in on their first European Cup success. But it was a 1-1 draw at home to Bolton in between those two matches which sealed our safety with three games to spare, to provide our absent gaffer with some tonic. QPR joined already relegated Birmingham City and Chelsea in going down. With safety assured, we finished the campaign with defeats against Coventry and Manchester United, when John Richards scored his ninth goal in 17 games since returning from a potentially career-ending knee injury. There's no doubt JR had a huge impact in helping us stay up. But we needed more quality like that. Now the new management team would have to start working on improving the team for the following season. Changes had to be made so we were all hoping we would remain part of the manager's plans.

21

Cup Heartache

With Richie Barker joining as John Barnwell's assistant, we had our own version of the Brian Clough-Peter Taylor management team and I wanted to be part of it, hopefully for many years to come. It was looking promising but first we had to escape relegation. Results started to improve and we had a great FA Cup run, with hopes high that we could banish memories of Leeds in 1973 and get to Wembley.

After beating Brighton away 3-2 in the third round we were rewarded with another long trip in the fourth round – to St James Park, Newcastle and another encounter with our Terry. I have described that game and the 1-1 draw in greater detail in an earlier chapter. Because of snow the replay was postponed 10 times and we had to wait almost a month – to February 22 – for the game. But it was worth it as we won with our striker Norman Bell scoring the only goal. Conditions were heavy again but we just about deserved the win. In the fifth round we had to play away at another Second Division side, Crystal Palace. It was another tough draw and it was going to be a hard battle for me as I was directly up against Kenny Sansom, who was about to become England's regular left back for the next nine years. He was one of the best left backs I had ever played against, and never stopped getting forward as I spent most of the game chasing him. He was a bloody fit guy as well, and we were fortunate to come away with a 1-0 win thanks to a Martin Patching goal in a very hard-fought tie. The game saw Bell break his leg against Terry Venables's team who ended up winning the title a couple of months later.

We were now into the sixth round and this time the draw appeared to be kinder to us as we were paired at home to Third Division Shrewsbury Town. It was like a derby as they were just down the A5. Swelled by some 14,000 visiting fans from Shropshire, there was a crowd of 40,946 to watch us do battle in the Molineux mud. Graham Turner's side played really well and took us back to Gay Meadow for a replay after a 1-1 draw. Billy Rafferty scored our goal and Ian Atkins netted theirs from the penalty spot, but they deserved a draw. The replay was tough again as Shrewsbury played their hearts out, but we had enough quality to get through and won 3-1. Rafferty was againon the scoresheet along with Willie Carr and a Peter Daniel penalty. We now had a semi-final to look forward to against Arsenal at Villa Park. Arsenal had our former player Alan Sunderland in their line-up having joined them from us 16 months earlier. He was a terrific player – quick, good in the air and versatile. Although he made his name first as a midfielder then a striker, he even played at right back a few times and enjoyed a good spell in that role for us in 1975-76. He came on in that position in an England Under-23 match with Scotland in 1974. He then won an Under-21 cap as a striker in England's first ever game in that age group – a 0-0 draw with Wales at Molineux in 1976. Sundy is one of only five players to be capped for England at both Under-23 and Under-21. Wolves' own JR, QPR's Phil Parkes, Joe Corrigan of Manchester City and the late, great Ray Wilkins of Chelsea and Manchester United were the others. Ray qualified by age at both levels but the other four were over-age players when they played for the Under-21s.

I had a lot of time for Alan. He loved a laugh and was a big mate of Steve Daley, who, like Alan, was another Yorkshireman who came through the ranks. When they were together it was fun all the way. I remember advertising Levi jeans with my wife Jane and Alan and his then wife Christine. We had such a laugh trying on all this gear, it took hours to get it right. Alan looked like the comedian Dick Emery, and when Alan started laughing he used to cry a bit, like Steve did. My wife had to sit down because the jeans she was wearing didn't fit at all. We eventually got the advert done but it was hilarious.

We really fancied our chances and were looking forward to our fans seeing us play at Wembley in an FA Cup final after the disappointment at the same stage against Leeds in 1973. We were all up for it, the build-up was good and our preparation couldn't have been better. Confidence was also high as we'd won 1-0 at Arsenal in the League back in February with a goal from John Richards on his comeback from a long-term knee injury, so we knew we could beat them. But for some reason the game just passed us by, we didn't perform at all well and we lost 2-0.

All the lads were gutted and our dressing room wasn't a good place to be afterwards. We were really pissed off with the way we performed and a few tears were shed. I was very proud to have led the team out as captain and had dreams of lifting the Cup, but after that performance I started to wonder if that was my last chance to get to another final. Looking back now I think the number of matches we'd played showed in our

115

performance. Back then we never made excuses about a fixture pile-up, but it was our eighth game in 29 days and I think it played a part in our poor display. We were often playing on thick mud every week, not like now where they play on good pitches all season. I'm very envious of them and would love to have had the same facilities. To make matters worse, Alan scored one of the goals. We missed him when he left Wolves. Our loss was certainly Arsenal's gain, and a few weeks later he scored one of the most famous and dramatic Cup final winners when they beat Manchester United 3-2 at Wembley. Alan continued to enjoy a fine career which also included one full England cap (he came on as sub against Australia in Sydney in 1980) and seven B caps.

22

Handy Andy And League Cup Glory Again

There was a feeling that things could really take off with the changes John Barnwell wanted to make. The manager, now fully recovered from his car crash, knew we needed to bring in players of quality but also knew it was going to cost a lot of money. Where that money was coming from only he and the board knew. We were building a new stand at a cost of £2.5m – a huge sum in those days – on the Molineux Street side of the ground which was supposed to be the first phase of a highly ambitious project to completely rebuild the stadium. The chairman Harry Marshall had been working on this for some time as the ground had been in decline. But there was a feeling we needed to re-establish ourselves as a First Division team again after just two seasons back in the top flight and having just avoided relegation. It was a team that needed investment because we weren't good enough to push for honours without it. But they ploughed on with the development. Because the ground had been so cramped and the fans so close to the pitch, the club had purchased 70-odd houses in Molineux Street and demolished them to make way for the new development, with the pitch moved towards it. But with the new stand still some 40 yards from the touchline, the ground was now lop-sided, and the atmosphere at Molineux, which had always been fantastic, was lost. Teams used to dread coming to us and back in the early 1970s it was regarded as a fortress. So the question was, 'Did we need a costly new stand before we invested seriously in the team?'

I felt our home form was in danger of suffering and I voiced my concerns to the manager. Early on, I struggled so much with my bearings on the re-aligned pitch that I was actually running out of play when I pulled wide for a pass; I just couldn't get used to it and this went on for some time. Also, the atmosphere disappeared very quickly because the once-tight ground was now so open. I said to the boss 'Playing on here the way it is will see us drop a lot of points at home'. Barnwell replied 'Don't say that – it could be costly at the end of the season'. 'I know,' I said. I remember talking with Ray Wilkins, who by then was playing for Manchester United but guested for Wolves in John Richards's testimonial against Moscow Dynamo in March 1982. He'd played for

Chelsea at our ground before the new stand was built and said 'Kenny, I get the feeling this place is a fortress no more. We used to hate coming here because we thought we wouldn't get a result, but now that feeling has gone and we are more confident now'. That was from a great player who had played at Molineux on several occasions. I believe the pitch should have been moved right up to the new stand and another new stand built on the Waterloo Road side before redeveloping behind each goal because the North and South Bank terraces needed updating as well. But the money wasn't there. We struggled to win many home games because the atmosphere wasn't the same. That's not an excuse for poor performances, but, deep down, I knew it was going to cost us points.

Initially, the team rose to new heights, just like the newly completed stand suddenly dominating the Molineux skyline. There is an old saying in football that managers like to make their first signing a statement of intent. Well John Barnwell certainly did that in June 1979. At just £90,000, he pulled off a great piece of business to bring in the Liverpool captain and England international Emlyn Hughes. I lost the team captaincy to him but that was fine. He was a top player and a leader on the pitch. Playing at the back, he could see what was happening in front of him and could change things if needed to. I was proud and honoured to have captained Wolves, but the decision to relieve me of the captaincy also gave me the freedom to concentrate on my own game.

With the arrival of Emlyn and the new stand, there was a real buzz around the club and the town. But even bigger events were about to happen which would see Wolves remain in the national headlines. To implement the changes he wanted, Barnwell had to sell one of our best players. There had been plenty of speculation surrounding Steve Daley for a while, but it still came as a shock to find out we were selling him to Manchester City. Less than two years before we had sold Alan Sunderland for a club record £240,000 to Arsenal and now we were selling another class player who had come through the ranks. Steve was sold for a then British record fee of around £1.44m, although Steve will tell you it was more! City manager Malcolm Allison's vision was to build a young side around Steve, who by then was 26 and coming into his prime. I don't blame Allison for buying him – I would have done the same. But it all seemed to happen so quickly and I was very disappointed and surprised, not just at losing a great player but a mate as well. I'd known Steve since he was an apprentice and together with another fine player, Willie Carr, it was the best midfield I'd played in since Mike

Bailey left. I knew City wanted Steve because they had showed an interest in me as well at the time before going all out for Steve. I don't blame Steve for going. He thought he was joining a better club and the chance to make a bob or two. Personally I never looked on Man City being a better club than Wolves and still don't. Anyway Steve signed for them on September 5, 1979 but within three days we trumped that by splashing out on one of the best strikers in British football at the time – Andy Gray from Aston Villa for £1,469,000, just a few thousand pounds more than Steve cost. It was amazing – in the space of three days we had sold the most expensive player and bought the most expensive player in Britain. Wow! It was all happening at Molineux. We were even given club cars – maroon Ford Cortinas with vinyl roofs, which were considered quite stylish at the time – for about twenty quid a month. Willie Carr was the only player not to have the saloon version – he opted for an estate. He'd got three kids by then and a fourth one was soon on the way. It was the first time we had been given cars by the club since we won the League Cup in 1974, when we had gold coloured Volkswagen Beetles for a fiver a month. I opted not to have one though because I couldn't fit my golf clubs in the boot!

It would have been good if we could have kept Steve and still brought in Andy. But Barnwell had to sell to get the money to change things. Andy's medical showed a problem with his knee and the chairman Harry Marshall didn't want the deal to go through but the manager dug his heels in, threatening to resign if he didn't sign. In the end it was a good piece of management and a great signing because we needed someone such as Andy to give us a spark and lift the club again. He certainly did. The likes of Munro, Bailey, McCalliog, Dougan and Wagstaffe were the backbone of our team in the early 1970s but they were never effectively replaced. We were desperate for an injection of new blood. Now we had captured a fine player who was a real winner, a goalscorer of the highest quality to help John Richards up front, and it got the whole club buzzing again. Andy was infectious too. When he walked in you just felt he wanted to win something and he was confident he could do that with us. Barney loved footballers and players with a good football brain and on away trips, he would walk down the coach and sit in the seat in front of Willie and I and talk football. Barney was the only manager I played for who discussed transfers with players and how he wanted to improve the team, and he revealed he wanted to bring in the Everton winger Dave Thomas, the ex-QPR and England international. He got his man for £350,000. Dave looked another terrific signing – he was surely the one to finally replace Waggy and supply the crosses for Gray and Richards. Things were taking shape, the new players had given everybody a huge lift, the dressing room was a happy place again and we were all looking forward to the games. I felt we could do really well and put some silverware on the mantelpiece again as long as we had that bit of luck and no serious injuries to key players. Another player Barney told me he was trying to sign around this time was Peter Reid. He was a good lad, a great character, and an excellent footballer who would have been a fantastic signing for us. But after protracted negotiations over several months, the deal fell through, and it would be two more years before he moved on, to Everton, where he helped them to so much success.

Sadly, Dave Thomas didn't have that luck – but it had nothing to do with injuries. Dave started well but unfortunately he had a massive fall-out with our coach Richie Barker. Our assistant boss told Dave to wear shinpads, pull his socks over them and wear studs, not rubber moulded boots. Dave famously always played with his socks around his ankles and wore rubber studs whatever the weather. Anyway, he told Richie he'd never had any problems in the past, saying: 'I've played for my country, and been successful at big clubs and you're telling me I have to change. B*****ks, there's no way I'm going to do that for you or anyone else!' The manager tried to solve the problem but to no avail and that was the beginning of the end for Dave at Wolves. It was a shame because he was a great lad and a superb player who could have done us a great job for us. I thought Richie Barker went over the top and was out of order; we'd signed a top player and he should have been left to wear what he felt comfortable with. I think I would have reared up if someone told me what to wear. After playing just 10 League games for us, Dave had now completely fallen out with the club and was told to train with the kids and play in the reserves. He did what was asked of him, but it was a shame and sad the situation was never put right by the time Dave moved on to Vancouver Whitecaps at the end of the season.

Talking of celebrating, we had another major success that season. The League Cup campaign was soon upon us, and with the excitement of the new signings and the eagerness to put the FA Cup semi-final defeat behind us, we really wanted to do well in this competition again. We felt there was no reason not to have another good cup run. But boy did we have to work hard for it! In all we played 11 games, with the third-round win at QPR and the final the only times we didn't play a team twice or more. Burnley was the first hurdle in the second round, which in those days was over two legs. Up against our old team-mate Steve Kindon, we drew 1-1 at Turf Moor and then won 2-0 at Molineux. Right back Geoff Palmer didn't score many but he netted in both legs against a team he later joined in between his two spells at Wolves. I got our other goal. Our reward was a trip to Crystal Palace, who were living up to their 'Team of the Eighties' billing at the time by setting the early pace at the top of the First Division after promotion. But again I was fortunate to score along with Mel Eves as we triumphed 2-1.

Fuelled by the arrival of Andy Gray and his burgeoning partnership with John Richards, this was a boom time for the club. Victory at Selhurst Park made it four straight wins after 3-2 successes at both Everton (Andy's debut) and Arsenal, sandwiching a 3-1 beating of Manchester United in front of a Molineux crowd of almost 36,000. Andy scored four times in those three League games. After we had overcome Palace the draw brought us another trip to the capital, this time away to QPR. Rangers were in the Second Division at the time but this proved to be a really tough game. We were 1-0 down with only seconds remaining after our recent team-mate Bob Hazell, who joined them for £100,000 at the start of the season, kept our strikers quiet and played very well. Almost at the death we had a throw-in. The ball reached Wayne Clarke, I ran behind him, Wayne backheeled it into my path and I hit it as hard I could with my left foot. It ripped into the net and was enough to earn us a replay. A week later we were through to the fifth round after Willie Carr scored the only goal at Molineux.

Grimsby Town were our next opponents and we were well happy with that draw. They were a Third Division side and we all thought we only had to turn up to reach the semi-final, but what a shock we got. They had done terrifically well to get to that stage, beating Everton along the way, and they held us to a 0-0 draw at Blundell Park, then 1-1 in the replay to force extra-time at Molineux, Andy Gray scoring for us. In those days ties went to a second replay instead of a penalty shootout, so we had to meet again, this time at the neutral ground of Derby County. The notorious Baseball Ground pitch in the middle of December proved a great leveller. Perhaps not surprisingly, we were a bit apprehensive, but fortunately we scraped through 2-0. We were 1-0 up through John Richards when we were awarded a penalty. I was so nervous about taking it because the mud was horrendous and the footing around the spot was awful. I knew how important it was to score because a two-goal cushion at that stage would have left no way back for Grimsby. I stood over the ball and my backside was twitching. I had never felt like that before taking a penalty. Thankfully it went in it and I was so relieved.

That put us through to the semi-finals where we were paired with another Third Division side in Swindon Town. It was the one we wanted as the holders Nottingham Forest had been drawn against champions Liverpool in the other semi, and we knew we had a great chance of reaching another League Cup final. The first leg at the County Ground was a lot tougher than we probably expected and they deserved their 2-1 victory in front of 26,000. Peter Daniel's goal for us turned out to be crucial to take back to Molineux. The second leg was just as tight and Swindon again played fantastically well and made us really work hard. Fortunately for us, John Richards was on top form and he scored twice in a 3-1 win, taking his chances superbly.

Powerful and as brave as a lion, John was lethal in the penalty box. I don't think many centre halves liked playing against him because he could handle himself as well. I remember him being sent off for hitting someone in retaliation when we played away to Portuguese side Belenenses in the UEFA Cup in 1973-74 and he gave Mike Doyle of Manchester City a right hook in the League Cup final that same season. Had it happened today, the FA would have punished him severely on video evidence. He was one of the best strikers I was lucky enough to play with and should have had more than the one full England cap he earned. Even then he was played out on the wing and I felt he wasn't treated with the respect he deserved from Sir Alf Ramsey. John played a major part in our success and was still producing the goods in the early 1980s. Mel Eves grabbed the second goal after his cross-cum-shot hit a defender's foot and looped inside the far post.

The final whistle was the cue for the vast majority of the 41,031 Molineux crowd to go wild. John Richards and myself were carried off the pitch by jubilant fans as thousands invaded the pitch. Willie Carr was in tears after reaching his first Wembley final and captain Emlyn Hughes was relishing his second League Cup final after being in the Liverpool side who lost to Nottingham Forest in a replay in 1978. The champagne was flowing in the dressing room afterwards and myself and the rest of the lads had a few drinks that night, I can tell you. Amid the celebrations afterwards we had a pleasant surprise when the great Eusebio walked into our dressing room. Our manager John

Barnwell must have had some contact with Benfica, who the Portuguese player had played for, and invited him over as a guest. He only spoke a little English, so there wasn't really a conversation, but he said enough to congratulate us and he shook hands with the lads. He was a bit of a hero of mine after watching him on television play for Portugal in the 1966 World Cup and for Benfica in the 1968 European Cup final against Manchester United. Some of the lads and I were determined to get a photograph taken with him, which we managed to do.

As for the celebrations, I think I needed the alcohol to dull the pain as I'd played on after tweaking my ankle ligaments after just five minutes of the game. But with a final to look forward to, I was determined to be fully fit for it, and, with four goals in the cup run, I was looking to score again at Wembley in the final against Nottingham Forest on March 15. Myself, John Richards and Gary Birtles of Forest were looking to become the first players to score in two League Cup finals, so there was that extra incentive.

Understandably with so much excitement and after six years without Wolves being in a Wembley final, there was a big build-up to the game. Along with the usual round of media duties, the players were also booked in for what had become a popular diversion for the cup final teams at the time – the recording of a song. For us that meant a trip out to the Old Smithy Studios in Worcester to record 'Wonderful Wolves', a single that had been written for us to sing along to. From what I can remember, the recording wasn't going too well so the producer decided to get among us to listen to who was singing well and who wasn't. He said 'If I put my hand on your shoulder, stop singing' and as he came round to where I was standing, John Richards and myself got the hook and were asked to button it. After we stopped singing, the producer said 'That's it – we've got it.' I'm pretty sure it was only us two – the two goalscorers in the final the last time Wolves had won the League Cup, in 1974 – who failed to make the cut. So for anyone who has a copy of the single, you didn't get to hear the 'dulcet' tones of John and myself!

Two weeks after the second leg of the semi-final, there was more evidence of us being in the big time when Emlyn was the subject of ITV's *'This Is Your Life'* at the end of our home game against Liverpool, which we won 1-0 courtesy of a John Richards special – our third successive League win and all without conceding. The show was recorded at our gym, hastily converted into a television studio. It was above the social

123

club next to the ground on Waterloo Road and we made our way to it after the game. Emlyn, who was the third Wolves player to be featured on the programme after Billy Wright and Derek Dougan, was a winner, a great captain and a top player. He was popular in his time at Wolves, but I don't think that was always the case at Liverpool and two or three of their players stayed on the coach rather than support him on his big night. On the short walk to the makeshift studio, I got chatting to Bill Shankly, the legendary Liverpool manager who was by then retired but had travelled down from Merseyside for the event. I asked him why when you played Liverpool, it seemed as if they had more players on the pitch than the opposition. He replied 'Son, all of my players are comfortable on the ball'. Whether or not I'd have excelled in their company I don't know, but Bob Paisley, who succeeded Shanks, once said I was one of the best strikers of a ball around and I always remembered that.

For the second time approaching a final, I was injured in the build-up after suffering a thigh strain a week beforehand. Rested for a 3-1 win at Aston Villa on the Monday night before the final along with John Richards, Mel Eves and the suspended Andy Gray, I stayed behind at Molineux for extra work with the physio while the rest of the players trained at Lilleshall. The sessions I was put through were rigorous but had to be done if I was to prove I was capable of lasting 90 minutes at Wembley. Fortunately I was passed fit and I was in the team for the final. I couldn't wait for the day to come.

Forest were about to successfully defend their crown as European champions and were red-hot favourites to make it three League Cups in a row after toppling Liverpool in the semi-final. We had plenty of experience in our team with Emlyn, Derek Parkin, myself, Willie Carr, Andy Gray and John Richards but were still massive underdogs against a team packed with internationals such as Peter Shilton, Viv Anderson, Kenny Burns, Frank Gray, Trevor Francis, Gary Birtles and John Robertson, as well as that unsung hero, John McGovern. And if we had to come up with a plan to even things up, then our success in the final was partly down to a tactical masterstroke that John Barnwell and Richie Barker agonised over beforehand. In an effort to nullify the impact of Robertson, one of Forest's most dangerous players, they decided myself and Peter Daniel would switch positions, which meant I moved inside to centre midfield and Pete switched to play wide right. 'Robbo' was a skilful left winger who could go past opponents with ease. Pete started his career as a right back and arrived from Hull City playing that position. He had pace and could help keep him quiet doubling up with

Geoff Palmer, whereas I wasn't the quickest. But the switch of roles would free me up a bit in the centre alongside Willie. Manager Barnwell was a very proud man that day leading his team out and it was a wonderful feeling to be walking down the Wembley tunnel again on to the hallowed turf. Barney had worked hard with us to get there and our determination to win came from him.

The tactical change worked a treat as Peter nullified Robertson and stopped him from feeding the strikers Trevor Francis and Gary Birtles. Peter also set up the only goal, scored by Andy Gray. His terrific long ball from the right saw their centre back David Needham and the goalkeeper Peter Shilton in all sorts of trouble as Needham tried to chest it back to Shilton not knowing his keeper had come out for the ball. Andy had read it superbly and ran around them to pick up the loose ball and tap it into the empty net. Our fans erupted and we couldn't catch Andy to celebrate with him as he took off around the back of the goal and over the advertising boards. It was a brilliant feeling. But we couldn't celebrate for long as we had to defend for our lives. As Forest piled on the pressure, Andy even dropped back to play as a third centre half alongside Emlyn and George Berry. There were numerous goal-line clearances and saves from our keeper Paul Bradshaw, who even ended up sitting on the ball for one block. But the defence were outstanding as we held on to win the League Cup once more in an excellent team performance.

Emlyn was a very proud man as he lifted the cup – the only domestic trophy he hadn't won in 13 years at Liverpool. We were just as ecstatic as we completed a lap of honour and showed the cup off to our fans. They again supported us brilliantly and played a big part in our success once more because it was a really tough game. Forest were a great team who were about to successfully defend their title as European champions so it was one hell of a result for us. At the final whistle I swapped shirts with Martin O'Neill, which made my day. Like me, Martin played on the right side of midfield and I really admired him for his industry and honesty. It was a terrific result for us but mostly for John Barnwell after nearly losing his life. We were all delighted for him.

I can't remember everything about the celebrations afterwards, but it seemed lower key than after we won the League Cup in 1974. Rather than stay in London, as we has done six years earlier at the Hilton Park Hotel, this time we boarded the bus back to Wolverhampton after celebrating by swigging champagne in the dressing room. We

125

briefly got to see our wives just outside Wembley at a hotel before they boarded their coach. Unfortunately for them though, the heating broke and they were freezing all the way back. Once we were back on our bus, we got stuck into champagne and a couple of crates of beer for the journey home. Back in Wolverhampton, a meal was laid on for us at The Mount Hotel where a three-piece band struck up, but our places were occupied by other people at the time so we had to wait a while until they finished. My team-mates Geoff Palmer and Willie Carr kept the band up until about one or two o'clock in the morning, but by then the rest of us were tucked up in bed.

Our victory at Wembley put the club on the map, but it was one of many on the road that season. Our away form in 1979-80 was superb, with 10 League victories to help us to sixth place, our best since finishing fifth in 1972-73 and still the highest Wolves have managed 38 years later. It was one of the three best away records in the First Division that season and the club's best since the glory days of the 1950s. Fourth-placed Arsenal and champions Liverpool also had 10 away wins but the Gunners, with six away draws to Liverpool's four, had most away points in the top flight with 26. Our total was 23.

One of our successes was at Manchester City, where we had our first reunion with our old mate Steve Daley. He might have gone but he certainly wasn't forgotten and we were all eagerly anticipating the game at Maine Road on December 1. To justify why he left, Steve wanted to prove he was worth his price tag and that City were better than us. But he didn't look the same player in that game. He looked a bit lost and you could see in his play he was carrying the burden of that huge fee on his shoulders. I don't know if facing his former pals put him off his game, but he wasn't playing with the same fluency he had with us. You know how some players just look better playing for certain clubs? Well, Steve looked like he belonged in a Wolves shirt. The sky blue City jersey didn't seem to suit him. We whacked them 3-2 with goals from Peter Daniel, Andy Gray and myself. The scoreline sounds close but we were superb that day. Steve won't like me for saying it but at the end of the game I felt a bit sorry for him. We hoped he would be a success at City and he was a strong enough person to succeed. There was no shortage of memorable away days that season and there was another one for me to remember fondly, this time in north London. It was during the penultimate away game that I had a reason to celebrate, when, for once, we managed to put one over our bogey team Spurs. I had the pleasure of scoring my 100th Wolves goal at

White Hart Lane in a 2-2 draw on April 23. It was also significant because strangely I wore the number 10 shirt that day instead of the number seven, with Andy Gray and John Richards out injured. Norman Bell, one of their replacements, scored our other goal.

After home games we would go for a meal out with some of the lads and their wives to an Italian restaurant called Ristorante Romagna in Tettenhall, Wolverhampton – but only if we had won. I couldn't bear going out after we'd lost. 'Romano's', as we used to call it, was a nice place to go and we didn't get bothered by too many people, although it was always a pleasure to sign autographs when asked. Sometimes the celebrations would go on into the early hours. Willie Carr liked to let his hair down on a Saturday evening after a game and he was usually among the last men standing. Quite often towards the end of the night he could be seen weaving his way back from the bar with a tray of flaming sambucas above his head, or he would disappear for a while, and just when we'd be wondering where he was, he would emerge from the kitchen with a mop and bucket and start dancing with it, as if he was holding a lady! One time when Willie was carrying the drinks, he lost his balance and the glasses started sliding off the tray on to the floor. As each flaming tumbler hit the floor, a small flame ignited on the carpet, which Willie tried to put out by stamping his foot on it. As he attempted to put each flame out, so the tray would slide and another glass would topple to the ground, giving him another one to extinguish. By the time he got back to our table the tray was virtually empty, and Willie ended up with a blistered foot from stamping the flames out! Imagine if that had happened today – phones would be out capturing the footage and it would be all over social media within minutes.

Thankfully this was well before the advent of mobile phones. The management saw the funny side and we didn't get banned! But with the new stand so far from the pitch, Romano's profits were in danger of being hit. Thankfully we won two out of our last three home games against Leeds and Nottingham Forest – both by 3-1 scorelines. I managed to find the net in both to take my tally to nine in the League and 13 overall. More importantly, those victories helped us finish just a point behind Nottingham Forest, who would successfully defend their European crown a few weeks later by beating Kevin Keegan's Hamburg 1-0 in Madrid.

23

The Accused

Winning the League Cup meant we were now back in Europe for the first time in six years and we were all looking forward to a successful new season and another good cup run. We had a good team with bags of experience to carry us into the European challenge. Our captain Emlyn Hughes had plenty of that from his years at Liverpool and we could learn so much from him. There was no shortage of that anyway from those still at the club who had helped get us to the UEFA Cup final in 1972.

However, things didn't quite go to plan. For a start, I pulled my thigh in pre-season training and ended up watching the VII Trofeo Villa de Bilbao 1980 from the stands. This was a four-team pre-season tournament that we were invited to take part in along with the hosts Athletic Bilbao, Borussia Monchengladbach and Czech side Bohemians Praha. This was the first chance we got to see our new summer signing in action, the Uruguay international sweeper or defensive midfielder Raphael Villazan. We paid £140,000 to buy him from the Spanish club Huelva. Rafa was a lovely guy and clearly at home with the ball at his feet, but he struggled with the physical demands of our game and didn't last long with us. The thing we remember him for was the phrase he shouted whenever someone fouled him: 'Hijo de puta!' which translates as 'son of a bitch'. I could have said the same about my own predicament. Whenever I tried to exert myself, I could feel my thigh pulling, and although I played in the first game of our defence of the League Cup, a 3-1 defeat at Second Division Cambridge United, I was taken off and missed seven of our first eight League matches. I had been doing exercises at home to improve my flexibility, but it made little difference.

Andy Gray had suffered a similar injury when he was at Aston Villa and he recommended me to see someone he had visited for a manipulation procedure. Andy drove me to Manchester for the appointment and when I described the symptoms, the doctor said 'Well, Andy, we know what we've got to do here, don't we?' I was told my thigh was like a piece of elastic with a knot in the middle, and when the knot is pulled from either side, it gets tighter, restricting the blood flow in it. The doctor proceeded to put me to sleep and I had my leg bent over my head and pulled in different directions. When I came round I felt no different, but when I got home, I lay in front of the fire and tested it out by doing the same exercises as before I'd had the manipulation, and I couldn't feel a thing. I shouted to Jane, 'I can't feel it, it's gone!' Within two or three days I was back in full training and ready to play again.

I made my comeback in our concluding UEFA Cup first round tie against the crack Dutch side PSV Eindhoven on October 1. I had missed the away leg in Holland due to my injury so was determined to make up for it at Molineux. We had a lot of work to do as we were 3-1 down from the first leg. I felt great playing pain free again and I was in the mood to make a difference. I could have had a hat-trick – I hit the post and their goalkeeper made a couple of great saves, but it wasn't to be and although we won 1-0 thanks to a Mel Eves goal, we went out 3-2 on aggregate. Sadly we couldn't repeat our successes from 1971-72 and we went out early, along with the Molineux floodlights following a power cut which held the game up for a while. We weren't as good a team as we were nine years before.

It was a similar story in the League Cup, where also we exited at the first hurdle to Second Division side Cambridge, also 3-2 on aggregate. This was the repeat of what we did after winning it in 1974, losing to Fulham on that occasion. The 1980-81 season wasn't the best for me in terms of goals – after notching 13 the season before (nine in the League plus another four in the League Cup) I only managed five (three in the League plus another two in the FA Cup). For the second year running I scored away at Stoke and Norwich, but the team didn't have a great season. We found ourselves in the bottom half of the table for most of it and just about stayed up, finishing 18th, just two points above the relegation zone.

But any disappointment at missing out on a few trips in Europe and failing to defend the League Cup was replaced by the excitement of another run in the FA Cup. We progressed to the semi-finals by beating Stoke and Watford – albeit after replays – Wrexham, who were then in the Second Division and possessed a prolific goalscorer in Dixie McNeill, then Middlesbrough in the quarter-finals after another replay. Our striker Norman Bell had earned the nickname of 'Super Sub' during the Cup run after coming off the bench – remember there was only one substitute in those days – to score two goals against Wrexham and one in the replay against Middlesbrough to help see us through. It was my third FA Cup semi-final with Wolves and I was determined to make it third time lucky. I received a little help along the way from an old Wolves favourite after going through a bit of a rough time. We weren't playing particularly well and I found I was also taking the problems at the club home with me. I was snapping at the wife and kids a lot, which wasn't right. Barney suggested I had a chat with a psychologist, Dennis Wilshaw, who had been a prolific inside forward for Wolves in their glory days of the 1950s. I never really believed in that sort of thing before but thought I'd give it a try. Through the sessions with Dennis, I developed an attitude of positive thinking and started to enjoy playing, training and life a lot more.

So when the time came to face our bogey team Spurs in the semi-final at Hillsborough, I was ready. Although we were having a poor season in the league, we went into the semi-final having won three of our previous five games and really fancied our chances this time. The referee that day was Clive Thomas, who was a controversial official known as 'Clive the Book' for his habit of booking players. Barney said to us 'If you get in the box, you never know what this guy will do'. Little did he realise how true his words were to be. It was a full house with 50,174 and the atmosphere was fantastic. 'This is it,' we thought, 'our best chance to get to an FA Cup final for our fans at long last'. They deserved it after the setbacks against Leeds in 1973 and Arsenal in 1979.

But Spurs reckoned otherwise. We had only been playing for four minutes when Steve Archibald put them ahead from close range. But six minutes later Wayne Clarke, who had taken the midfield place of Peter Daniel after he broke his leg against Aston Villa a couple of months earlier, controlled Geoff Palmer's crossfield free kick and centred from the left, Andy Gray nodded it down about 20 yards out and the ball bounced lovely for me to volley it with my left foot into the bottom left corner of Spurs keeper Milija Aleksic's goal. Scoring that made me feel just like I did in the 1974 League Cup final and I jumped on Andy's back and wrapped my legs around him. My equaliser came just at the right time but we couldn't rest on our laurels as Spurs came back at us.

I felt if we could get to half-time level we could have a really good go at them in the second half. But in the 38th minute George Berry fouled Ossie Ardiles on the edge of our penalty area. George still denies it was a foul but I don't believe him – if you make untidy tackles you get punished. And we did as Glenn Hoddle struck one of his bending free kicks into the top left hand corner of the net. Our keeper, Paul Bradshaw, was bloody good but he didn't move, knowing it was in, and we went in at half-time 2-1 down. I thought 'Here we go again' but Barnwell and Barker got us going and stressed Spurs were looking tired so they told us to get the ball into their box and they might make a clumsy tackle on us. With that in mind we went out for the second half believing we could win it. The minutes were ticking away though and we were still behind. In the final seconds I broke away with the ball from our left-back position and played the ball to Emlyn Hughes, who was playing in midfield for us that day. I carried on going forward towards the right, and the ball came to me about 35 yards out. Playing a one-two with Norman Bell on the edge of the box, I took it beyond Steve Perryman and I just took it a little too far left of the goal. I was just wondering if I could get a shot in when Hoddle made a terrific challenge from the side and played the ball out for a corner. I fell over his foot tucked under him as he slid in – my foot caught it, and having just ran the length of the pitch and it being the last minute, I fell over exhausted.

We were attacking the famous Spion Kop, where most of the 20,000 Wolves fans were packed in. As I lay on the ground a big cheer went up and I thought 'That's a big cheer for a corner'. Just then John Richards came over and said 'Hibby, get up – it's a penalty and you're going to take it!' I said 'You can get to, I ain't taking that!' It was the first time I'd ever refused to take a spot kick. You could say I bottled it but I felt so tired and I wasn't confident enough to take it. Willie Carr and I always agreed if I didn't fancy taking a penalty he would step in. Anyway he slotted it away, cool as you like, in stark contrast to me. I didn't even look and I had to wait until later that night when I watched it on *Match of the Day* to see it for the first time. Nobody was more surprised than me to see us win a penalty.

No sooner had we got back to the centre circle and Spurs kicked off afterwards that Thomas blew the whistle for the end of normal time. Spurs were so hurt and disappointed that I always remember Archibald picked the ball up and tried to kick it out of the ground. None of their players said anything to me at the time but their manager, Keith Burkinshaw, was quoted afterwards as saying I should have been in the Olympic Games for diving. Many years later Burkinshaw became a Premier League delegate with me dealing with referees. The penalty incident cropped up in conversation and I told him what had happened and he accepted it. We pressed hard for the winner in extra-time and went home very disappointed not to have won. I was absolutely knackered but it took me a long time to get to sleep when I got home that night. I kept playing the game over and over again in my mind, thinking 'If only this or that had happened'. These are the things as players you think of after games, win or lose. But if I'd known what was to follow I might never have slept that night.

I woke up the following morning still feeling really tired and gutted, while Jane went downstairs to make me breakfast in bed. She brought up a tray with tea and toast and the *Sunday Express*. I always go straight to the back page and wanted to read about our game. Well I nearly dropped my cup of tea when I read the headline. HIBBITT: 'I DIVED' it screamed. My heart nearly stopped. Jane said 'What's up?' I said 'Look at this'. I felt sick to my back teeth. I started to swear and Jane had a job to calm me down. I couldn't stomach my toast. I just couldn't believe what I'd seen. I'd only spoken to the local press, not the national papers. John Barnwell had told me not to speak to anyone other than our local guys and the television interviewer Gary Newbon, which is what I'd done. They asked me if it was a penalty and I said 'I thought it was a corner at first then I heard a big cheer and thought "That's a big cheer for a corner". The next thing I knew John Richards ran up to me as I lay on the ground and said "Hibby, it's a penalty, get up, you're taking it". I said "You can get to, I'm not taking that!" We had a laugh about that, then someone asked if I had to go down, I said 'Yes' because I'd tripped over Glenn Hoddle's foot. Then I was asked if I knew it was the last minute and I said 'Yes' as I knew it was near the end of the game. That was all I said to the locals but I think some national press guys were listening in and quoted me quite wrongly. Their version went something like 'Yes, I had to go down because I knew it was the last minute'.

That was totally untrue and so wrong of them to write such rubbish. I felt so bad about it that I went to see Barnwell on the Monday morning to see about taking it further. I was very unhappy about it because there was no way I said what I was quoted as saying. I want to make it clear I never dived and I never would. I was so tired after 90 minutes of a very hard-fought semi-final on a heavy ground you could have knocked me down with a feather. I didn't go into the box to dive, or to gain a penalty, I went into the box to try to get a shot on goal. I looked at the footage and highlights and the way I fell doesn't look great, but that's what happened. From the position referee Clive Thomas took at the time I can see why he gave it. He was behind looking at the backs of Glenn and myself. He didn't see Glenn play the ball out, and I tripped over his back foot and went down. Thomas didn't think too long about it before he blew his whistle for the penalty, but that was his decision, not mine. I told Barnwell of my concerns and he just said 'Forget about it – let's get on with it'. The replay was at Highbury, home of Tottenham's north London rivals Arsenal. It was almost like a home game for Spurs so we were always going to be up against it. In the event they won 3-0 in a game where we never really looked like winning. We were really down because we never turned up as a team. After getting back to Molineux Jane drove me home where her mum and dad were babysitting for us. We got them up and we shared a few Scotches to drown our sorrows, not getting to bed until about 4.30am as I released my anguish at our performance.

For about a month afterwards, I received some horrific abuse in letters from Spurs fans. They wished all sorts of things would happen to me. It was a really bad period for me and I worried about it for a long time. I didn't show Jane all of the letters at the time because she was already very upset from what she'd read about me in the papers. Nobody knows me better than her and she knew I'd never dive in the penalty area, or anywhere else on the field for that matter. I think it's awful even now how a fellow professional can cheat another by trying to get them booked or sent off, and occasionally even hurting them deliberately. All players are trying to make a living in the game and that's hard enough itself without someone trying to harm that on the pitch.

Almost a year later, in February 1982, we went to White Hart Lane and I remember getting loads of abuse from Spurs fans. I was getting plenty of stick so I pretended to trip myself up in the warm-up before the game just to take the sting out of it. When I came out of the ground after the game to board the coach, there were about 10 or 12 Spurs fans waiting to give me a bit of grief. They weren't being aggressive but they were claiming I'd cheated to win the penalty in the semi-final. So I asked if I could have a word with them because I wanted to put my side of the argument across. I said something like 'Hey come on lads, let's have a chat and I'll tell you exactly what happened'.

I got off the bus and sat down with them on the wall and they joined me and I spent 20, 25 minutes with them saying what happened. I told them about the press and that I never said I dived. Bearing in mind there were no stewards or police around maybe it was a brave thing to do, but I just took it on myself to speak to them. I was a bit panicky about it because I didn't know how they were going to react, but I was pleasantly surprised to find they listened and took everything on board. I felt better for it afterwards and shook hands with them.

Just recently I was at a charity golf day at Essendon Golf Club near Hatfield in Hertfordshire to raise money for John Lacy, the former Tottenham player who has been diagnosed with cancer and I saw Ossie Ardiles there. Ossie and I were the celebrities and the three guys I played with were all mates of his so they all had a £10 bet on the outcome of the game. Afterwards, Ossie came up to me asking where my £10 was, as they had won. I said 'I didn't bet you' and he said 'Come on, you dived!', meaning to win the penalty in 1981. I replied 'I've got a lawyer here!' but it was all good banter and great fun – he's a lovely man.

24

For My Benefit

In 1981 I was granted a testimonial, which Wolves gave me for a decade's service. Benefit years are not so common nowadays because so few players stay that long at one club and players make so much money anyway that testimonials don't have the same significance as they once did. Players who moved on made money from signing-on fees so clubs rewarded those who stayed loyal with a benefit year. We had a few players at the time who had had testimonials such as John McAlle (1978) and Derek Parkin (1979), while Phil Parkes (also 1978), Derek Dougan, Dave Wagstaffe (both 1975) and Mike Bailey (1976) had them in recent years and John Richards was also due one (his came in 1982), so I had to get in line and wait for my turn. I was thankful to the club for allowing me this but sadly, the impending recession bit hard and many people had lost their jobs and budgets were tight. That made it difficult to ask people to support me and I cancelled a lot of functions my committee had put together. However, I did go ahead with a folk evening held at the Wolves Social Club next to Molineux and what a great night it was. Several singers, including Harvey Andrews and Geoff Bodenham, put on a marvellous show. Harvey was in fact singing for the first time since a serious car accident. He'd surgery on his nose and face and was worried whether it would affect his singing, but he was as good as ever.

We continued with all the darts matches we'd organised in the pubs because we felt it was important to share the hard times with the fans. It was a chance for players and supporters to socialise and we enjoyed plenty of laughs. The players were great and came along to support me. We were a team on and off the field who enjoyed each other's company. Our captain Emlyn Hughes used to stay at the Mount Hotel in Tettenhall several days a week up until he left us to join Rotherham United as player-manager in the summer of 1981. So coming to the events helped him relax and I was very grateful to him for his support as he attended all of them.

I was sharing my testimonial year with the Worcestershire cricketer Norman Gifford, so our respective committees got together and arranged a joint floodlight cricket match. It was to be an England XI versus a Rest of the World team under the floodlights at Molineux on April 28, with the idea to share the proceeds. This was the first time a

135

footballer and a cricketer had joined forces in such a way. At the time floodlight cricket was just taking off and the interest was amazing. The MCC representatives said they would keep a close eye on how it went. Brilliant, I thought, some of the world's best players had agreed to play and I was going to get a close-up of them, something I had always dreamed about. Ian Botham, who had been injured, was coming to get some practice in, and there were others such as my old school friend David Bairstow, Clive Lloyd, Viv Richards, Alvin Kallicharran and Malcolm Marshall of the West Indies, plus England batsmen David Gower and Derek Randall, fast bowlers Bob Willis and Graham Dilley and South Africa players Mike Procter and Graeme Pollock. The weather looked like it would be just about OK.

Tickets were selling extremely well – in fact better than for our next home game against Arsenal, who we were playing three days beforehand. It looked like it was going to be a full house. But most of all I was looking forward to seeing world-class cricketers and I could hardly wait for the day to come. I loved my cricket and here the sport was coming to Molineux, which with its now wide, open spaces was ideal for some big hitting and fiery bowling on a plastic wicket. People were coming to watch from all over the country to see these brilliant cricketers and everything was in place for a great night. But on the Saturday night of the Arsenal game – remember we're almost into May – there was heavy snow and by the Sunday morning we woke up to around four to six inches of the stuff! I couldn't believe it when I opened the curtains. 'Oh no' I said to Jane. 'What's up?' she replied. 'Look at this', I said. We were both gutted; the cricket match had to be cancelled and I felt sick. But worse was to come – after we'd cancelled everything, the sun came out and it was dry! I was so disappointed the game never got played.

My testimonial game was on Sunday, August 23 against Derby County, six days before the start of the new season. John Barnwell promised me a big-name team as the opposition. He mentioned many glamour clubs in Europe and reckoned he could persuade Benfica to come. I thought that would be great, but it didn't happen. I want to stress I was grateful to Derby for playing and supporting me, as they're a big club who had won the League title twice in the decade before, but it was a big disappointment not to have a European team for the fans. I only found out we were playing Derby while I was on holiday in Portugal with my family. I read it in the newspapers while we were on the beach and was shocked because no one had told me and I felt Barnwell let me down. But beggars can't be choosers and I'm sure the 6,221 fans who came to watch had an enjoyable day. I was grateful to all those who supported me, especially during the recession. Derby were great too and I was able to play against Kevin Hector, who had been with me at Bradford Park Avenue all those years ago back – no doubt payback for me for all those wayward shots he had me chasing when I was an apprentice!

Peter Knowles had asked via a third party if he could play and I was delighted. Apparently he enquired because I hadn't invited him and I thought that was lovely because I didn't want him to feel exploited by me asking him. I got a call saying 'Mr Knowles has asked me to give you a call saying he would like to play in your testimonial'. I thought 'I'll have a bit of that!' and he came and played. We had some lovely pictures taken together in the dressing room with a Wolves number eight shirt, which Peter had worn with such distinction and I later donned as well. Peter replaced another Peter – Daniel – and played for half an hour or so in a game we won 2-1. Steve Powell put Derby ahead but our central defender John Pender, who was then a second-year apprentice, headed the equaliser and later started the move that brought the winner from Andy Gray 13 minutes from time.

Knowlesy still displayed lovely touches and glimpses of the natural skill he had – and he showed he hadn't lost his enthusiasm and desire as well. One of the Derby players pulled him back by his shirt to try to get the ball off him and Peter swung his arm round to have a go at him. That told me he still had that passion about the game, and it was great to see him in a Wolves shirt again. I think he was sorry about that incident afterwards, but if he was, then he certainly hasn't regretted his decision to turn his back on the game at the age of 23. Having encountered him a few times since, he is the most contented man I've ever met, always smiling. He's a smashing lad and I'm just glad I got to play with him in a game at Molineux again, even though it was all those years after he'd retired. It meant an awful lot to me.

25

Relegation Again

Boosted by two signings, we had high hopes for the 1981-82 season. We had snapped up winger Alan Birch from Chesterfield for £180,000 and long-serving central defender Joe Gallagher from Birmingham City for around £350,000 in a deal that could have seen John Richards move to St. Andrew's, but he turned it down. Our manager John Barnwell had pushed hard to sign the 18-year-old St Johnstone striker Ally McCoist, who was tipped to be the new Kenny Dalglish according to many people in Scotland, but he rejected a deal to join us and signed for Sunderland instead. A £350,000 fee had been discussed and McCoist had even spent a few days' training with us. It was a shame he didn't join us because he would have been a terrific signing.

Another player who trained with us for a short while was Rene van der Kerkhof. A World Cup finalist with Holland in 1974 and 1978, the right winger was a household name and the pursuit of his signature was typical of the profile of player Barney loved to attract to the club. We were also linked with a move for Michel Platini, who was then with St Etienne and went on to become one of the world's greatest midfielders, but nothing became of it. As for van der Kerkhof, a deal worth around £350,000 was struck with his club PSV Eindhoven – our UEFA Cup opponents a year earlier – and personal terms were agreed. But the club cooled their interest after he had trained and played a practice match against Chesterfield at Castlecroft. He was only just short of his 30th birthday but he didn't seem physically fit enough and suffice to say, he didn't impress. Instead we signed Alan Birch, whose younger brother Paul later played for Aston Villa and Wolves with distinction. Alan was a good player who could play in several positions, but mostly wide right, and he was quick with two good feet. Things needed to change because of our poor finishing position in 1980-81, just two points above the drop zone. We also lost two experienced central defenders that summer in Emlyn Hughes and John McAlle to Rotherham and Sheffield United respectively, so the manager knew he had to make some new signings if we were going to progress.

We beat Liverpool 1-0 at home in the first game with a goal from Mick Matthews, a promising young midfielder who had come through the ranks. That result gave us a real boost because it wasn't often you beat a team like them. But then after a 4-1 defeat

138

at Southampton, we lost 3-0 to Leeds at Elland Road. That brought us back down to earth. Having finished ninth the previous season, Leeds were still a very good side, not quite as good as they were in the early 1970s but they still had quality players and were still difficult to beat on their own ground.

That month's papers reported that Leeds, Newcastle and Manchester City wanted to sign me and that I would cost them up to £250,000. It played on my mind for some time thinking the club may want to sell me. It was the same feeling I had when Bill McGarry told me a club was willing to pay £100,000 for me back in the early 70s, but no one at Wolves had told me of the interest. Our young striker Wayne Clarke told me his brother Allan, who was in charge of Leeds at the time, wanted to sign me but that was all I heard about it.

All sorts of things go through your mind when the speculation starts, particularly at home and with young children. Schooling is very important for children but they tend to adapt to change more quickly than adults. My wife was a local girl but it wouldn't have stopped us moving. However, nothing came of the interest and as far as I was concerned I was very happy at Wolves. If at any time you find the club no longer need your services then that is the time when you look elsewhere. I had been fortunate over the years at Wolves as the new managers that had come in still thought I was a player they wanted to be around and to help them achieve some success. I was very settled at Wolves, even when relegation came I never thought about leaving a great club. There was also the fact I had been part of the relegated team and wanted to stay to help them back to the top flight as early as possible. No player wanted to leave a sinking ship back then.

The team were changing very quickly with youngsters coming through like John Humphrey, Colin Brazier, Mick Matthews, Wayne Clarke and Hughie Atkinson. But we had plenty of experience as well, with Paul Bradshaw in goal and Geoff Palmer, Derek Parkin, Joe Gallagher and George Berry in defence while in midfield we had Peter Daniel, Alan Birch, Willie Carr and myself to choose from. Andy Gray, John Richards, Mel Eves, Wayne Clarke and Norman Bell were all fighting for places up front, so on paper it looked fine, but we were not functioning right for some reason. It was about to get worse for me and the team. On October 17 1981, I picked up a knee injury in a 0-0 draw at home to Middlesborough. At first I thought I had just tweaked a ligament but after a few days it was diagnosed as a cartilage problem and I feared the worst as this was just the kind of injury I had experienced early in my career as a 19-year-old. I knew this was going to be a long-term injury and I would be out of action for three months, if things went well. I hated being injured and not playing; it was at a time when we needed all the players to be fit as we struggled to get any momentum going. Coincidentally, I found out through our mutual pal John Richards that our old team-mate Steve Kindon suffered exactly the same injury at the same time. By this time 'Kindo' was playing for Huddersfield and before we had our respective operations – mine on the Tuesday and his on the Wednesday – we exchanged telegrams wishing each other good luck.

It was my bad luck that we had one of the worst winters in 1981-82 and the adverse weather didn't help my rehabilitation. The cold and snow on the ground made it awkward to keep pedalling my bike around Wombourne and Castlecroft with our physiotherapist Toby Andersen, who was back at the club after a hugely successful spell with us in the 70s. The big freeze also meant there was a lack of games for me to make my comeback. Toby was doing a great job helping me in my recovery and spent many hours with me, listening to my moans and groans. Frustration was creeping in at not being able to force my way back into contention because of the weather and Toby must have been brassed off with me during that period. Thankfully he didn't show it. He was very patient and a great guy who did so much good work for me and the rest of the players. One of the things I'll never forget is his handshake. It was so strong, it was like putting your hand in a vice. If ever you crossed him or took the mickey he would have you on your knees begging him to let go. You didn't mess with him from close range!

At the turn of the year into 1982 my recovery seemed to be taking forever and the manager was keen to arrange for me to get some match practice to test out my knee. It is always easier to train with an injury as you can work within yourself, but in a match situation it is completely different. You forget about it when you are chasing the opposition or going into a tackle and that will tell you if you are ready to start playing. So I was waiting patiently for a game but the bad weather meant it was very difficult to arrange anything for me. The plus side – if there was one – meant I was able to enjoy and join in the festivities of Christmas. It's the time of year when the games come thick and fast so the players cannot afford to over-indulge, but this one was very enjoyable and I could let myself go for a change without feeling too guilty. My children had a great time as we could all spend Christmas together as a family.

But being injured meant I couldn't impress the manager to win a new contract, which I needed to do as mine was running out at the end of the season and I was concerned about my future. I was out but desperate to get back playing to prove to the manager John Barnwell I was good enough to warrant a new deal, but the team were not doing well at all and the punters were getting a bit restless with Barney. He needed some wins and quickly. We had no money to buy real quality players so we had to dig deep with what we had available, and with me sitting in the bloody stands not being able to help, it was very frustrating indeed. I wanted to stay at Wolves and hoped to play for them for the rest of my career but I could understand the club's reluctance in re-opening contract talks because of my injury. I was desperate to assure them I was 100 per cent fit and all I needed was a couple of reserve games to prove it. I just hoped I figured in their plans. If I didn't, then I did not want to wait until my contract ran out before they told me. It was all very unsettling for me and my family. I would be 31 in January so I wanted something to be sorted out quickly but I understood the way the club were delaying any further talks on a new deal. The manager was having problems with the chairman Harry Marshall and he was also waiting to be offered a new deal but he had to improve results first.

I finally made my comeback on January 23, 1982. But while I was relieved to be back playing again, it wasn't a happy experience as we lost 3-0 to Everton at Molineux. The fans were so disgruntled they were shouting for the chairman's head and invaded the pitch in a sit-down protest. It was the worst show of bad feeling I had seen in my near 14 years at the club, but this was their frustration coming out. We were really struggling and to lose at home in the way we did was just too much to take and they showed their disgust. Those fans protesting weren't hooligans, they were caring Wolves fans who felt they needed to show their feelings. I played in this game – or at least I was out there – and the harder we tried, the worse we got as we crashed to what was the fourth defeat in a row in a run of eight straight losses – a club record.

But if I was gutted at the way things at the club were going, then I only had to look at Steve Kindon to realise things weren't so bad after all. While I made a full recovery, poor 'Kindo' was still in hospital eight to ten weeks later after his surgery failed, with his leg in a sling watching me play on *'Match of The Day'*. In fact, he never played again and was forced to retire at the premature age of 32. Ultimately he had four operations on the same knee after being told that the original wound had become infected. Our rehabilitation had been different; while I was told to stay in bed and recuperate before putting any weight on my leg, Steve had been instructed to get out of bed almost immediately. We shall never know whether the different approaches had any bearing on the subsequent outcomes, but all I know is I got to continue my playing career while his reached a sad end.

It was a terrible time for us and I think the situation was far worse than when we got relegated with Bill McGarry in 1976. There was something not quite right off the field; you could feel it in the dressing room and in the club. It was something I had never felt before in all my time since joining Wolves. There was a really big problem that wasn't going to be solved very quickly and if we went down again I could see us not getting back into the First Division for some time as the playing staff were just not good enough. Looking back I don't think the board and the chairman were very supportive of the manager and in fact Barney resigned on January 8, 1982, in a dispute over the terms of his new contract. I think he'd had enough with little backing and he thought it best he left to try to give someone else a chance to pick us up and lead us to survival. It was very sad to see him go after what he had achieved with us, a League Cup win that took us back into Europe and two FA Cup semi-finals. He was a cat's whisker from taking us back to an FA Cup final for the first time since 1960 and I never got that close again. Soon after Barney resigned, Wolves interviewed a manager who had made his mark north of the border. After talks with chairman Harry Marshall, he decided to stay with Aberdeen. Thank you, Alex Ferguson!

I had grown a full beard at the time because I vowed not to shave until I scored. That was before my knee injury so I had to carry on my promise until I had recovered and played again. My kids thought I looked scary with it and some might think I did without one as well! But it came off not long after our new manager Ian Greaves replaced Barnwell. Ian had come in to try to keep us up having been successful with Bolton Wanderers and Oxford United and he was a very experienced manager. I had heard some great things about his man-management style and he had managed Peter Reid and Frank Worthington in his time at Burnden Park so he knew all about big-name players and how to get the best out them. At Bolton he also worked with big Sam

Allardyce, who was a tough centre-back who we remembered when we beat them 1-0 at Burnden in May 1977. That was nearly five years before but our new gaffer hadn't forgotten it. One day not long after Ian had taken over, Willie and I were leaving the dressing room to go training and we said good morning to him and he replied the same. Then he suddenly shouted at us: "You're the f*****g two that kept us down, you b******s, come here!" and we just ran down the corridor and out on to the pitch to escape. His first fixture for us was away to our bogey team Tottenham, so it perhaps wasn't the ideal game for him to start with. We got battered 6-1 and I got the consolation goal from a free kick, a week after scoring in a 2-1 defeat at Arsenal, which at least meant I could finally get rid of the beard! After the Spurs game we got back into the dressing room, our heads all bowed in disgust and feeling sorry for ourselves. You could hear a pin drop as we waited for the manager to make his entrance and we were in for the biggest bollocking ever – or so we thought. He came crashing in and shouted: "You think you have f*****g problems, I have a b*****d wife at home taking me for every penny I have!" and with that he smashed a ball at the dressing room wall. Whether or not that was true, I don't know – I think he may have just said it to get us going again – but it seemed to have the desired effect.

He changed the atmosphere completely with that remark. But that was what he was about. He wanted us to get our heads up, stop feeling sorry for ourselves and get on with our jobs. Then he told us to have a bath and get on the coach home. I knew from that day we were going to have a chance of staying up. He treated us like men and completely changed the feeling around the place. He picked us up and gave us belief again with his management skills. He seemed to drag the best out of each and every one of us. He loved the game and he just loved being around the players. But one thing he hated was anyone trying to kid him or shirking their work. He asked for hard work and nothing else and he could soon tell if someone was trying to pull the wool over his eyes. He loved ball players who had a football brain and he loved hard tacklers, but most of all he liked grafters who put 90 minutes of effort in.

The players in the team fighting for First Division survival were good enough to stay up but unfortunately because we had played so badly in the early games it was going to take a lot of hard work or even a miracle to stay up. Better players were needed before the start of that season and if that meant me moving on to make way, so be it. A few more could have moved on as well. When you lose players like Wagstaffe, Bailey,

Munro and Dougan they take some replacing, but players should have been in place ready for the change because as a squad we were getting old together. Looking back I also think Phil Parkes was the best goalkeeper I played with although Paul Bradshaw came close. 'Braddy' was in inspired form that season and won the club's Player of the Year award for the second year running. The performance of Gary Pierce in the 1974 League Cup final was one of the best I had ever seen. John McAlle was the most under-rated player outside the club, closely followed by Derek Parkin, who left us to join Richie Barker at Stoke City in March 1982 after becoming our record appearance holder. We had many very good players but nothing lasts forever and changes should have been made for the long-term benefit of the club after winning the League Cup in 1980, or following the FA Cup semi-final defeat against Spurs, to bring in better players and build on that successful team. Some may not agree, but that was the way I felt at the time.

Something was drastically wrong within the club that wasn't spelt out to the fans. The board could – and should – have been more transparent and let everyone know the truth about the dire financial position of the club. When I was trying to negotiate a new deal, even though we were on the verge of relegation, I wanted to be part of the set-up to help bring them back up like I had done in the past. I didn't want to run away like some players do, but the club couldn't offer anything at the time as they were in deep financial trouble. They were the words of Ian Greaves who didn't want to lose me or the other six or seven players whose contracts were ending. I know it was not bullshit from the manager because he was an honest and terrific bloke for whom I had 100 per cent support.

We still had half a chance of staying up when we went to play West Ham away on April 6. To prepare for the game we had an overnight stay in a hotel in London and all the team and staff had a meal together. Afterwards the manager took Willie Carr and myself to one side and said: 'If you fancy a pint, you can have one. I know you don't sleep well before games', pointing at yours truly. So we said 'OK boss, that would be nice'. What we didn't know was that he was setting us up to ask a few questions about the club. We had both been there some time and he wanted to get the full SP from us. We had a great couple of hours with him and we were offered a second pint – which we had – but it didn't go down well with the coach Jim Barron. He said 'Gaffer, it's 10pm and they have to go to bed'. And with that the manager turned to him and said 'If you want to go to bed, p*** off, I am talking to my boys'. I couldn't believe it, but that is how Ian Greaves worked. He knew we would go out there the next day and give it all we had, but he also knew I would sleep and rest better with the couple of beers.

I slept like a log, but even though we played well next day and dominated the match for long spells, we lost 3-1. Our problem was that we just couldn't find the net enough times and that had been the case all season. It's easy to point the finger but the real problem was the managers, both Barnwell and Greaves, should have had more support from the board to strengthen the squad. With players, including myself, enjoying new-found confidence under Greaves, we fought hard right to the end and had some decent results against good teams. We won 1-0 at Nottingham Forest with Andy Gray's diving header from my free kick, and followed that up by battering Manchester City 4-1 at home with all of our goals coming in an amazing 17-minute spell in the first half, before drawing 1-1 at home to Birmingham to make it three defeats in 11 games to climb to 17th. But our rivals had games in hand on us. I wasn't to know it at the time, but my goal against City on April 12, 1982 was to be my last at Molineux. After that we lost 2-1 at Stoke after leading through my goal at the break to make it two in three games but two of only four I managed all season. Then a controversial penalty saw Andy Gray sent off for dissent against our old mate Derek Parkin. We lost the Black Country derby 2-1 at home to Albion and went down 2-0 at Brighton before grinding out a 1-1 draw at Everton, but it wasn't enough to save us from relegation. Our sorry tally of just 32 goals was one of the lowest totals of a top-flight team that century and told its own story, Mel Eves being our top scorer with a modest seven.

Now the manager had to make the decision on whether to keep eight players and start to rebuild the team. He told me he wanted to keep me as I could be the player who could help the youngsters on the field as well as off it. I'd had a reasonable season playing-wise – apart from the time I was out with the knee problem – and I played every game once I returned from injury. So it was good to hear he wanted me at the club. However, the down side was he could not offer me anything at the time as the budget had not been discussed by the board.

He asked me if I was interested in playing in the United States which could be a solution for us both. I could go over there and make a few bob which would take the weight of the summer wage bill off Wolves and when I came back he would give me a two-year contract as the club would be in a better financial state by then. I wasn't too keen on going to the USA. I was only 31 and I thought the only players who went out there were in the twilight of their careers and I was nowhere near it. I still felt good and fit, so I said 'Maybe in a couple of years, boss, I might think of it, but not at the moment'. He said 'It's the only way I can keep you, Kenny, and I really need you next season playing here, you are in my long-term plans for the future of this club'. He meant every word of it, again it sounded like it was no bullshit and I went home to have a word with Jane. I always discussed things with her and we had two children to think of. She was shocked when I told her what the manager had said but she understood the reasons behind it. She always said she would support me and go anywhere where football took me. Some big decisions were going to have to be made – and quickly – as the summer was about to begin and my contract was close to running out.

26

American Adventure

Sitting at home one day in late May 1982, I received a telephone call from Vic Crowe, the former Aston Villa boss who was then manager of Portland Timbers, who played in the North American Soccer League. He asked if I would be interested in joining them for the summer and maybe longer if it went well. It came as a shock really and I didn't know the answer to give him. It surprised me how quickly the news had got out that I was available, albeit on a temporary basis. I didn't want to leave Wolves but somehow the word was on the street. Vic was a very good, experienced manager who knew what to say to me, but all I could blurt out was 'I will think about it when I speak to the manager tomorrow'. Jane and I were now deep in thought about which way my future was going as Wolves had no money, my contract was running out at the end of the next month and we had two children to think about. Our heads were spinning.

The next morning I went to see Ian Greaves and asked him why Vic Crowe was calling me. He said Vic was very keen on taking me for the summer, that he would pay well and by the time the three months were up Wolves should be in a better position financially to offer the two-year contract I wanted. He added that he had eight players who were out of contract and he wanted them all back at Molineux next season. I expressed my doubts because I had a wife and two young kids to look after and obviously I wanted the best for them. If I had been single I would have said 'Yes' there and then but he told me to go away and give it some more thought – adding it would be a great experience for me and the family. We talked it over yet again and eventually Jane said: 'If that's what we have to do Ken, let's do it, but let's see what Portland have to say about the offer first and where we will be living'.

That same day Tony Penman rang me. Tony was the English scout for Seattle Sounders, managed by former Wolves, Nottingham Forest and Derby County winger Alan Hinton. Steve Daley was playing for them at the time, having moved there from Manchester City where it didn't go very well for him and he had a tough time of it. Steve was one of the best players in the States and I had always rated him very highly. Another of their star players was Alan Hudson, someone I had admired for several years from his time with Chelsea, Stoke City and Arsenal. Just watching him gave me a buzz, and with him and Steve there, I decided that was the club I wanted to join. Tony, who had been a school teacher in Wolverhampton and a scout for Wolves who recommended John Richards to them, admitted Seattle had had an indifferent start to the season and knew of Portland's interest in me. Alan Hinton told him he had to get me as he was desperate for a midfield player who could score goals and balance his team on the right hand side. He invited me for talks and I knew they had other good British players who would make me feel at home. There was Ray Evans, the ex-Tottenham full back, one-time Crystal Palace keeper Paul Hammond, Roger Davies, the striker from Derby County, and Peter Ward and Gary Mills from Nottingham Forest. I told him I was definitely interested and he said Alan would be in touch soon.

However, next day Vic Crowe rang again and offered me a very good deal which sort of put the cat amongst the pigeons. Let me say one thing before I go any further: Although as a kid we had no money at home, my mum and dad brought us up well and money never really motivated me, but the sums they were talking about were way beyond anything I had earned before in my career. However, the move still had to be right for the family so my mind was now drifting towards joining the Portland Timbers. After all it was a nice place to live, they were doing OK in the league and why should I not make some money in the process? That move was on now and I told Tony Penman the Timbers had offered me a really good deal. We were getting our bags ready for the trip to Timbers when Tony called me again and said he had spoken to Alan Hinton and the chief executive of the Sounders and they offered me something I just couldn't turn down. Toronto Blizzard had also shown a bit of interest as well but at long last we as a family decided Seattle was the place. It felt right and not just because the money was good for the three months I was there but because of the English contingent who would help us to settle in. I had to telephone Vic Crowe to tell him I was going to Seattle and that was not an easy call to make. I heard he had called me a greedy b*****d because the Sounders had offered me more.

Now we were packing to go to Seattle, we made arrangements with the school about the children not having to attend for three months. Julie, who used to babysit for us and wanted to sample the experience, came along for the trip. We didn't have a clue where we were going in terms of the area where we would be staying but it wasn't far fromwhere a lot of the players lived. Our accommodation was a new, three-bedroom apartment which was lovely, situated on the second floor of a three-apartment block.

The kids thought it was great and loved it, not just the house but not having to going to school for three months! They must have thought it was going to be one big holiday for them, but Jane had taken their school books with us so they could do a little bit of home tutoring. Jane was very busy with the kids as I was often away, but it was also tiring for me at times because of all the travelling. I was contracted to Nike during my stay with the Sounders and they gave me all the clothes I wanted, and for the family. They were all kitted out with some great gear from trainers to jumpers and coats – so much so that we had to buy two extra suitcases to get all the stuff home when we came back.

For my first game I was on the substitutes' bench. I had only had a couple of days' training with the team so I wasn't surprised about not starting and I felt OK about it. I got on for the last 20 minutes and the pace of the game surprised me. The standard was first class with some fantastic players and the teams could have all done well back in England. I was really looking forward to playing with the players Seattle had but also realised what a good team they were, although they were in the bottom three at the time and only getting 4,000 supporters into the Kingdome Stadium. It held around 60,000 when the Mariners (baseball) and the Seahawks (football) played there so it felt pretty empty and not the best atmosphere. We had to start winning some games and climb the table before the fans returned – a bit like here in many ways – as fans want to see success and the Americans don't like losers.

Away games were always three-day affairs – travel one day, play the next and travel back on the third day – and it was the first time I had left Jane, the kids and the babysitter alone. That first night Seattle was hit by thunder and lightning strikes; anyone who has experienced the extremes of weather in the States will know how powerful it can be. It was an electric storm but it was actually a bit exciting for the family. Well, that's what they told me when I got back. They all hugged and cuddled up together in bed and listened to it. They couldn't ring anyone as the phone lines went dead, so they just had to bear it out until it subsided. It was so frustrating not being able to talk to Jane. We watched the weather forecast on TV in our room in Edmonton and could see Seattle was being battered by the storms. I was concerned for the family but I couldn't do anything about it. It wasn't a good feeling for me and I was thinking it was all my fault because I'd brought them to the States. Because of the storm, I was worried about leaving the family again because we had another six or seven away games still to play. But I needn't have worried because Jane and the kids adapted very quickly. The next away game was 10 days away so it was a chance to spend some time together and see a bit of Seattle, which is a beautiful place. Steve Daley and his wife Lynda really helped us. They were great and the children got on well. On our days off we would often go to the pool and Alan Hinton was good at man management. He knew when the players needed a rest and time with their families. It was so important we spent as much time with them as we did in training.

During this break we had a bit of down time and Steve Daley drove me to a local Mexican bar, where we had a few beers. The drink-driving laws weren't as strict as they are now and Steve drove home afterwards. On our return journey, our car mounted the pavement and the next thing we knew, we were hitting a row of saplings, one after the other – bump, bump, bump. I was screaming at Stevie to stop but he seemed oblivious to what was going on. Thankfully we were close to where we lived and we somehow got away with it, without getting into trouble with the police or the club.

But the whole experience, on and off the field, was great. It was wonderful for the players' families too. Peter Ward, the ex-Forest and Brighton striker, helped our son Rod learn to swim. He spent a lot of time with him and it paid off handsomely as our son could swim quite well by the time we left. In fact the cheeky little monkey would do for Peter what he wouldn't do for me when I tried to teach him, probably because he was a lot more patient than me. Our daughter Kelly could already swim and she had a great time.

Our training ground was out of town right next to where the Boeing aeroplane engines were tested. When they started up you couldn't hear a thing the manager was saying or anyone else for that matter. It was so loud and when two jet engines were being tested you had to put your hands over your ears, they were so loud. When we trained in the Kingdome some of the lads would take the kids to training. They loved it and the facilities we enjoyed were five star. On the field we started to win a few games and as a result we were now getting thousands more coming to watch us as we had climbed into the top three and Jane heard a lot of the fans praising my contribution and saying what a good signing the Sounders had made. She was well chuffed to hear the fans praising her husband for the hard work I was putting in and chipping in with a few goals as well, but they mostly liked the effort and determination I was showing for the whole game and as a result I became very popular with the fans. It was refreshing for her as she had to put up with some criticism of me early on when a lot of the fans thought I was there just for the money. It was cruel for her to hear that knowing I would never do that. Before every game the national anthem was played or sung by someone and we had to face the American flag. It made the hair on the back of my neck stand up. Before every home game the owner Frank Calluccio would say to me in his American accent: 'Go get 'em Kenny.' It made me feel so good to hear him say that; he was a great guy who I liked a lot and he was desperate for success for the Sounders. One day we went to a barbecue with the Sounders' supporters club, called The Booster Club. It was a fantastic day, the weather was great and when the Americans put on a barbecue they do it in style. All the players were there and their families and the children ran riot but as newcomers it was great for us to meet some fans. They made us so welcome and were very friendly. In fact some of the fans wanted me to sign for longer than just for the summer.

Having won the NASL Western Division, we played in Toronto against the Blizzards, in the first round of the play-offs, and as we arrived the day before the game at mid-day, about five or six of us went out into the city for some lunch. We started our order with a beer each, but suffice it to say lunch turned out to be a long and liquid one! We had been drinking for about five hours and came out of the bar at about 5.30pm with training due at 6.45 for 7pm. We were steaming and just about managed to get back to the hotel for half an hour's rest or to try to sober up. Some of the lads could see what we were like and tried to protect us from the coach and manager. It was only a short session thank God but the boss seemed to be unaware of what we had done – or was he?

We had been busy with matches and the travelling was exhausting, and we had had a good run of results. I think the manager turned a blind eye in the belief it was a one-off and that we deserved to let our hair down a bit. The next day we weren't feeling great but we knew we had a match to win. We went behind to a superb goal scored by a great player in Teofilo Cubillas, an attacking midfielder who was known as the 'Pele of Peru'. There were only seconds remaining and we were knackered and just wanted to get off the pitch as quickly as possible when Steve Daley hit a shot from the edge of the penalty box that flew into the bottom corner. On any other day we would have been happy with a draw but we just looked at Steve and said 'What the hell have you done?

Now we've got to play an extra 30 minutes, you plonker!' However before the match could go into overtime Blizzards scored again to nick the victory. That was the first and only time we had a drink before a game. It had backfired on us big time and it was a lesson to be learned.

The next day I got a call from John Bond, who was manager at Manchester City, asking me to join them when my contract finished at Seattle. I said I would talk to him when I had played my last game for the Sounders, knowing Wolves still wanted me back. I wasn't sure what was happening back home as the club had been in financial trouble when I left and our former striker Derek Dougan, who headed a consortium that bought the club after it went bankrupt, was filling me in how much the club had changed and how the new owners were going to take the club forward. Graham Hawkins replaced Ian Greaves as manager and although obviously I knew of him – he had played with Derek at Wolves in the late 1960s and had recently been assistant to Graham Turner at Shrewsbury Town – I didn't know him very well and I was surprised at his appointment.

No disrespect to Graham, but I thought Derek was giving me a load of bullshit at first. I wondered how a club could change so much in just a short time and why they had got rid of one of the best managers I had worked with in Ian Greaves. I had a long chat with Jane and was in a bit of a quandary. My heart was still with Wolves but it was sad to see the way it was going before I left for the States. We decided to carry on at Seattle, so all of my concentration was on the task in hand before making any other decision about my future.

We ended up winning the league on goal difference, and with nearly 30,000 fans now pouring into the Kingdome, it was a special place to be. We had turned things around completely and the fans thought I had played a big part in it. Everything seemed to go one way when I arrived and the American fans thought I was 'the man'. It was an amazing feeling and I scored the overtime winning goal in Fort Lauderdale in the second leg of the semi-final. We had lost the first leg 2-1 in Seattle and nobody gave us a chance away from home and it was 3-3 with only seconds to go when the ball was played out wide. The cross came over to the far post where Roger Davies was waiting. I could see the space to run into and gambled that Roger would head the ball across the six-yard line, but he did better than that. He put it across the goal-line and I dived in to head the ball into the net from all of two inches – as the Press said – but they all count don't they? When we got off the plane back home in Seattle the number of fans there to greet us was unbelievable. I was besieged by TV cameras and reporters and of course the fans and I had to talk to them all. I was even presented with bouquets of flowers. It was just incredible.

My last-gasp goal made it 5-5 on aggregate so we now had to play Fort Lauderdale a third time, this time back in Seattle to reach what the Americans call the Soccer Bowl. We were very confident of beating them, but they were also hopeful after beating us 2-0 earlier in the season. Over 35,000 fans flocked to the Kingdome and the tension was high in the build-up to the game. I was very busy with interviews, having scored in the last game in Fort Lauderdale and the rest of the lads were just as busy. The game soon came around and the buzz was unbelievable. We were ready, the fans were really up for it and as we walked down the tunnel you could hear the fans chanting 'Sounders, Sounders' over and over again. Then the national anthem started and boy was I nervous, but as soon as the whistle blew, all of the tension disappeared.

Both teams missed chances and the match went into overtime, 15 minutes each way. It was in the second period that we finally got the breakthrough, following a corner on the right. It was headed out to where I was lurking on the edge of the penalty area, and, as a defender came to close me down, I went to hit it with my right foot but swivelled and thumped it with my left into the bottom left corner of the net. The keeper got a touch but couldn't keep it out and that was it – we were off to Soccer Bowl and the fans went wild. I turned and ran towards our manager to celebrate with him before the rest of the lads could catch me. He believed in me and said I was the last piece of the jigsaw in his team to turn an indifferent start to the season into a winning team. He was spot on with his team selection and deserved to take us to the final. It was a fantastic night for the Seattle fans and especially for the owner. As I watched a replay of the winning goal, I remember the commentator saying: 'Hibbitt has come through every time.' I really felt good and after that game the joy was almost as good as winning the League Cups with Wolves – not quite but it was close. We would go on and meet the New York Cosmos in San Diego the following week. They had a good season as well and the last time we played them, we lost at home. I had a broken coccyx, courtesy of the former Tottenham defender John Pratt who played for Portland Timbers. He caught me from behind with his knee and it was bloody painful. I had to sit on a plastic ring for a few days but I did play against the Cosmos about five days after I did it – only a broken leg would have stopped me playing against a great team who included the Dutch player Johan Neeskens. The night before the final we had a banquet with the Cosmos team and for the first time in my life I was fortunate to meet the best player I have ever seen – Pele, who had retired from playing by then but was there to watch the game. I had my photograph taken with him and he was such a gentleman. He was willing to spend time with me even though he had no clue who I was other than a Seattle player. It is one of the best photos I have and regard it as a piece of treasure. He could play a bit too!

Before we went to the dinner Steve Daley and I had been measured for our tuxedos but mine wasn't fit to wear for an evening of this nature. I put it on and found the sleeves were so short. They just about went past my elbow and the trousers were six inches too small. I looked like the comedian Max Wall and I told Steve I simply couldn't go looking like that. He asked why and I said: 'Look at the f******g state of this suit, there is no way I am going wearing this.' With that he burst out laughing and couldn't stop. He was actually crying with laughter but it wasn't funny to me and I went crazy. I mean there I was, just about to meet some world class players and hopefully Pele who was the guest of honour, looking like a right fool.

When Steve did eventually stop laughing ages later he came up with a plan. He said if the rest of the lads surrounded me, nobody would see the horrendous state of the suit and they would be none the wiser. I was still unsure about this but eventually succumbed and agreed to go along with the idea. When we got to the entrance to the banquet the lads were standing around me, protecting me – until they all walked off, leaving me all alone and looking like a right scruffy idiot! 'You b******s!' I shouted to them – but what a laugh and thankfully a few beers helped take the embarrassment never got my own back for that, but there is still plenty of time, Steve, so beware!

The build-up to the game was pretty nervy for a few of the lads, particularly the American players in the team who were experiencing a final for the first time, but none of us was exempt from the nerves. This was a big game against a top team who had several great players in their ranks – Carlos Alberto, the Italian star Giorgio Chinaglia, Romero, and Steve Hunt, the former Aston Villa and Coventry City midfielder, to name but a few. The game didn't go too well for us, and, although we created a few half chances, they were too good for us and we lost 1-0 to a Chinaglia goal. It was disappointing to get so far after winning the league. It would have been the icing on the cake for me in particular as I was only a loan player and it would have been great to go back to England knowing I had helped them to win the double.

It was while I was in Seattle that the FA brought in a new rule stating any player leaving the club they were attached to couldn't return to that club for 12 months if he had gone abroad to play. My contract at Wolves was due to finish on June 30, 1982 so I just didn't know where my career was going. My head was full of thoughts, most of them negative. All I could think of was my family and what the future held for us. It was a hectic and uncertain time as I had to be back in England within three days of my last game in the States, and we had to return to Seattle from San Diego the next day, pack everything up, close the bank accounts in Seattle and arrange the flight back to London. The club were brilliant and helped us all the way. All in all it was a terrific club and I have to say it was very tempting to ask if I could stay, especially knowing things at home were so uncertain.

By the end of July, Wolves had new owners, a mystery consortium fronted by my former team-mate Derek Dougan. Soon the Doog was trying to persuade the FA to agree for Wolves to take me back, claiming the deal to Seattle was done before the new rules came into place. How long this was going to take we didn't know. My wages had ended at Seattle and I had no contract at Wolves so it was a worrying time for us. I had been paid well in the States so we were able to survive financially for a couple of months. Just as we were ready to leave I had a phone call asking me if I was prepared to stay with the Sounders and when I said I was, I was asked to go to a place in town for talks.

The building was absolutely huge and I was interviewed by three men who were sat at a desk which seemed 30 feet away from me. I reckon you could have sat 50 people around it comfortably. Outside Peter Ward was also waiting to see the same guys. It transpired they were taking over the franchise of the Sounders and wanted Peter and I to sign two-year contracts. Peter had had a great season scoring plenty of goals alongside Mark Peterson, an American player, and Roger Davies. They asked me what I wanted in terms of salary. This was new ground for me because I hadn't conducted any negotiations myself before. Previously when a manager said he wanted to sign me,

I just signed the contract but here I was now in a position to name my own price. It was all a bit surreal and although I was nervous I said 'Just pay me what I am getting now over the two years.' They looked at each other as if to say 'Is that all you want?' quickly followed by 'No problem Kenny – leave it to us, we will be in touch when everything is sorted with the takeover'. It was the shortest interview I had ever had. I shook hands with them and said I would see them soon. As I walked out, Peter asked if it had gone well. I don't know what the outcome was with Peter as we flew back to England the next day. It was very unsettling for my wife and children, but Jane was brilliant through it all and supported me 100 per cent on any decisions I made.

Manchester City were still interested in me and Stoke City were now keen also as I could be a free agent when the FA made their decision. The journey home was a long haul and all we talked about was what we were going to do. Is it Wolves, Stoke, Man City or Seattle? It was going to be the biggest decision I had to make. Wolves were always top of my list for many reasons – Jane was a local girl, my children was settled at school and of course I had played for Wolves for 14 years and they were, and still are, in my heart. We just had to wait for the FA to make a ruling before any decision could be made. It was frustrating but eventually the news came that I was OK to return to Wolves. I was a free agent as my contract had ended with Wolves but that more or less made my decision so much easier.

The day after we got back Derek Dougan rang to arrange a meeting with me. We met up the next day and he talked about how the club had changed, the team had had a good start to the season and were in the top three in the table. When Derek had called me in America saying 'The club has changed so much you wouldn't believe it' I thought he was trying to pull the wool over my eyes and he was just saying it to get me back. But as soon as I walked through the door you could sense a feeling of real optimism and it felt so much better than three and half months before. That time had been the lowest I had known at the club and I couldn't see a great future unless someone was willing to get hold of it and turn it around. Well it felt like it was ready to go forward again, the team had some good youngsters mixed in with a few old heads around to help them. Wolves could go straight back up to the First Division again and I felt I wanted to be part of it. We talked for about an hour about which way the new owners wanted to go. As the ex-chairman of the PFA, Derek was always a good talker and negotiator and he sold the club to me. We soon agreed on a two-year contract, but before we shook hands he asked me if I would like to call Jane. Naturally I said yes because it was important she was happy with the deal but when I called her she told me to ask for an extra few bob spread over the two years. Derek thought about it, looked at me for a couple of seconds and said 'OK – do we have a deal?' We shook hands and I couldn't have been happier going back to the club I love. The Doog agreed to give me a signing-on fee which I was delighted with, but less so when the first cheque – which he signed – bounced! In the end I had to pursue the payment through the PFA and it took their intervention to get the money directly from a TV payment owed to Wolves, who were then paid the remainder. But I still felt I had made the right decision to return home because the franchise in Seattle I had spoken to had broken down so that was a non-starter. Jane and I were both very happy to get my future sorted out and the children were settled back at school.

Everything in the garden was rosy – now all I had to do was force my way back into the team as they had made an excellent start, with six wins and two draws from their opening eight games and just one goal conceded to top the table. The manager Graham Hawkins said I would have to work hard because I couldn't simply walk back into the side, and he was right – and I wouldn't have it any other way either. Things had worked out brilliantly for me. Here I was back at Molineux after a great adventure in the States where I had thoroughly enjoyed the experience. They love their statistics in America and here's a few I left with:- I had been voted player of the week twice and won 11 of the 14 games I played in, scoring four goals – half of them with my head – and a few assists as well. The one stat I do cherish is simple – if you score more goals than the opposition you will win matches. Simple. But Seattle was a wonderful place to be and I am so glad we went. It was very educational for the children as well and we still talk about it now as if it all happened just recently, even though it was over 30 years ago. Frightening how time goes so quickly, eh?

27

Back Home And Promotion Again

I was determined to make my mark after rejoining Wolves, but ill health prevented me from making my comeback earlier. Due to be our substitute at Carlisle on Saturday, October 2 – remember there was only one replacement allowed in those days – the night before the game I developed a temperature and a sore throat. I went to see the doctor and he put me on antibiotics. As a precaution I was put in a room on my own. But as the evening wore on I got worse, despite stuffing myself with pills. It was a long night and I felt dreadful, my temperature had risen and there was no way I could be involved in the game. So I stayed in bed until after the match and the doctor picked me up and drove me all the way back home. It felt like the longest trip I had experienced. We couldn't have been much further from Wolverhampton and feeling so bad made the journey feel twice as long. The doctor thought the change in the weather may have had some bearing on my illness, having come from the warm climate of the States. I didn't care too much about that, I just wanted to get back home and get into bed after a bloody nightmare trip.

A week later, I was back on my feet again for my first game back for Wolves, away to Sheffield Wednesday. It was a big game as both sides had enjoyed cracking starts to the season and it was a top-of-the-table clash – well, third versus first anyway. The manager put me on the bench, but that was fine as I didn't expect to start so soon coming back from being ill and from being in the States. I was well pleased to be back in the squad. I got on late in the second half for Billy Livingstone, our young striker, and it felt great to be back. We drew 0-0 and on reflection the result was about right. Neither team really created that many chances but we got a point away from home. The important thing from my point of view was I was back in the mix and looking forward to the rest of the season.

Although experienced lads such as George Berry and Willie Carr had left – George joined Richie Barker and Derek Parkin at Stoke, while Willie had been sold to Millwall – we had some decent young players who had come through the ranks such as John

Humphrey, John Pender, Bob Coy, Mick Matthews, Billy, Paul Butler and Wayne Clarke alongside the senior players. Gordon Smith, a midfielder, had arrived just after the start of the season and was very experienced having had spells at Aston Villa and Tottenham and Alan Dodd, a vastly experienced centre half, was soon to join from Stoke for £40,000. The goalkeeper John Burridge, who came from Queens Park Rangers for £80,000, had replaced the injured Paul Bradshaw, who was to miss the whole season with a back injury, and stalwarts such as Geoff Palmer, Peter Daniel and Mel Eves were all regulars. Geoff was our new captain, having switched from right back to left back to accommodate Humphrey and replace Parkin. Then we had great players like Andy Gray and John Richards to come back into the squad. Andy was on his way back from injury at the time, so the future was looking pretty good.

When I left for Seattle, Wolves were in dire straights financially, the future looked very grim and it was at death's door after 105 years, but the club breathed again under new ownership. I wasn't there to see the takeover but when I came back I couldn't believe it. There was a good feeling in the club again, the players were talking to each other in the right way, and the fun was back around the place. You've got to have a good dressing room with plenty of laughter between each player. That is where you build the team spirit. Without it you have no chance of being successful. I wasn't too bothered about going back to Wolves from the States when I left as it was so bad. But after walking back through the doors it felt right again and I was excited about the season ahead with a good blend of youth and experience in the squad.

Graham Hawkins had become our third boss in the space of eight months after John Barnwell and Ian Greaves. The latter was unfortunate in that he was a victim of circumstance following the takeover of the club. A lot of people said 'Graham who?' when the Doog went for Graham as he wasn't well known. But he wasted little time in putting his own stamp on things, introducing fines for any player who was booked for dissent. That rule brought problems for Andy Gray and I as we were both a bit mouthy towards referees. Andy was the first to be fined – and it wasn't a light fine, I can tell you. I thought to myself 'No way am I going to be throwing money away so easily', but it happened to me and I was done the same as Andy. It is difficult not to voice your anger towards the referee if he has failed to give you a free kick when you're getting kicked, pulled and shoved and you're in the heat of battle. He is the first person you look to for support. But I have to say Andy was a far worse offender than me. He just

159

couldn't bear losing at anything. And if he felt he wasn't getting enough protection from the referee – and there was precious little of it about in those days – then he was happy to take matters into his own hands.

I remember we were playing Tottenham at Molineux and Graham Roberts, their central defender, was giving him a bit of stick. Everyone had their battles in those days, particularly Andy and big Robbo, who was a hard player who could bloody tackle. Andy could rough it, though, and Robbo knew he was in for a battle against him. As a centre half, you're generally positioned behind the strikers you mark all of the time so they're always within your sight, whereas forwards often can't see where their markers are. Anyway, Andy shouted to me, 'Hibby, just f****** toss the ball up to me, will you?' So the next time I got the ball, I just floated it on top of his head, because he knew by me playing the pass like that, Roberts would be on top of it. If I had drilled it into his head, he wouldn't have had a chance of heading it. So I chipped it up to him with my left foot, and the next thing I knew, Andy's elbow had come out and Roberts was on the floor with his nose smashed across his face. There was no sending off – the referee didn't see it and Andy claimed they had both gone for the ball. I said to Andy 'What did you do?' He said 'He's been at me all f****** game!' He would have been done big time nowadays but you could get away with it back then.

Andy's winning mentality wasn't just confined to the pitch but off the park too. He is a big mate of mine and we have spent a few holidays together with our families. We used to go to Portugal and one night when the kids were all in bed we played a game where you had to guess a famous person's name from a number of letters. When his then other half Jan came up with someone he hadn't heard of, he stormed off and that was the end of the game. It lasted 10 minutes. But that's Andy – he's a winner whatever he plays.

Andy could be feisty and wasn't one to back down easily in an argument – as I found to my cost. One time we had boarded the coach to return to Molineux from our training ground at Castlecroft and the lads were discussing FA Cup final tickets, as each player had an allocation, whichever teams got to Wembley. How senior a player you were dictated the quality of seat you were allocated, so if you were one of the experienced lads, you were given more expensive tickets. Suddenly George Berry, our defender, started piping up from the back seat. George could be quite outspoken if he wanted to and the gist of his argument was he thought that system was unfair and he thought we should all have the same seats. Andy disagreed and soon they came together in the middle of the coach, squaring up to each other. Sensing things were about to turn ugly, I dived in between them to try to split them up but only succeeded in having the top of my head smashed against the luggage rack above us. I can't recall whether it was Andy or George who pushed me, but it left me with a painful bruise and thinking that if it happened again, they could get on with it!

Another time I remember nutmegging Andy in a five-a-side game and I had a laugh about it. I soon found out it was the wrong thing to do. He gave me some stick and warned me if I did it again he would "Knock my f*****g head off'. I can assure you I didn't go anywhere near him after that. But as soon as the final whistle went he came running up to me and said 'Come on Hibby, let's go and have a beer, mate'. That's his way and if you don't like it then tough. But he is the most generous person I know and I had to stop him spoiling my children on holiday, or I attempted to anyway. The kids loved him because if we denied them treats, we would find he had bought them what they wanted – be it an ice cream or lilo.

We used to do a bit of training early in the morning and collect the papers so our other halves could read them around the pool then we would find a local bar and have a late breakfast. We did this most mornings. I'm not sure whether they knew we had a beer or not, but it was good to spend time together to talk football. This was during the summer of 1981 – little over a year after lifting the League Cup in which Andy had scored the winner in the final against Nottingham Forest. At the time he was talking about the club and was worried we weren't going anywhere. He could sense Wolves were struggling financially and couldn't see too much of a future for himself or the club. It turned out he was right because all the things he was saying came true. We got relegated, the club went bankrupt and we sacked a fine manager in Ian Greaves.

Fast forward to the following season when I'd got back from the States and we were trying to get out of the Second Division at the first attempt. Graham Hawkins was doing a great job with the team, we were playing fairly well and getting some good results and we were right up there with a great chance of promotion. I was really enjoying my football again and felt so relaxed, something I hadn't done for some time as the nerves used to take over. I still had a few nerves before games which is always good, but it wasn't as severe. I think the time in America had helped me a lot. I was going into matches without feeling so much pressure and found how to relax more beforehand. I can't put my finger on why but I felt that spell helped me enormously. I was still as committed as ever and always give 100 per cent, but I had conquered my nerves to a great extent, and it was a good feeling.

We were playing good, passing open football and my understanding with Andy Gray was getting better. We used to talk before matches about what we were going to do on set-pieces as the manager wanted me to take them. So Andy and me made eye contact and he would tell me where he wanted me to put the ball. If he dropped his right shoulder he wanted it down the left and vice versa. Or it could be a little finger point by his side. If he put his finger one way he wanted the ball to go the other way – anything he could do to lose his marker, and it worked well. It was great having him in the team.

It was no secret he wanted to leave at the beginning of the 1982-83 season after relegation and the takeover, and he was linked with several clubs, including Manchester United. But he was a great professional and always gave his best. Like any striker, he loved scoring goals and loved celebrating them. But I was again reminded of his hatred of losing – this time in a different sport. We played snooker before we beat Crystal Palace 4-3 on November 27. I beat him by the same scoreline in frames but there was a dispute in one of the games and he just wouldn't accept my point of view and stormed off to bed early. His enthusiasm is second to none but the incident didn't seem to affect him as the next day he led us to a great hard-fought win, scoring one of the goals.

That win at Selhurst Park marked the debut of Alan Dodd, who helped bolster our defence. It also gave the manager options with John Pender and Bob Coy playing centre half but Alan was the difference at the back we needed with his experience. He was a very good player and he brought us a bit more quality alongside Pender, who was a young kid. We also had another youngster in Ian Cartwright in central midfield along with Wayne Clarke, who had been waiting in the wings to establish himself for some time. Wayne had great feet and could finish just like his famous brothers Allan, Frank and Derek. Their other brother Kelvin had a terrible injury and had to pack the game in unfortunately, but they were a real footballing family and one my wife Jane is distantly related to. Her maiden name is Clarke and they hailed from Willenhall, not far from the Clarke footballers in nearby Short Heath.

By the turn of the year, we were flying and we led the table ahead of Terry Venables's Queens Park Rangers. I remember we played Blackburn at Ewood Park on January 15, 1983 on a big but very flat pitch. We ended up drawing 2-2, which sounds OK but we had a really good chance to beat them with excellent opportunities going begging. Our fans had been fantastic from the first day of the season and they gave us great support as always. Hopes were high and so they should have been with the quality in the team and they were expecting us to go straight back to the First Division.

At one point we were awarded a free kick just outside the penalty area on the left at the end where all the Blackburn fans were and they were giving us some right verbals. Andy Gray, Geoff Palmer and myself had worked on a free kick during the week. Andy was to get himself lined up at the near post, where he always had a couple of defenders around him as he was so dangerous in the box, especially in the air. I was to feign to swing the ball in with my right foot at the same time as Geoff was to play it with his left, but we would both run up to the ball together as if we were both going to take it.

Anyway it looked as if we had cocked it up as we both ran over the ball thinking the other was going to play it, Andy would wave his hand at us giving us a b******g and turn away disgusted, and the defenders would switch off for a couple of seconds. The Blackburn fans jeered us and took the mickey but when Geoff and myself looked at each other and we pointed the finger, I would then hit the ball to the near post with my left foot, and, in the confusion, Andy had got away from his markers. He stole a yard on their defenders to head the ball towards the top corner of the net, but instead it hit the outside of the post, with their keeper Terry Gennoe static, having switched off as well. So it nearly worked and I just looked over to the fans and put my finger up to my lips to ask them to 'Shush'. They actually fell silent for a couple of seconds and a few of them applauded us for it. That was good banter and they really appreciated it. We never tried it again and I don't know why because it nearly worked and it was a good way to unsettle a defence. January 1983 was a good spell for me. I was voted by *Daily Mirror* readers as player of the month and was presented with a silver-plated tray and a framed picture. It felt really great to be recognised by the media. The team remained top, and a 2-1 win at home to Chelsea on the 22nd made it 10 unbeaten in the League from that victory at Crystal Palace. We had taken 26 points out of a possible 30, we were 15 points clear of fourth place – remember only the top three went up in those days, with no play-offs. But we all know how quickly things can change. Times like that are when managers earn their corn and Graham Hawkins did everything right. We had great training sessions, and there was laughter and enjoyment. It was what we needed, while being totally relaxed yet totally focused on what was required to win promotion.

Earlier that month we had been drawn to play Tranmere Rovers from the Fourth Division at Prenton Park in the third round of the FA Cup. Despite the two-division gap, it proved to be a tough tie and we were fortunate to get a 1-0 win. Yours truly scored in the 69th minute in what proved to be my last goal in the competition for Wolves. Mike Dean, the Premier League referee who I work with now in assessing referees, was only a teenager at the time but he remembers me scoring the goal that knocked his team out of the Cup and he gives me so much stick for it now!

We didn't want the Cup to get in the way of our target of promotion, but the FA Cup is special and was treated as it should be – with respect, not like it has been in recent years. The competition gives the smaller clubs a chance of making some money with a good run. It was also great for the players from smaller-sized teams to get a good draw as they wanted to be tested against the best. As a top club the players had to have the correct attitude or you could get turned over. It was always a dream for players to play in an FA Cup final.

Around this time Graham Hawkins started to experiment with me playing in a sweeper role. I found it interesting as I was able to get more time on the ball, and because I was a half-decent passer, it worked quite well. I could break out of the defence with the ball and play it up to the front men or put it out wide then drop back, and from there I had a good, open picture of things. In many ways it was slightly easier than in midfield where it gets a lot more congested. But I still missed what attack-minded players like doing best – scoring goals, particularly from midfield, or creating chances for others. It was a new role for me but I enjoyed every minute of it and I think it is good for players to be able to play different positions. It gives you an insight to what your team-mates have to deal with during games. Playing sweeper, the marking is different and you have to cope with high crosses from all angles. Set-pieces were always difficult for me to deal with because I was up against some big strikers who were coming in on top of me, especially if the ball hung up in the air. I must admit heading wasn't my forte, so I more or less marked space or stood guarding the goal post like I did when I had done in midfield.

Off the field, I was suddenly having to use my head in a different way. One day Derek Dougan called me into his office and asked me if I would give evidence in a case against the long-serving former club secretary Phil Shaw, who Dougan had sacked. Shaw was claiming he was unfairly dismissed by the club and took them to an industrial tribunal. Dougan said in evidence the club didn't tell the new owners that 'The club's best player might be prevented from turning out for them again' – his words not mine – and was using my transfer to Seattle Sounders as the reason to sack him. I knew nothing about what had happened to the secretary as I was in the States and wasn't really interested in how the transfer was dealt with and by whom. Derek was saying the club could have lost a valuable player. As I mentioned earlier, the rules had changed slightly for a player moving abroad just after the agreement was made with the Sounders, in that a player couldn't return to the same club for a year, which is what all the argument was about.

So it meant when my time in Seattle was up, I would have been a free agent and could sign for any other club for nothing. Dougan thought my value was around the £150,000 mark. I was asked to stand in front of the tribunal as if I was in court and forced to answer some awkward questions. It was the most frightening thing to experience. I felt sick and wondered what the hell I was doing there. They put questions to me about things I had no idea about, then they asked me about the payments I had received from Seattle and what wages I earned. I looked at Dougan before I answered because he told me they wouldn't ask me anything about my wages and payments.

The guy putting the questions shouted at me and said 'Do not look at Mr Dougan, Mr Hibbitt, look at me and tell me what your payments were'. I felt like saying 'What the f**k has it got to do with you?' but I composed myself, although I got a feeling of guilt as if I was the one on trial. I was only there for back-up and there I was feeling like that, it was terrifying. Afterwards I told Derek he had better not put me through anything like that again or I would be out of there. I was like a nervous wreck for a few days afterwards. By the start of April, we were on the verge of promotion. I was suspended for a game and was disappointed at not playing, but I had a bit of a lift when I was voted into the PFA's Second Division team of the year along with team-mates John Burridge, Andy Gray and John Humphrey. It was a great feeling being voted for by your peers. A certain Mick McCarthy of Barnsley was also in the team of the year. My suspension came on the back of a couple of indifferent performances and I was left out of the team on my return, but I looked at it with a positive attitude and had to work hard to regain my place. I probably needed a rest as I had played continuously through the summer and maybe I was a bit fatigued. But I always hated being out of the team for any reason. A couple of reserve games is sometimes good for a player to get his sharpness and confidence back and that's what happened. I came back raring to go. The team could see the finishing line but we were getting a bit anxious to get the necessary points. We needed to slow down and steady ourselves, and this is where the experience of the senior players helped.

We finally made it back to the First Division at the first attempt, just like we did in 1977, although rather than going up as champions, we had to settle for the runners-up spot, 10 points behind QPR, who had my old Wolves team-mate Bob Hazell in defence. We had led the table for half of the season but we ran out of steam a bit. A run of two wins in the last 13 games – with 10 draws in that spell – put paid to our title hopes, and we finally clinched promotion with a 3-3 draw against Charlton at The Valley on May 2 with two games to spare. We had led 3-0 with two goals from Billy Kellock, who we signed from Luton Town for £20,000 in the March. He had previously played under Derek Dougan at Kettering. The other goal came from Mel Eves, his 18th League goal of the season and final one of the campaign, before Charlton hit back. Mel finished as our top scorer for the second season in a row. Talking of last goals, I scored what was to be my final strike for Wolves in a 1-1 draw at Rotherham, on April 9. It was almost a year to the day since what turned out to be my final goal at Molineux, against Manchester City. I suppose it was fitting that it came in my native Yorkshire, albeit in the south of the county rather than the west where I was from! A week later, in a 0-0 draw at home to Bolton, John Richards and myself played in a Wolves team for the final time in a competitive game in what turned out to be John's last for the club. He had struggled to get into the team all season and had had a loan spell with Derby. Soon he would be leaving for good, and for a new adventure as it turned out, with a spell playing for Portuguese side Maritimo based on the island of

Madeira. Having joined the club in July 1969, eight months after me, John was my longest standing team-mate and we had been through so much together. I felt sorry that his time was coming to an end because he had been such a tremendous player. He had everything you could wish for in a striker – he was strong, brave, fast, two-footed, in the air and he saw things quickly. He was a goalscorer and he scored all sorts of goals – I've seen him score from 35 yards and from tap-ins so he had a lot of skill as well.

It was just sad that he suffered from knee injuries which not only almost ended his career early but cost him half a yard of pace. When he finished at Wolves he was the club's record scorer with 194 goals in 486 games, which when you consider some of the greats that he surpassed, tells you all you need to know about what a class act he was. I felt John suffered after Waggy and Doog left because he didn't have the service he deserved, but he still scored plenty of goals and was our top scorer in the League on six occasions when players such as the Doog, Andy Gray and myself often reached double figures as well. He also deserved far more than the solitary England cap he earned, but he played at a time when there were several other strong candidates such as Kevin Keegan, Allan Clarke, Malcolm Macdonald, Martin Chivers and Frank Worthington and later Trevor Francis, Tony Woodcock and Paul Mariner.

28

Down Again

Going back to the First Division, I felt we needed to sign some quality players to compete at the top. We were good enough to get out of the Second Division but, deep down, I knew in my heart we weren't good enough to stay there with the squad we had. The players were thankful that the new board had saved our jobs when the club was taken over by Derek Dougan and his consortium, and grateful to the manager Graham Hawkins who had done a wonderful job getting promotion at the first time of asking. But it was now time to move on and for the club's owners, the Bhatti brothers, to make that next step and take the club forward. I even offered Derek the chance to sell me, not that I wanted to leave, but I thought it might give them the chance to make way for new players if Graham thought I wasn't good enough for the First Division. We'd had a hard nine months trying to get back to the big time and after celebrating promotion with champagne and lager it was time to reflect on the task ahead, which was going to be really tough unless good players were brought in.

In the past the club had made mistakes. When we had that bit of success in the 1970s, more money should have been invested in the team but the board ended up borrowing from the bank to build a new stand. A new stadium is no good if you haven't got a good team to play in it. The fans would rather be in an old ground watching them win than a new one seeing them struggle. At that time we had several players who had given everything to Wolves but we had all grown older together and you can't go on for ever. It's cruel at times for players who are forced to leave but the club and its future is the most important thing. Players and managers come and go but the fans will always be there. The club needed to look to the future. That's the way it is in football, you're always looking over your shoulder.

Pre-season training came around very quickly. It didn't seem two minutes since we had been celebrating promotion. But now it was time for the hard work of getting fit in readiness for what looked like a bloody tough season. No one knew what to expect over the following nine months and questions such as 'How do you think you will do this season?' were always being put to us. But it was one question I struggled to answer positively. We needed to buy some quality players, players that had seen the First

Division before and knew what it was all about. When I looked back at the squad we had in the early 70s and right up to the time we won the League Cup in 1980, we had some great players – lads who could win matches by putting the ball in the net on a regular basis, defenders who defended with their lives and a team who played for each other. It looked like we were going straight back up from halfway through the previous season so I hoped the management had been planning ahead and I thought they would bring in at least five top players. That's what we needed if we were going to move forward and that meant spending some money. When you have success you can't stand still, you have to move on. That's why I said to Derek Dougan I was willing to step aside if he thought I couldn't help take the team forward, and I was serious. I wanted to stay as I loved the club and they gave me my big chance way back in 1968.

That summer I read the paper every day looking out for new signings, hoping for some quality players. We bought Tony Towner, a winger from Rotherham, for £60,000. I had heard about him. He'd had a good season and had played against us in the Second Division. I thought he was a good addition. He was quick and had the pace to go past defenders and put crosses into the box. He was the kind of player we needed at the time.

Going back a few years, John Farley and later, and sadly briefly, Dave Thomas were the last real wingers who tried to replace Dave Wagstaffe, but how do you replace someone of Waggy's ability and skill? I don't think we could because he was extremely gifted. He had a great career but even then he didn't achieve what he was capable of. He should have been an England player for years but he probably didn't have that ambition top players need to have. I would have loved to have had his pace and ability to go past defenders with the ease that he did.

We now waited to see if Tony could help fill that gap at wide right and provide Andy Gray with the crosses he loved to get on the end of. We probably played too many straight balls into Andy and not enough were put into areas where he was most dangerous, which was balls from wide positions. So Tony was brought in to provide that for him. How long we were going to hold on to Andy was another matter as we all knew he wanted to move away, and probably needed to for the sake of his career. It was going to be a sad day when he left, not only for his playing quality for which he would be missed, but also in the dressing room. Infectious, he lifted the spirits of everyone and was a real character. When he walked in you thought, 'I'm glad he's with us' and we hoped he would stay.

We went to Sweden for pre-season training again, the eighth time we had done so during my time at Wolves, but I didn't mind as it was a place I loved going to. The people were always welcoming and we were in the company of the Swedish Wolves fans club. We were based in Vasteras, a great place where our former coach and gaffer Sammy Chung had managed. While we were out there I was given the club captaincy and Andy Gray was appointed team skipper. That night we went out to celebrate. We were given a curfew of midnight, so it wasn't too late.

On our way back we walked past a McDonald's restaurant and Billy Kellock said he was hungry. It was 11.45pm so we thought eating a quick burger wouldn't leave us late. Alan Dodd said to Billy: 'I'll bet I could eat more burgers than you.' That was it, the contest was on in what could have been a prelude to TV's *'Man Versus Food'*. They ordered two each but they didn't last long and another two each were soon called for. We were in stitches watching them devour these burgers. Another two each were ordered, and by now everybody in the restaurant was watching and even the chef was falling about. The staff eventually said they wouldn't charge us for any more and the chef just kept cooking. It got to a stage where they both couldn't swallow any more without a drink but their mouths were full so we had to get them straws and thread them through the food into their mouths. I think it ended up as a draw six burgers each. That is a lot of food but what a laugh. It was brilliant but the time was now getting on for 1am and we had to rush back to the hotel and sneak in somehow without the management seeing us. But we had bargained without the coach Jim Barron, who was waiting for us and wasn't happy. The next morning we had to explain ourselves to the manager Graham Hawkins. It wasn't a good start to my club captaincy and we were all fined, quite rightly too as we had broken the curfew. But it was well worth it and I think the management had a laugh later in the day, and it was good for team bonding in our books.

Billy Kellock was only with the club for a short while but he was quite a character and made his mark – in more ways than one, leaving Jim Barron in a rage again. On another occasion, we returned to our hotel after a night out with a few drinks. I was rooming with Tony Towner, who had been feeling tired so stayed in and was in bed when we got back. Billy came back to our room, and, being slightly jolly after the evening's refreshments, starting swinging a chrome bar stool-type chair around his head, saying he could throw it through our large plate glass window. Unfortunately, just as Billy pretended to throw it, Tony put his head up out of the bed and the chair leg caught him flush on the head, causing quite a nasty gash. All hell broke loose, with claret everywhere and an angry Jim soon back on the scene going berserk at Billy as we cleared up the mess and Tony was despatched to get stitched up. I tried to defend Billy, saying it was an accident, and luckily he was able to stay on the tour without being sent home as a punishment.

The build-up to the season had promised much, but like a lot that happened in the sorry Bhatti era, delivered so little. Desperate to inject some quality into a team that limped over the finishing line to promotion, Graham Hawkins drew up a wish list to strengthen his squad. Graham never discussed potential signings with me, but in the years since, it has crept into the public domain who he was trying to land that summer. His list read like a 'Who's who' of top 1980s footballers, when you consider what they went on to achieve in the game. Goalkeeper David Seaman, then with lowly Peterborough United, and his Posh team-mate Micky Gynn, then aged 22, Mick McCarthy, who was then a 24-year-old centre back at Barnsley, an attacking midfielder Paul Bracewell, who at 21 was impressing in Stoke City's midfield, and Gary Lineker, then a 22-year-old striker beginning to make a few waves at Leicester City – these were the players Hawkins identified to turn Wolves into a First Division force.

But rather than force it quickly looked like farce when it become clear the manager wouldn't have the funds he wanted. It wasn't as if he was asking for the earth – Gynn was sold to Coventry City for just £60,000 that summer. The little-known Mike Bennett, a left back who came in on a free transfer from Cambridge United, was our only other summer signing. Bracewell went to Sunderland for £250,000, while McCarthy joined Manchester City, then in the Second Division, for £200,000 in December 1983. Seaman had joined Peterborough for just £4,000 a year earlier from Leeds and was sold to Birmingham City for £100,000 in October 1984, and Lineker stayed another two years at Leicester, who he had helped to promotion in third place, one behind us (remember there were no play-offs then) on the back of being the Second Division's leading scorer with 26 League goals. Despite the lack of transfer activity, the season started OK with a 1-1 draw against the champions Liverpool, but

171

things quickly went downhill and we slid to what was Wolves' worst ever start to a season. We got a fair few good hidings – 4-0 beatings against Luton and QPR and 5-0 at Nottingham Forest. That day at the City Ground we at least had a new signing in the ranks with the arrival of Danny Crainie on loan from Celtic. A slight but skilful left winger, Danny impressed so much in his temporary spell that the Bhattis somehow scraped together the £25,000 required to oblige the fans and make his move permanent. Danny came in shortly after we signed the midfielder Andy Blair on loan from Aston Villa. But the performances of Andy and Danny were rare beacons of hope in a season of despair. In fact we set a sorry club record of 19 League games without a win. That was finally ended on November 26 when we upset the odds by beating arch rivals West Bromwich Albion 3-1 at The Hawthorns in the Black Country derby. Crainie was inspired that day, scoring twice in front of the BBC TV cameras with Wayne Clarke grabbing the other, so the fans could revel in the rare but welcome combination of seeing a Wolves win on *Match of the Day* that night! That victory picked us up a bit and we needed it because we had sold our record signing Andy Gray to Everton for a knockdown price of £250,000 earlier in the month, just to get some money in because of the club's dire financial situation.

With my mate Andy gone, I wondered who was going to score the goals and help us survive. Andy was a big player and one that could have helped us in our quest for survival, but you couldn't blame him for moving to Everton, who were a good team and a big club who went on to enjoy tremendous success with him leading the attack. He had to look after his own career and his future. He had been unsettled for some time but he always gave his best. Andy was John Barnwell's biggest signing and was the most expensive player in Britain until Manchester United paid West Bromwich Albion £1.5m for Bryan Robson just over two years later. I felt Andy was a great signing; for him to pick Wolves instead of a more successful team at the time was a great piece of management by Barnwell. After his exit, we were a sorry state of affairs and it shows how good Andy still was and how far the club had fallen that he was sold for such a low fee and yet he ended that season as an FA Cup winner, scoring with a header in the final as Everton, who finished seventh in the League under Howard Kendall, beat Watford 2-0. I remember Jane saying we should have been at Wembley that day. Andy had promised us tickets for the final but we couldn't go as she was still in hospital with septic arthritis. Lying in her bed, she actually looked up at the clock at kick-off time and thought 'I should be at Wembley'. Playing alongside better players, Andy enjoyed a

Cheers lads! Celebrating our League Cup win with some bubbly. Interesting choice of headgear for yours truly, Andy Gray, Peter Daniel and Geoff Palmer, who seems like he's having a snooze! George Berry (top) looks like he's raising a toast to the trophy.

Mixing with the stars . . . it wasn't just Robert Plant who we rubbed shoulders with from the world of showbiz. Bev Bevan, drummer from ELO is a big Wolves fan and brought us some copies of their greatest hits LP, along with Britt Ekland, the Swedish actress, who is holding her calendar. I'm still wondering how Britt was persuaded to come to Castlecroft!

Pirates of the Caribbean – with my Wolves team-mates, from left John Richards, Paul Bradshaw, John McAlle, Andy Gray, me and Willie Carr putting our faces in the frame on a trip to Disney in the summer of 1980.

Hitting the bar . . . in Magaluf letting our hair down on end-of-season trip are, from left, the bar owner, a waiter, me, Geoff Palmer, Colin Brazier, Paul Bradshaw, Norman Bell and Willie Carr, with a rather oversized glass!

Up for the Cup . . . team-mate Mel Eves gives the thumbs up as we prepare to depart for our hideaway before the FA Cup semi-final against Tottenham at Hillsborough in April 1981. Little did we know what drama lay ahead as I became the story and made the national headlines. *(Express & Star)*

Top: FA Cup semi-final drama . . . Glenn Hoddle's challenge brings me down and referee Clive Thomas (right) and Tottenham players Steve Perryman and Graham Roberts look on. *(Dave Bagnall)*. Bottom: John Richards and substitute Norman Bell congratulate me on winning the penalty. I wasn't taking it, though! Emlyn Hughes calls for the ball and Hoddle protests it should be a corner instead. Perryman and Ossie Ardiles walk away in disappointment. *(Dave Bagnall)*

Willie Carr (left) scored the last-minute penalty against Spurs that earned us extra-time then a replay at Highbury, which we lost 3-0. Here we are working on one of our free kick routines. Willie was one of my favourite players and we shared a great relationship both on and off the pitch. *(Dave Bagnall)*

I've got your number . . . I was honoured to have Peter Knowles play in my testimonial against Derby in 1981. His decision to retire at the age of 23 was a loss to Wolves and to England. We could have enjoyed more success with him in the team, but he has never regretted his decision and is the most contented man I know.

On the ball Stateside. Top: A picture of concentration for the Seattle Sounders in the Soccer Bowl final against New York Cosmos in the summer of 1982. Bottom: Three is the magic number . . . playing in an unfamiliar shirt number for the Sounders. I really loved my time over there.

Hands up if you're the player of the month! February 1983, receiving a silver salver and framed picture as part of the *Daily Mirror's* award for January. I gained a new perspective from playing sweeper and was voted into the PFA's Second Division team of the season as we won promotion at the first attempt.

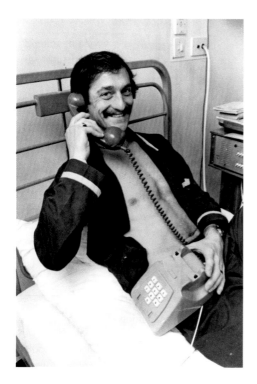

Hanging on the telephone . . . calling Jane from my hospital bed. She was also in hospital, but a different one on the other side of town – talk about bad timing! It was just as well we had a good family to look after the kids. *(Express & Star)*

'How many do you want in the wall, Budgie?' That seems to be what I'm saying to goalkeeper John Burridge, with John Humphrey, Billy Livingstone (hidden), Paul Dougherty and Martin Bayly. This 0-0 draw against West Bromwich Albion in April 1984 was my last competitive game at Molineux. They were also my first Molineux opponents for my Wolves debut back in April 1969. *(Dave Bagnall)*

Sent to Coventry . . . I spent two more years in the top flight with the Sky Blues after leaving Wolves in 1984. Here I am getting a shot in ahead of Newcastle's David McCreery in October 1984 on a mixed day for me. I gave away a penalty for handball and Peter Beardsley scored from the spot, before I equalised with a 25-yard free kick. *(Jim Brown)*

Sign here please Andy . . . a picture 'exclusive' as Andy Gray signs for Aston Villa for the second time. Chairman Doug Ellis (right) had tracked Andy down to our villa in Portugal, where we were on holiday in the summer of 1985.

A hero's homecoming . . . I've never known a reception like the one when I was welcomed back to Molineux in March 1989 with Bristol Rovers. It was the first time I'd been back for a game since leaving five years earlier. That will stay with me forever.

Making a splash by the pool. . . I think I was the only one to have been on holiday that summer. I am looking tanned, third from the left of this Bristol Rovers' Third Division title-winning squad in 1990. Devon White, our big striker, is missing from the picture.

Having a ball with Barrie Blower, the then Walsall chairman who appointed me as manager. It was my first job in management and I couldn't wait to get started. I will always be grateful to Barrie for giving me my big chance. *(Express & Star)*

Ken the builder. Here's me putting the finishing touches to the Bescot Stadium after Walsall moved there from Fellows Park in the summer of 1990. *(Express & Star)*

A penny for my thoughts . . . I soon found out life was no bed of roses in the dugout, with little money, no scouts and no assistant to bounce ideas off.

'I'll wring your neck if you cheer for them.' That's what I seem to be saying to my son Roderick before Walsall played Chelsea in the League Cup. He's a Chelsea fan! Mind you, some might say you can see his point. They hammered us 9-1 over two legs in 1990-91 and beat us 4-0 on aggregate in 1992-93. *(Express & Star)*

Pleased to meet you Your Highness . . . greeting the Prince of Wales as Cardiff City manager. I was proud to have managed such a big club with a passionate fan base, but was disappointed with the way I was treated after becoming director of football.

All smiles at Rod's wedding to Katie in Florida, with our oldest friends, Phil and Janet Brookes, who live there. Janet is an old school friend of Jane's. They have been pals for over 50 years. Phil and Janet were delighted to join us on the big day.

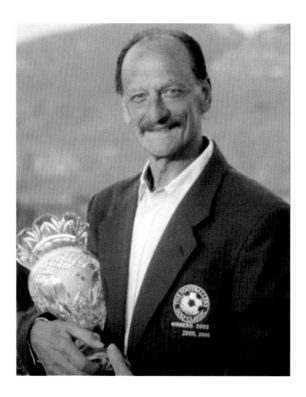

My proudest moment on a golf course . . . winning the La Manga Golf Footballers Classic in 2015. It is the most competitive golf tournament for retired footballers, with about 45 of us playing each summer in Spain. It turned out to be lucky 13 for me as I won it at the 13th time of asking. This year will be the 16th time I have played in it.

Sharing the limelight . . . with our niece, Emilia Clarke. To us she's just Milly, our lovely, very smiley, happy niece who dons her party hat at Christmas. But to millions of viewers, she is Daenerys Targaryen from *Game of Thrones*. This was taken at a private screening in Soho of the latest *Star Wars* film, *Solo: A Star Wars Story*, where she plays Qi'ra, the female lead.

My squad . . . from left, me with grandsons Tom and Jasper, son Rod and his wife Katie, grand-daughters Lucy and Ella, daughter Kelly, Jane and Kelly's husband Eddie. We are an extremely close family and have made a happy life for ourselves in the beautiful Cotswolds.

I'm pleased to say the sporting tradition in the family has continued to my grandchildren. Here Kelly's daughters Ella, aged nine, and Lucy, six, are preparing to go riding.

Kelly's son Tom (right), aged 16, and Rod's lad Jasper, 11, are pictured at Cotswold Edge Golf Club's presentation night. Tom is holding the trophy he won as junior club champion and Jasper won the junior captain's day. I'm proud of them all.

new lease of life in his new surroundings, going on to win the League and the European Cup Winners' Cup the following season and reaching another FA Cup final, where this time Everton were denied a treble as Manchester United beat them 1-0. For us, the win at Albion proved a false dawn as we conceded 10 goals in two games at the start of December, losing 5-0 at home to Graham Taylor's Watford when their new striker Maurice Johnston hit a seven-minute hat-trick, then getting thumped 5-1 by Leicester City at Filbert Street. The Watford setback was the biggest defeat I had been involved in – the result was humiliating and the fans deserved to have a pop at us. Things on the pitch were looking very miserable again. Although we won three League games out of four either side of Christmas against Everton and Norwich at home and bizarrely Liverpool away with a lone goal off Steve Mardenborough's shoulder, our situation was so bleak that we were still bottom and five points from safety. The shock win at Anfield was the club's first there for 33 years but it was a rare highlight. Our second away win of the season proved to be our last.

Shortly after that, in the February, the club decided to take us away for a few days – and to a place with a difference: Kuwait. It was a long way to go for a brief trip and a couple of friendlies but I guessed the club was making a few bob out of it. As it was somewhere I hadn't been to before, it was pretty exciting. A couple of weeks before the trip I had suffered a stomach bug, or so I thought. I took some medicine to get rid of it and thought no more about it. We stayed in a magnificent hotel. It was luxurious compared with some of the places we had been to and the food was out of this world. But in the first game I only managed to stay on the pitch for a short time because my stomach ache came back very severely and I had to leave the field. I could hardly breathe because of the pain I was in. It was worrying and from then on, I was advised to eat only potatoes and bread with water. So it wasn't a good time for me. I couldn't go home, I was always on the toilet, I couldn't leave the hotel room and I had to put up with considerable pain.

Tony Towner was my room-mate again and I felt so sorry for him having to put up with it. But he was brilliant and helped me a lot. He knew I was very concerned about the pains I had but he was so comforting and understanding. I know a lot of players wouldn't have put up with it and would have demanded to be put into a different room, but Tony stayed with me and helped me through it while we were out there. On the way back to Wolverhampton from the airport, our coach Jim Barron wrapped me in a blanket to keep me warm. The pain was excruciating and I didn't know where to put myself. I still kept needing to go to the toilet and it was becoming embarrassing. It was eventually diagnosed as ulcerative colitis, as I have described at the start of the book.

Over 20 years later, Stoke City midfielder Darren Fletcher – then at Manchester United – suffered with it. Darren's case seemed more serious than mine. He was diagnosed in 2008 then took a complete break from football in December 2011 and was finally operated on in January 2013. As for me, I was only out for a matter of weeks, missing just four games before making my comeback on March 24 in a game away to Arsenal as a substitute. But I had to continue taking medication for the next 30 years, with up to 17 tablets a day, along with annual check-ups, even seeing two specialists into retirement! I had to cut out any pork product and pastry, as well as watching my diet to try to prevent any flare up, and woke up every day wondering when the next episode would be. A flare up would see me suffer excruciating cramp-type pains in my abdomen.

When I started playing again, I made little impact on our fortunes as we went down 4-1 away to Arsenal on an afternoon when teenage defender Stuart Watkiss, who I later signed for Walsall, made his second and final appearance for the club. By now, Mark Buckland, a utility man who had worked as a scaffolder, had signed from non-league AP Leamington, and striker Scott McGarvey had arrived on loan from Manchester United. But the club was in a sad situation and the team were struggling big time, with relegation looking more likely with each passing week. The lads still tried hard but the quality was missing and it became a big uphill battle. Relegation was the biggest inevitability. This time there was no fight to the bitter end like we did in 1976 or a prolonged battle against the drop like in 1982. We still had six games left when our fate was confirmed after a 3-0 defeat at home to Ipswich. Just 6,611 were at Molineux to witness it. There had been 26,249 there on the opening day against Liverpool, but now with seemingly no hope, the fans had deserted us in droves. Who could blame them though? Statistically, we went down as one of the worst teams to have played in the top flight and were 21 points from safety when the season ended, after winning just six games and scoring only 27 goals. We were 12 points adrift of the next-placed team Notts County and a further seven behind Birmingham City, who were also relegated. The future looked grim for Wolves. I wanted to stay and try to help the club back up at the first attempt like we did the previous season and in 1976-77, but the financial problems were much greater than we all thought.

29

Sent To Coventry

The disappointment of relegation for the third time in my 16 years at Wolves was a nightmare. Worse was to follow in the next two years as the club entered the blackest period in their history with consecutive relegations to fall into the Fourth Division by 1986, when they went bankrupt for the second time in four years. But I would have no part to play in the rest of that sad fall from grace.

I turned down a new one-year contract when our coach Jim Barron was put in temporary charge after the sacking of Graham Hawkins. Jim called me into the manager's office and told me about the club's financial problems and that he could only offer me a 12-month deal on half the wages I was on. He slapped it on the table and said 'Take it or leave it, it's up to you'. My reaction was to tell him to stick it where the sun doesn't shine, so I said I would leave it and walked out.

The cold manner in which the offer was delivered by Jim must have been a reflection of what the chairman and owners thought. Jim had obviously been given the orders, and I knew they weren't going to offer me the same money as I'd been on during the two-year contract I signed when I returned from Seattle because of the problems the club were going through. So I knew I would have to take a pay cut to stay. They actually offered me the same money as I ended signing for at Coventry City but it was the way it was done. If he had discussed it in the right manner and said 'We want you to stay Kenny, but unfortunately we can't offer you the wages you have been on for the last two years, but we can offer you this', I would probably have remained and helped try to build the club up again. But he threw it on the desk. There was no attempt to persuade me to stay. I felt that was the least I deserved after 16 years' service, but it was done in a way that told me they wanted me off the wage bill, which for me was so disappointing and hurtful.

The writing was on the wall for me at Wolves, and, although I didn't know it at the time, a 0-0 draw at Watford on May 5 was to prove my last game for the club. It also proved to be Mel Eves's last match for the club, though in much more unfortunate circumstances than mine. Mel had ruptured his Achilles tendon, which was then a

175

career-threatening injury. I remember he ran past me, changing pace to chase a goal kick from John Burridge, and I heard a snap like a dry twig. The way he went down was like someone had shot him in the leg. He was carried off the pitch and we came back into the dressing room after the game and Jim Barron said 'I don't believe you, Mel!' They had just left him on the bed. I felt sorry for him because Jim could have been a bit more sympathetic towards him.

Tommy Docherty took over as manager that summer and he saw me in the dressing room after showering from a training session I had done to help keep in shape just in case I was wanted back in the United States. He asked me if I was leaving because of money, but I said it had nothing to do with that. I told him money didn't motivate me, but after 16 years at the club, I didn't like the way I was spoken to by Jim when he offered me the contract. He asked if I fancied a player-manager's job and I said I might do if I couldn't get fixed up at a decent club as a player. He told me to leave it with him for a couple of days and he would be in touch. The next day he called and said he'd arranged a meeting for me at Swindon Town. They were looking for a player-manager and said they were very interested and would like to talk to me. At this point the old nerves kicked in again. I said 'OK boss, when do they want to see me?'

He told me someone would be in touch and I got a call from the Swindon coach Danny Williams saying they were keen for me to join them and that the chairman Brian Hillier and the board wanted to arrange an interview with me as soon as possible. They were also meeting other candidates as well. Driving to Swindon gave Jane and I chance to discuss our plans without the children interrupting us. She asked if it was what I wanted and I said yes but I admitted going into management might be a bit too early for me. But if they offered me the job then I would seriously have to think about it. We arrived 10 minutes late due to traffic and not knowing exactly where the ground was. Lateness is my pet hate as I would rather be an hour early than a minute late. Anyway Danny Williams met us as we got out of the car at the County Ground, where the press and TV were there to greet us as they knew the club was holding interviews that day. Danny showed us around the ground and said they really wanted me but they had to go through the process of seeing other candidates who had expressed their interest before I got involved. The meeting went well and they offered me the job but I needed a little time to think about it as it had all happened so quickly. But that night I had even more to ponder as I got a call from my former Wolves team-mate Bobby Gould, who was now managing Coventry City. Bobby offered me the chance to stay in the First Division as a player and my decision was made. The offer – a two-year deal with a signing-on fee – took away all the doubts I had about taking over at Swindon as player-manager. Not only that, but it felt right for me to continue playing at the highest level. It was what I wanted, and to have the chance of another couple of years at the top at the age of 33 was a great opportunity, albeit not playing every game. But I was excited about the prospect of playing for Coventry and it also meant I remained in the West Midlands and so wouldn't have to move house as the kids were settled at school. That night I called the Swindon chairman Brian Hillier to thank him for the interview and the offer and expressed how very professional they were in the way they treated us, but said I couldn't turn down the opportunity to carry on playing in the First Division. I went on to say that had Coventry not called that night I would have accepted their kind offer. He said he understood and wished me all the best and said maybe one day we would work together. He eventually appointed the former Manchester United and Scotland star Lou Macari, who led them to the title within two years with a record Football League points total at the time.

So I was sent to Coventry, but I was in good company as one of the new boys. Around the same time Bobby signed Steve Ogrizovic, Kirk Stephens, Brian Kilcline, Martin Jol and Cyrille Regis, and they already had Stuart Pearce, Trevor Peake, Terry Gibson, Micky Gynn, Micky Adams and Dave Bennett. The squad Bobby was putting together looked good. But after all that I nearly didn't sign for Coventry. As I was putting pen to paper, Bobby said he couldn't give me the full signing-on fee we had agreed and instead offered me half of the amount. I was very disappointed. I stopped and said 'What? I have turned jobs down to come here'. Why did he not tell me before instead of waiting until I was putting pen to paper? I felt cheated but I decided to sign anyway. I was already annoyed and disappointed before I had even had my first training session, but at no point did I wish I'd taken the Swindon job or was going to pull out of a chance to play for Coventry. I'd asked my mate Willie Carr about the Sky Blues where he started his career and spent almost a decade and he told me it was a good club. I was raring to go for the new season after a hard 12 months at Wolves and the disappointment of relegation. Sitting at the foot of the table for long periods and getting some drubbings and then suffering the drop takes its toll on you. The atmosphere at the club is so awful – players are having a go at each other and people are pointing the finger. But this was a new challenge for me at a new club and I was looking forward to a good season. The training ground, called the Sky Blues Connexion, was immaculate with three pitches, while the facilities were something I hadn't experienced at Bradford PA or at Wolves. It had everything, even a solarium and best of all a cupboard full of brand new boots. But I thought it was too comfortable for some players and I think that was part in the reason why they hadn't done particularly well in previous years.

We kicked off the new season at Aston Villa and I found myself on the substitutes' bench. But I was not too unhappy as it gave me chance to see from the outside the quality we had, how Bobby wanted the team to play and how the players performed in a real game. We lost 1-0 but did well and I managed to get on for the last 24 minutes and thought I did OK. It was a hot day and Villa Park looked at its best. It's a wonderful stadium to play at, although I didn't win many games there. It wasn't the start we were looking for but it was a tough opener and I was looking forward to our first home match in front of new supporters for me. I had to try to win them over with some good performances.

The squad looked good on paper but performances on the pitch get the points and we didn't do that too often in the first few months. In fact we were bottom of the table when we had to go to Sunderland on September 22. Roker Park wasn't an easy place to go – even though they were having a bad time – and they had an experienced manager in Len Ashurst. But it was a good chance to get off the bottom and we played very well in a 0-0 draw. It moved us off the bottom by a couple of places and we thought we could feel some confidence coming back after an awful start. I didn't expect us to be so low in the league, but the table doesn't lie and it looked like it was going to be a long, hard season.

The games were coming thick and fast and we headed into October with a home game against Arsenal. We took the lead through Terry Gibson and then he was pulled down for a penalty. I was going to take it and I felt comfortable as I stepped up to take the kick, despite one of the best keepers in the game Pat Jennings standing in front of me. I thought if he was going to save my shot, he would have to do something special. Anyway I ran up and put the ball right into the corner of his right-hand post where I put most of my successful penalties. But as I looked up, big Pat's enormous right hand pushed it out for a corner. I don't believe any other keeper in the league would have got to it. That would have put us 2-0 up against a very good team. I sensed it could have been a costly miss and so it proved as Tony Woodcock and Paul Mariner scored to beat us 2-1. I felt disappointed afterwards but Pat's penalty save was outstanding. We brought in Peter Barnes, the ex-Manchester City and England left winger. He was a player we needed. He could turn a game with his pace and he was a good crosser. Players such as Cyrille Regis and Terry Gibson would relish his service and hopefully score a few goals that would spark our season. With those lads, Dave Bennett and Micky Gynn, who was also quick, we had a good forward line with a good balance. On October 13, we played Newcastle at home, a team I had done really well against in the past, so I was hoping for another good day against them. I was really looking forward to the match but in the 60th minute the game changed. After making all the running, we suddenly had some defending to do and the ball bounced up on to my arm and the referee blew for a penalty. I was angry with his decision and was cautioned for dissent, very unlike me! My mood only worsened when Peter Beardsley scored the penalty and we were now chasing the game. I felt sick inside for a while but when we were awarded a free kick on the right of the Newcastle area, I thought 'Here's my chance'.

Several players stood over the ball but I was determined I was going to take it. I stepped back and could see the Newcastle keeper Kevin Carr not quite where he should have been in relation to his defensive wall so I bent it over the wall and just under the bar to the keeper's right for the equaliser. Carr tried to get to it but it flew into the net, and, my goodness, I felt good! It was my first goal for Coventry and it made up for conceding the penalty. That night on TV the commentator Martin Tyler said 'That will make him feel better' in a loud voice. I can still hear him now after all these years. We drew 1-1 but we played well enough to have won.

In the Milk Cup (also known as the League Cup), we were drawn to play Walsall from the Third Division and although we won 2-1 at Fellows Park in the first leg, we approached the game in a poor manner. We thought we only had to turn up to win, but worse was to follow as the second leg became one of the most embarrassing games I'd ever played in. The manager Bobby Gould played a 4-2-4 formation with only Micky Gynn and myself in midfield. We got battered in there and our performance was pathetic as Walsall deservedly won 3-0. They were awesome, and, a season after they memorably reached the semi-finals where they were narrowly beaten by eventual winners Liverpool, they took First Division Chelsea to a third round replay. We were shocking that night and got what we deserved. Again we took them for granted and thought we only had to turn up to win. Our attitude was crap and we had some work to do if we were going to stay up.

Bob Latchford, the former Everton and England striker, joined us, to boost the attack as an experienced head, although a few of us were in the autumn of our careers and our best days were probably behind us. We were also there to help the younger players develop, but improvement was hard to come by, and after being beaten 6-2 at Chelsea and 5-2 at West Brom, we were still struggling near the foot of the table. Bobby Gould was now under pressure to keep his job. The inevitable happened in December 1984 when he was sacked after we had lost seven games in 10. His assistant Don Mackay took over, bringing in Frank Upton from Wolves to help him. I knew Frank and he liked discipline in the ranks, something lacking under Bobby. Gouldy was a great guy and I was very disappointed he lost his job, especially as he had brought me to Coventry. I had a lot of respect for Bobby after playing with him in his two prolific spells at Wolves and we got on really well, but he was too easy with certain players.

I remember once he substituted me at half-time for smiling with an opposition player as we walked off. It had nothing to do with the way we were playing. It was a remark from the player about being lucky over something that happened and I just smiled and agreed with him. But Bobby took exception and hauled me off. I was absolutely raging so I went to see him on the Monday and he said he was trying to set an example to others. I have never treated a game like it doesn't matter and I felt he was wrong to use me as an example. I was a senior professional who always had pride in the job I did but Bobby could be very unpredictable and did many unorthodox things that made the senior players smile at times.

Back at Wolves – remember we still lived in Wolverhampton – things were getting worse on and off the pitch. Results were very poor and the club was in real financial trouble. I was sorry to hear that but I wasn't surprised. I didn't feel good about what was going on but I could feel and smell the problems in the club before I left. It was sickening to see a great club going downhill so quickly but I couldn't see them putting the brakes on the big slide heading their way. The players didn't perform in the season we were relegated and I include myself in that. But you could use the phrase made infamous by former Liverpool defender Alan Hansen on *'Match of the Day'* when he said 'You don't win anything with kids' to sum up that season at Wolves. The youngsters weren't to blame for the poor results as the club had no choice but to play them because the money had run out. But to see it fall from grace so quickly was frightening and heartbreaking for me and they ended up in the bottom tier of the Football League, the Fourth Division, where I'd started my career back in 1966. If someone had told me in 1980 after we won the League Cup that little over six years later Wolves would be in the Fourth Division I would have suggested locking them up and throwing away the key. It couldn't happen – or so we thought.

At Coventry, it looked like we were heading in the the same direction as Wolves. We had big-name players who were just not producing the form they should have. Players always look for excuses when things go wrong – they point the finger at each other and blame others. We all had to look in the mirror and ask ourselves if we were giving our all because we had no drive, but I think that comes from the management. They should have been showing the way, not by shouting all the time, but sometimes by showing more support and belief in the players. We were all good players individually but collectively we were poor and that had to change if we wanted to remain a First Division team.

The papers had reported I was going to join Shrewsbury Town or Swansea City but I knew nothing about it. Sometimes you wonder where the stories come from because I was very happy at Coventry, although we were in danger of going down. The manager Don Mackay was aware of the speculation surrounding myself, but he insisted nobody was leaving, especially the senior players, given the position we were in, so that was that and we continued to try to help Coventry survive.

The two years I spent at Coventry were hard going. We had to fight to stay up in both seasons, which I hadn't anticipated when I left Wolves and it was taking its toll on me physically and mentally. I was taking the disappointments home with me and that was not fair on my family. The travelling didn't help either; I was sitting in my car for two hours every day back and forth. In my first season, 1984-85, we survived the drop on the last day by beating Everton 4-1. It was our third win on the bounce after beating Stoke away and Luton Town at home, both 1-0. By the time we played Everton, they had been away celebrating winning the League and they also won the European Cup Winners' Cup and were denied a historic treble when they were beaten 1-0 in the FA

Cup final by Manchester United. My mate Andy Gray and a few other top players were left out of the team to play us so it made our task a little bit easier. There were questions asked about Everton playing a weakened side and I felt a bit sorry for Norwich City because our win meant they were relegated and not us. They had won the Milk Cup earlier that year but it turned sour (pun intended) for them just a few months later. After the game we were all delighted with the result but most of all because we had stayed up for at least another season.

My family were in North Wales on holiday waiting for me to join them. We always went to Wales around this time of year, and as I was driving there, the ex-Southampton, Manchester City and England striker Mick Channon was on the radio talking about the disappointment of being relegated with Norwich. He sounded really unhappy about our result as much as them getting relegated and was asking for an enquiry because of the weakened team Everton fielded against us. I didn't blame him because I would probably have felt the same. As he went on, there was a real bitterness to his words but all I could think was 'Up yours, mate'. We were staying up and I was still on a real high, even though I'd been driving for a couple of hours. When I arrived in Wales we all celebrated our tremendous win and our survival, which kicked off a great summer.

Later, when the kids were off school, we went on holiday with Andy Gray and Jan, hiring a villa on the Algarve. What I didn't realise was how the next chapter of Andy's career was to materialise before our eyes. One day there was a knock at the door and standing there was Doug Ellis, the Aston Villa chairman, and his associate Dave Ismay. They wanted to speak to Andy so we invited them in, gave them a drink and Andy had a good chat with them. They then took Andy and Jan out for a meal while we looked after their baby daughter Amy. The next day Doug and Dave took us all out for lunch in Vale De Lobo and Andy signed for Villa there and then. After the negotiations were completed, I took a photograph of us all together. Doug turned to me and said 'Unfortunately we can't do anything for you, Kenny!' I don't know whether he said it tongue in cheek or whether he meant it, but it felt like he meant it. I don't think Everton knew about the deal at the time but even after they signed Gary Lineker that summer, there were petitions protesting at Andy being allowed to leave because he was so popular and had been such a big part in the most successful period in their history. Villa weren't the only club to knock at our door that holiday either. In the same week, representatives from PSV Eindhoven called at our villa as well – remember this was in days largely before agents existed – so a few people had clearly been doing their homework on where we were. I can't remember which club came first, and Andy apologised for the disruption, but he didn't know they were coming because it was out of the blue.

The following season was going to be my last year of my contract so there was a bit of pressure to do well enough to gain another deal at Coventry. But things change quickly in football and you never know what's round the corner. My old club Wolves were now in the Third Division and still in dire financial trouble. I was still living in Wolverhampton and it was breaking my heart to see them struggling so badly. But the hardest thing was thinking how low could they go before someone put the brakes on and stopped the rot. Tommy Docherty had been sacked there and speculation grew that I was one of the favourites to take over. I went to see our manager Don Mackay and he said he wouldn't stand in my way if Wolves offered me the job. He also said if he was there I would be top of his list. How serious he was I didn't know, but he looked and sounded genuine enough.

Anyway I was thrilled to be invited for an interview and went to Molineux to meet the Bhatti brothers. I was desperate to get back to Wolves and to manage them would have been my dream. I was very nervous as I went upstairs to meet them but I was totally relaxed when we got under way. I was straight to the point in saying the club needed a lift, an injection of money to freshen it up and give the fans something to look forward to. It wasn't going to be an easy path but we had to stop the rot very quickly and settle the club down and rebuild. That all sounds very easy but if we pulled together we could achieve our goal and start looking towards a brighter future. But at that moment things weren't looking very clever from the outside looking in and the fans had had a very rough time over the last three years. That is what I said – no bullshit, just plain words. I spoke from the heart like I always have done, but I wasn't convinced the board liked what they were hearing. I love Wolves and I wanted to give something back for the great years they gave me. If I'd got the job it would have been the toughest task of my working life but I was willing to have a go. A lot of my friends, family and supporters asked me if I was sure about it because they said I could fall flat on my face and the fans would have a go at me if I didn't succeed and I might lose credibility with them. My reply was this: 'Look, what if I do change it around and I start to take the club forward? The fans will love it and they will support me, I'm sure about that because they know how much the club means to me'. I had told the Bhattis what I felt needed to be done because of the mess it was in and the years I had spent there. In truth I knew I wasn't going to get the job – deep down, there was something telling me it wasn't right for me and there was no positivity coming back from the Bhattis whatsoever from the moment I walked in. The interview didn't last long, so I decided to put it down to experience. Derek Dougan, who had been chairman and chief executive, had left by then and I was seen by the two brothers and someone else. It was very rare that the Bhattis were actually seen at the ground so it was all done very discreetly, in an executive box in what is now the Steve Bull Stand. But I never heard anything after my interview and they appointed Sammy Chapman, who was their chief scout, then Bill McGarry again for a very brief spell before giving the job to Sammy again.

I returned to Highfield Road and was knuckling down at Coventry trying to help them stay up again when one day a reporter asked me if I was interested in becoming assistant manager to McGarry. I was delighted to hear that and said I would love to be his assistant. I was now excited again to at long last get the chance to go back to my beloved Wolves. It wasn't long after Bill returned to Wolves in September 1985 when I got the call from him. He always sounded the same. He was blunt and straight to the point. 'Hi,' he said. 'These b******s here don't want you here with me and thought it only right I tell you son. I want you, and I think we could be good together, but not these people, it's diabolical.' I said: 'What have I done wrong to these people, boss?' He answered: 'I haven't got a clue, son.' With that I wished him well and hoped he could turn the club around. I was gutted to say the least but I couldn't understand why the Bhattis didn't want me near the club as I would have definitely taken the job. They were his words not mine but it was worrying from my point of view. I couldn't understand it and felt sick about hearing that. Maybe someone had stuck the boot in on me but I hadn't been critical of them. Anyway, I got on with trying to keep Coventry in the top flight, even though by then I wasn't playing a lot of games.

In April 1986 Don Mackay left and the press picked up from somewhere that I wanted the job. It was an interesting thought but this was a big First Division club and I had no managerial experience. But I thought 'What the hell – you never know, and if they advertise it, I will put in for it'. In for a penny in for a pound I thought as I was leaving as a player anyway at the end of the season. As it turned out, John Sillett and George Curtis got to take over until the end of the season. They were both experienced which was something the club needed in the short term. They said if we survived relegation they would take us to Spain as a reward.

We thought that would be great and the players were surprised but were definitely up for it. It worked too as we survived again. But the downside for me was being handed a free transfer, even though it had been reported in the press that I was going to be asked to be John Sillett's assistant, as Curtis held some other job in the club. I wasn't shocked by their decision but I was when Curtis rang and invited me to see him at the ground. He told me he wasn't going to take me to Spain with the rest of the lads. I was the only player not to make the trip and I was gutted. I had played my part and deserved to be given the same opportunity as the rest of the lads. I just got up and went home wondering about my future and not happy with the way Coventry had handled my situation. Not being able to say goodbye to the players in the proper way was awful. I heard some of the lads weren't too happy I didn't make the trip, particularly the senior ones like Trevor Peake, who was a fine player but also a great lad, Brian Kilcline and Dave Bennett. But I had plenty to keep me occupied in wondering where my next job was coming from, so it was a very worrying time for me and the family.

30

Go West

It was a World Cup summer, with England in Mexico for the 1986 tournament, but it seemed every bit of the several thousand miles away for me. I was now sitting at home a bit brassed off with Coventry City and George Curtis who told me I wouldn't be travelling with the boys to Spain. I accepted the free transfer they gave me and that they wanted to move forward and bring in younger players. But I felt I didn't deserve to be the only one left at home. Some of the boys called to see where I was and they were as disappointed as me. They couldn't believe how I'd been treated. They gave me great support but I never got chance to say my goodbyes to them and the staff. I felt like I'd just been shoved aside. It was a horrible feeling, probably the worst I'd had in football.

What was I going to do next? For the first time since I left school at 15, I had no club and nothing in the pipeline to look forward to. I knew I had still something to offer the game, I still felt fit and good enough to help some team out that needed experience to help the younger players. I accepted it wasn't going to be in the top flight any more but there were clubs in the Midlands I could have done a good job for.

Looking back I'd been very fortunate to have had a successful time from when I joined Bradford Park Avenue as an apprentice. I never thought I'd play in major cup finals when I was sweeping the ground and nearly getting the sack for watching my idol Geoff Boycott bat against the West Indies in 1966! It was hard to believe I was now sitting at home with my family wondering where I was going to end up next. It had gone more or less full circle now but I was determined to stay in the game. I wanted to coach and eventually manage.

Then a phone call from Bobby Gould, who was by now managing Bristol Rovers, gave me a lifeline. He still thought I could do a job for him at Rovers on and off the pitch. I was excited at the offer of player-coach, it was something I wanted to do after playing. The only downside was the couple of hours each way travelling every day, particularly before games. The alternative was to go into digs for a couple of nights a week. My kids were settled at school and I didn't want to disturb their education. It was going to be a huge decision for Jane and myself. The offer was pretty poor financially and I would have to take a big pay cut from what I was earning at Coventry. But I thought 'Beggars can't be choosers' and I asked Bobby to give me a week or so to think about it. Typically, a manager wants an answer pretty quickly as they usually have other options waiting in the wings. But this was going to be a massive decision for us as I had been fortunate enough to have played most of my career in the Midlands. We talked it over for hours before I decided it was the best for us both and the kids long-term future to take the offer and move to the West Country. I was given a one-year contract and Bobby said I could stay over at his house at times to ease the cost of travelling. His wife Marjorie was a lovely lady and she didn't mind me staying over.

Our immediate futures settled, there was time for us to enjoy a lovely holiday in Portugal before pre-season training started in July 1986. I was looking forward to a new challenge and to play at Eastville, the home of Bristol Rovers. I had played there a few times and it always had a good atmosphere and was a reasonable pitch to play on, muddy at times but then most pitches back then were like that. When I reported for the start of training, Bobby got the squad together and I was introduced as the new player-coach. A few eyebrows were raised from some of the lads because I had come from a First Division team to a club that had been struggling in the Third Division. I knew it was going to be tough having played in the Fourth Division when I was at Bradford Park Avenue, but we got on pretty well once I gave my reasons as to why I'd joined them and told them I wasn't on big money, because most of them must have thought I'd gone there for big bucks. We were soon sorting out our pre-season schedule and Bobby asked me to go to Bath City and have a look at the ground and pitch to see if it was OK. I said 'We're not playing Bath in pre-season, so why do you want me to go there?' He said 'That's where we're playing our home games this season.' I said 'What? Why Bob?' He told me the club had no money and they had to leave Eastville so Bath was going to be our home for some time. You could have knocked me down with a feather, I was so disappointed. I was looking forward to playing at Eastville, not Twerton Park, the home of non-league Bath City.

That first season was tough. A lot of home games were postponed because the pitch was waterlogged – it seemed as if you only had to spit on it and it was unplayable. The groundsman, a former player, Jackie Pitt, and his assistant Roger Ford, did their best, which was just as well as we didn't have the proverbial pot to pee in. But it was a tough job for them with hardly any money to improve things. Bath City weren't the wealthiest of non-league clubs but they were kind enough to let us share their ground. The meagre budget was also reflected in our pre-match preparation.

Before away games for our meal on the coach we used to snack on cold toast that our kit man Ray Kendall had warmed up at his home a couple of hours before we travelled. At least we could wash it down with a hot drink as we had a tea and coffee maker on board, which came in handy! How things had changed from the comparative luxury I enjoyed at Wolves and Coventry City. This was like going back to where I started in 1966-67 at Bradford Park Avenue. They had nowt as well. We just had to make the best of it and we did with no complaints from the players. Most of them had come from non-league so they were used to it, but it was tough. Thankfully, I got off to a dream start, smashing one into the top corner from 25 yards on my debut, away to Walsall, as we won 3-0 on the opening day of the season, on August 23, 1986. On the same day, Wolves kicked off their first ever season in the Fourth Division, in a game which ended in a 2-1 home defeat against Cambridge United.

Although I was registered as player-coach I didn't do much coaching, which was disappointing. Bobby liked to do it all but at least that meant I could just concentrate on playing. The travelling from Wolverhampton to Bristol was tough enough without using a lot of my energy doing some of the coaching as well.

One night I met up with a couple of the players to do a presentation for some youth team and afterwards we went out for a few pints just to get know them a bit better. It gave me chance to find out what characters they were and an opportunity to hear where some of them thought the club was going. It's amazing how people open up after a couple of beers, and a few of them said 'Not very far'.

Afterwards I got in my car to go back to my digs in Winterbourne where I was staying with Phil Purnell, one of the players who was single but was buying his own house. But I hadn't got a clue how to get to his place. I got on the motorway but didn't know which direction I was going. Then saw a sign saying 'The Midlands' so I drove back to Wolverhampton. We didn't have mobile phones so I couldn't call Phil for directions which meant the easiest thing for me to do was go home. I got home about 2am and had to throw small stones up at the window to wake Jane up. It frightened her to death and she gave me a real telling-off. Then I was up at 7am to get back to Bristol for training. When I told the lads what had happened they were in stitches. The season was a struggle, and, after three defeats in a row following three wins in four, we needed a point from our last game at already relegated Newport County to stay up. We were virtually safe as we were three points above the drop zone and our nearest rivals Bolton, and had a big goal difference in our favour. But the tension among the Rovers supporters was high, and, such is the intense rivalry in the area, the Bristol City fans were hoping we lost and Bolton won by the required big margins so we went down. It was one of the biggest games in the club's history and we had a meeting at our training ground a couple of days before the game as Bobby was very worried about how we were going to approach it, pondering what formation to play and who he was going to pick. He never consulted me on any issues building up to the game, which surprised me as sometimes you bounce things off your staff before the manager makes the decision. So I just sat there with the other players. The room went very quiet as Bobby started to make his points and how important it was to get the right result to secure the future of Bristol Rovers and our own futures. Then he came out with a real beauty. He said: 'After giving a lot of thought we're going to play a formation I think will get us a result. I'm going to play a 1-4-5 formation'. I was aghast. I'd never heard that formation in my life, and the other players nearly fell off their chairs. Some looked at me looking for a reaction. I was stunned and just didn't know what to think or say.

After a few moments I think Bobby got the message the players weren't too happy and started to re-think it. We all thought he was being funny at first but he was deadly serious. In the end he changed his mind and we played our usual 4-4-2. Bobby was a thinker and full of enthusiasm but his mind got the better of him on this occasion. We won with our winger Phil Purnell scoring the only goal late on. It was a great time to score after a hard battle from start to finish and Newport gave it their all but we just edged them. In the last couple of minutes we kept the ball in their half to waste time. I probably had one of my best games of the season. I was right up for the challenge and we controlled the midfield. We celebrated retaining our Football League status with a few beers back at the training ground at Hambrook. It was now time to have a break – and boy did I need it after one of the toughest seasons of my career. My contract was up on June 30 so I was waiting for the club to decide what they wanted to do. I thought having helped them achieve their League status they would offer me another. We needed a holiday so we went to Portugal again. On the way to the beach one day I read in the paper that Bobby Gould was set to leave Bristol Rovers for Wimbledon as their new manager. I knew nothing about this and the norm is you keep your coach informed about something like this happening. I got straight on the phone and he said he was going and that had I been in England he would have taken me with him. I said I would be home in six to seven days, couldn't he wait until I got back? He said they wanted it all done straight away. I wasn't too happy about that and it played on my mind for the rest of the holiday. On my return I wanted to see if Rovers wanted me or even take over from Bobby as manager. I had heard nothing from the club, and as I was getting closer to the end of my contract, I was worried. So I called Ron Craig, one of the directors, who I was friendly with. I played a lot of golf with Ron, he was a great guy and we got on well. He asked if anyone had been in touch. I said no and that I was bit concerned. He told me to leave it with him and he'd get back to me. I knew some of the other directors weren't too sure of me for some reason. But I'd done nothing wrong, I was on a small wage, I helped them preserve their League status in my first season, I was still one of their best players and had still a lot to offer on the pitch.

I was still travelling up and down the motorway as often as I could to be with my family and maybe the directors didn't like that. But there was no way I was going to uproot them for one season and find we were stuck somewhere we didn't know too much about. And the children's education came first. I commuted when I could as I was missing them so much. Ron said they wanted me to stay but on condition that we'd move to the West Country. I asked him if it was a one-year deal or two because I wasn't moving my family for 12 months. Ron told me they were appointing Gerry Francis as manager. Gerry had a brief spell of management at Exeter City before he became a part-time player at Rovers under Bobby Gould and they wanted me to be his assistant. I asked if Gerry was happy with that and he said 'Yes of course'. Now big decisions had to be made, but it became a little easier as my daughter Kelly was now getting bullied at school about my football past. So we thought this just might be the chance to get away and start a new life somewhere else. Jane, as always, said she would support me but was concerned whether it was the right move. We had many sleepless nights agonising over it but a decision had to be made. We decided to move to the Cotswolds, a lovely place and only a couple of hours from the Midlands. I signed a two-year deal and became assistant manager to Gerry. I was looking forward to working with him ashe had played under some top managers and coaches, including Dave Sexton, who was recognised as one of the best tacticians in the game and had led QPR to finish runners-up in the League in 1975-76. Gerry had captained England under Don Revie, and then played under future England manager Terry Venables at Crystal Palace and QPR. I felt if I couldn't learn from Gerry about coaching I wouldn't learn from anyone.

We put our house up for sale and started to look for somewhere to live in the Cotswolds. The prices were very high compared with the Midlands and we were finding it difficult to find anywhere suitable. We didn't know the area well but I was helped by a few players who lived locally. It was 1987 and the housing market went mad with prices in the West Country rising at nearly £1,000 a week, so it was a crazy time. After plenty of searching, Jane called me at the training ground one day in August with news of a house she liked. She had driven with our children to have another look around and saw somewhere in a village we had liked while we were looking earlier that month. I met her and the children and parked outside the house. I took one look and said 'No, I am not buying that – look at it. We've just sold a nice house in Wolverhampton and you want me to increase the mortgage for that?' The house had no central heating, no double glazing, a 1950s kitchen and hardly any carpets. She said 'Yes – but just look at the potential: Good grounds, a nice driveway and it's in a lovely area'. The children seemed a bit bemused but excited at the same time. So we went across the road to a restaurant for lunch to talk it over. It was now November 1987 and we decided to buy it and soon after, we moved in. But all wasn't quite what it seemed.

When we were moving in, our dog Seve, a golden retriever named after the great golfer Seve Ballesteros, ran into the house but within ten seconds he had galloped out like lightning and was crouched down on the back seat of the car. He clearly didn't like the house for some reason and refused to move. We literally had to drag him inside. It was very unlike him so something wasn't right. With no central heating and it being winter, that first night it was so cold I had to put on all the rings on the hob to get some heat, but within a couple of minutes the whole oven blew up! So now we had no heating at all, and all we could do was go to bed early to get some warmth. We had a new fireplace put in with a coal fire only to notice smoke appearing from the sides as we ate our tea. All of a sudden the room started filling with smoke and we rang the fire brigade. While this was happening, the phone rang and Kelly answered. It was Jane's mum. Kelly said 'Oh Nan, the house is on fire!' Jane grabbed the phone and told her she would ring her back. We ran outside and waited for the fire service to do their bit as apparently the back of the fireplace had been incorrectly packed with paper, which

191

had caught light. On the football side we had a lot of work ahead of us to instil some belief into the players. But first we had to make changes to the squad to avoid another season of struggle. They just weren't good enough to take the club where Gerry and I wanted to take it. We had a few lengthy conversations about players who might be available to us. The PFA list of free transfers was comprehensive and we spent a long time going through it. Changes had to be made but they had to be cheap as we had no money to buy players. Those coming in had to want to play and be hungry to play for us, while we also had to make decisions on the current squad. We wanted good characters and honesty with a good work ethic. Some of the current squad were good lads and half decent, but they just needed some guidance and a lot of hard work on the training ground to improve them. It was going to be tough, but with hard graft we could get the club going forward again and give the fans a lift and a brighter future.

It was around this time that Rod became very good friends with a lad called Jim Rollo, a handy footballer who I later took to Walsall as an apprentice and then later signed for Cardiff City. He is now heavily involved with Bath City.

We spent a lot of time working on players' fitness and pattern of play. It may have been a bit boring at times for them, but it had to be done and we were a very fit team. Gerry and I did a lot of what the players did so I know they were a fit bunch. Gerry introduced a run called 'box to box' which was a really good workout. You could change how you wanted to do it by using the halfway line. It went something like this: Start on the goalline in groups of four, five or six, run to the halfway line and back to warm up, then the next group and so on until they had all done it. Then they had to run to the opposite penalty box and back to the halfway line and back. You doubled it or even trebled it if you needed to. That was hard but it was replicating what you did during a game. We would then go into some ballwork and finish with some pattern of play. We trained for 90 minutes most days, to get them working at that intensity over the duration of a match.

31

Armstrong Leg Break – The End For Me

Things were starting to go our way at Bristol Rovers, but just when you think everything is rosy, football has a nasty habit of kicking you in the teeth, and I was no exception. For several months of the 1987-88 season, I had been suffering problems with my calves. I had picked up a calf strain in a reserve game at Aldershot when Gerry also played. I bent down to take a corner and felt it go 'ping'. I got back to the halfway line and told Gerry my calf had gone. I made a few comebacks, and I remember having to come off at Wigan in a game where I won man of the match despite playing only 60 minutes. Ultimately I had three cortisone injections in my calf to try to get back on the pitch, so I felt I had done everything I could to continue playing. I have never feigned an injury in my life and never would. But that view didn't appear to be one that was shared by everyone at the club. However, the concerns with my calf were soon replaced by a much bigger worry as my playing career was effectively ended.

Playing Sunderland at Twerton Park in a night match on February 24, 1988, we kicked off and the ball was played long up to Devon White. I raced forward to get the knockdown, but the ball went over my head and as I turned to control it, the Sunderland midfielder Gordon Armstrong came in with a high tackle with his studs showing. Fortunately I saw it coming and managed to get out of the way. I thought at the time 'Bloody hell, that was a close one' and carried on. Soon afterwards, however, I wasn't so lucky. Controlling a ball on my chest, I tried to play a one-two as the ball dropped. I played it with the outside of my right foot so my weight was all on my left, my standing leg, when Armstrong came in again and caught me just below the knee with a nasty tackle. He caught me with his foot up and got me good and proper. My leg buckled and I fell in agony. I knew before I hit the ground I had been seriously hurt. He got yellow-carded so was able to carry on, while I didn't see the end of the match and instead ended up being stretchered off and rushed to the hospital in Bath. The X-ray showed I had a broken ankle. The bony bit on the inside of the ankle had broken off completely and the ligament had more or less disintegrated. I have got pictures on my phone showing how I was hit in stages. He should have been sent off for what I felt was a disgraceful and unprofessional tackle. To this day I still don't know if it was premeditated or not, only he knows. We won the game 4-0 but I was more concerned about my leg, and whether I was going to be able to play again.

My close mate Mike Garland, who was watching the game, came straight to the dressing room and followed the ambulance to the hospital. Mike, who unfortunately is no longer with us, put me in the back seat of his car after the X-ray and drove me home. The next day I was booked into Frenchay Hospital on the north east side of Bristol, near our training ground at Hambrook. The hospital was really nice and was a lot closer to home than where we played at Bath, which made it convenient for Jane to visit more easily. I underwent surgery to have two pins inserted into my ankle, to hold the joint together because the damage to the ligaments and tendons was so severe. I was allocated a private room but found the treatment from one member of staff who brought me my breakfast and cup of tea terse to say the least. She would bark out 'There's your tea!' and just plonk it on the side table. I wondered why she was behaving like that and concluded she either resented me being in a private room, she was a Bristol City fan, or both!

Lying in hospital, I had plenty of time to think and I reached the conclusion that I wanted to take action against Gordon Armstrong. But I didn't receive any support from the club. I pointed out to them that I'd had my ankle broken by a nasty tackle and the game didn't need that kind of stuff. Deep down I knew my playing career was more or less over and the press had arrived at the same conclusion, but I decided they weren't going to tell me when I was finished and thought I'd show them. Once I was discharged and back home, I was still in discomfort and I was a total pain to be around, not knowing what to do with myself. But the desire to prove people who thought I was finished wrong made me determined to try to make a comeback. It wasn't going to be easy but it gave me a target and helped keep my spirits up and motivated me to work hard when the plaster came off. My broken ankle came 10 years and nine days since I suffered the same injury on the other leg, my right one, playing for Wolves against Norwich in March 1978, so I'd been in this situation before. On that occasion it was purely accidental, but I'm still not convinced even now that this one was. It was a long slog, but I did everything I could to get back playing again. The team coped well without me, the win over Sunderland one of 10 victories and four draws from our last 17 games as the team finished eighth, missing the play-offs by nine points. After reporting back for pre-season training in the summer of 1988, I pulled a calf muscle in a pre-season friendly at St Blazey in July before breaking down in training in early August. Returning to play in a friendly against Backwell on the 16th of that month, I was still struggling and so saw a specialist in November after injuring my calf in another friendly, against Weston-super-Mare. From there I underwent a cortisone injection and played alongside Gerry Francis in a friendly against Taunton in the December. In all I was out of the first-team reckoning for a year and had tried everything to get back playing but with the ligaments and tendons so badly damaged, every time I attempted to come back, I broke down. I did manage a first-team comeback though, on March 11, 1989 as a substitute in a game at home to Chesterfield. But even if I wasn't convinced I was bowing out there and then, it turned out to be my last match as a professional footballer. At least I went out on a winning note, as we enjoyed a 2-1 victory. And there was some symmetry about the fixture as it was against Chesterfield that I made my Football League debut 21 years earlier playing for Bradford Park Avenue.

While my struggles to play again went on, at least on the management side things were looking up. We got a half decent team together, and, after a couple of difficult, hard seasons where we finished 19th in the Third Division (now League One) in 1986-87 – three below where Bobby Gould had led us to the previous campaign – we significantly improved our position to rise to eighth in 1987-88, then fifth in 1988-89, before winning the title the following year. But it wasn't an easy process and it took a lot of work from Gerry and I behind the scenes.

Gerry asked me if I could get hold of Andy Reece, a midfielder who I saw playing for Goodyear on a Sunday morning in Wolverhampton. We took him on trial towards the back end of the previous season and Gerry liked him so I got in touch and he came in. He played well and ended up earning a contract. One of Gerry's other early signings was another midfielder called Ian Holloway. In fact Gerry was so keen to land him that he loaned the club the £10,000 fee that he cost from Brentford. But he had to wait two years, until we sold Nigel Martyn to Crystal Palace for £1m in 1989, before he was reimbursed. Gerry mentioned a big striker who he recalled had caused Exeter a lot of trouble when he was there and who had played for Lincoln City but had moved on. His name was Devon White. It turns out he had stayed in Lincolnshire after his spell with the Imps but had moved on to their neighbours Boston United before short spells with

Shepshed Charterhouse and Grantham. We managed to track him down and signed him. It was done very quickly and the squad were starting to take shape. He was also an electrician by trade so I used him to fix our house as an added bonus!

We already had some good players that Bobby Gould had brought in, such as the captain Vaughan Jones, John Scales, Nicky Tanner, Gary Penrice and Phil Purnell, but they needed help. Jones was a Wales Under-21 international who also played for Newport County and Cardiff City before joining Rovers for a second spell. Scales was a youngster Bobby signed after he was released by Leeds and he was soon looking good at full back and pushing for a place. Tanner could play anywhere across the defence or as a sitting midfield player, Penrice was a prolific goalscorer with a great touch and pace and Purnell was a lightning winger who could go past defenders and whip the ball into the box. Amazingly, all of those players apart from Scales, came from a local team called Mangotsfield United. We also had a youngster Steve Yates who had come through the ranks and was knocking on the first-team door and we knew it wouldn't be long before he made his debut.

Probably the best signing we made was a goalkeeper from Cornwall. His name was Nigel Martyn, who was playing for St Blazey. In stark contrast to the sophisticated set-ups nowadays of worldwide scouting networks, I-pads and laptops, Gerry was approached by our tea lady Violet Harris at the training ground who said she knew of a goalkeeper who was worth having a look at, so he invited him in. Looking overweight and not the most agile, we decided to put him to the test. Getting a bag of balls out, Gerry suggested we gave him some shooting practice. We were both still playing at this time so we could strike a ball pretty well and accurately. We peppered Nigel with some very hard shots, aiming for the top and bottom corners of the net. Undaunted, he threw himself around the goal and pulled off save after save to leave us looking at each other open-mouthed. Without a shadow of hesitation, we took him on board, paying him £125 a week, which was a 25 per cent rise on the £100 a week he was earning working in a warehouse at the time.

After a hard pre-season but armed with a first-class attitude, Nigel quickly shed a couple of stones and became our first-team keeper. He really wanted to be a professional footballer and worked his socks off to become one. At the time we had no goalkeeping coach so Gerry and I continued to work with him every day. Another young player who caught the eye was David Mehew, and he could play wide or up front. We also brought in Robbie Turner, a big striker who could look after himself. Robbie probably used his elbows too much – even in training. One day he went up for a high ball with Geoff Twentyman and caught Geoff in the face with his arm, breaking his nose. He also saw red in games on a few occasions, but he was a real handful for defenders, particularly at set-pieces which Gerry worked on tirelessly in training. Although I was assistant manager, I played a few games in our first season together and at the age of 36, I was happy I had some good players around me who could also do a bit of my running for me. Ian Holloway could run all day long and had bags of energy and passion for the game and Andy Reece was a Wolves fan so he didn't mind doing my running for me!

Through those astute signings and hard training sessions, we did very well and in 1989-90, we had the chance of going top of the table if we beat our arch rivals Bristol City, and, with plenty at stake, there was a big crowd at Twerton Park. City could still win the title if they beat us, but Ian Holloway was determined not to let that happen. They weren't Olly's favourite team and he wound our players up so much before the game that we went out and battered them 3-0. What a night for the Gas heads. With the rivalry so intense and losing to their arch enemy, it was all too much for some of the City fans behind the goal. Their manager Joe Jordan decided to walk towards the fans in an attempt to calm them down, but it only seemed to provoke them and he ended up with a soaked suit for his troubles after some of them spat at him. Poor Joe returned to the dugout with his clothes showered with spit. I know it was crucial derby where passions run high but to do that to the manager who led them to promotion was totally uncalled for. Joe had been a fearsome player in his time with Leeds, Manchester United and Scotland and I thought it was a disgusting way for his own supporters to treat their manager.

We also got to Wembley in the Leyland DAF trophy (now Football League Trophy) that season to complete four years of hard graft. But it was worth it to see players we had developed progress. Several of them – Nigel Martyn, John Scales, Nicky Tanner, Ian Holloway, Gary Penrice and Devon White – all eventually made it to the top flight. But coming from the modest beginnings of Twerton Park and cold, leathery toast, they remained seriously grounded. Mind you, perhaps that was not surprising after we had our pre-match meals scrapped. We only ever carried a small squad and with injuries beginning to bite just when we were looking to push on in the spring, Gerry had been trying to persuade the board to loosen the purse strings to sign a couple of players. Unfortunately he was turned down on the basis that the budget would no longer even stretch to provide scrambled eggs on toast for the players before games. Gerry later admitted that was one of several occasions when he had seriously considered resigning.

On one occasion we had to go to York, some 220 miles from Bristol. I sat at the back of the coach in the card school and said to Nicky Tanner, 'Liverpool want you'. Nicky, a West Country boy, refused to believe me and told me to stop taking the mickey. He was normally a centre back or left back, but the week before we had played at home on the Tuesday night and he had played on the left side of midfield. Ron Yeats, the chief scout at Liverpool at the time, was there to watch Gary Penrice. But I got a phone call from Ron the next morning asking 'Who was that boy playing the left side of midfield?' I could have dropped the phone. 'What the big tall boy with the blond hair?' I said. 'That's him,' answered Ron. 'Is he available?' I nearly dropped the phone again before saying 'I'm sure he will be but I'll have to go through the manager'. Anyway, Nicky ended up at Liverpool for the princely sum of £20,000.

I watched him at Anfield one Wednesday night spraying the ball around from the back. This was a player who, like Penrice, came from non-league Mangotsfield and within three years or so was playing for one of the biggest clubs in Europe. It was a massive move for him but it was the same with John Scales. He was already at the club when I joined in 1986 after he had been given a free transfer by Leeds without playing a game. But he established himself as our left back under Bobby Gould, who took him to Wimbledon where he won the FA Cup in 1988 and went on to win League Cups with Liverpool – where he moved for £3.5m – and Tottenham, where Gerry Francis was now manager, as well as gaining three full England caps. But in those days it was anything but the glamour lifestyle with Scalesy.

I used to stay in digs with Gary Penrice before we moved to the West Country and John used to stay with us, while Phil Purnell lived around the corner. Penrice lived with his wife but he always stayed with us on Friday nights and we cooked spaghetti bolognaise – just like we had when I was with Wolves. The following morning Scalesy used to drive us in his battered old Datsun Cherry with the windows and the glass on the front headlights taped up. We used to be freezing because there was no heating in the car either. I thought to myself 'This is how I started my career, back to basics, and this is how I'm ending it.' But it just shows how things can change in football, because some of these lads went to the very top of the game.

Of all the players we had at Bristol Rovers, I always felt Ian Holloway would go on to become a manager one day. He always had a lot to say for himself and always spoke out but was a really nice chap. He lost his father, Bill, at a young age and had been very close to his dad but he had a determination and the qualities about him to do well in the game. So I wasn't surprised to see him become a successful manager. Olly hasn't had it easy – he suffered glandular fever during his time at Brentford prior to rejoining Rovers yet he missed only five games in four years with us. He then enjoyed five years in the top flight after Gerry Francis signed him for QPR for £230,000 in 1991 – a handsome profit on the £20,000 he paid out of his own pocket to take him to Bristol Rovers. He ended up back at Rovers for a third spell, eventually becoming player-manager, but he has enjoyed long careers both as a player and now as a boss, and he is fast approaching 1,000 games in management, which would be a wonderful achievement if he does it.

32

A Hero's Welcome At Molineux, Then Promotion

By March 1989, I had been left Wolves for nearly five years. But it didn't seem that way as I prepared for my first competitive return to Molineux. Unfortunately I couldn't play for Bristol Rovers that day as I had only recently made my comeback from my badly broken ankle and was destined never to play again, so I had to be content with my assistant manager duties from the dugout. But going back to Molineux, my home ground for 16 years, was always going to be special for me. It felt strange to be getting changed in the away dressing room for the first time since I had been a reserve-team player in the late 1960s and I was concerned at what sort of reception I would receive as the club had been relegated when I was last there. It proved to be the start of a spiralling decline which led to the darkest days in the club's history, with three successive relegations and another bankruptcy before they were rescued in a deal with Wolverhampton Council, ASDA and a new board in the summer of 1986.

I knew some fans would welcome me back but I got the shock of my life at the reaction when I walked out of the tunnel from the now disused and crumbling Waterloo Road Stand. I never thought for one minute that the fans would react the way they did. The reception from the crowd of 20,913 – Wolves' third biggest in the league that season and quite remarkable for the third tier then – was just unbelievable as I walked out on to the track towards the bench. There were chants of 'One Kenny Hibbitt, there's only one Kenny Hibbitt' and the noise and support they gave me brought tears to my eyes. It was so loud it was like when I used to score at Molineux, or it certainly felt like it anyway. Even some of our players felt it as well. Ian Holloway said it was the biggest welcome he had seen for anyone returning to a former club and that it even brought a lump to his throat. It was an amazing, fantastic feeling and one I will always remember for as long as I live. I never expected that kind of reaction and it goes to show that fans don't forget about players who have played for their great club. I'm just sorry the cameras weren't there to record it because it had to be seen to be believed and I would love to re-live the footage.

200

Graham Turner had assembled a hungry side at Wolves and with Steve Bull and Andy Mutch terrorising the division and chasing a second successive promotion after they had romped to the Fourth Division title the season before, they were in ruthless mood and had been despatching allcomers. They had been top of the league virtually all season and hadn't been beaten for 12 months at Molineux, going 29 matches without defeat at home in all competitions, including 21 in the league.

But unfortunately for the home fans, we won 1-0 with a goal from Dennis Bailey. It was to be Wolves' only home defeat that season as they went on to win the title, eight points clear of Sheffield United. They were the best team in the league and not surprisingly, we were very happy with our win. But when the final whistle sounded, there was only once place for me to go, and that was to the Wolves fans to thank them again for the support they showed me. A few gave me some stick because of the result, but I knew they were gutted, just as I would have been in their situation. But the support they gave me before the game and afterwards will remain with me forever.

The reception and being back at Molineux made me think back to all the good times I had enjoyed at Wolves. I had the best 16 years of my career there and I just loved playing at Molineux. To me they were the best crowd in the land; I put them on a par with the great Liverpool fans. They gave me great support through the good times and, for a couple of seasons or so, the bad times as well. Like all players, I had my off days, but I always tried my best for the fans and the team, and I suppose the support they gave me from a young age made me feel like I never wanted to leave.

We couldn't emulate Wolves that year and win automatic promotion – but we gave it a damn good go. That win at Molineux was our fourth victory in five games and part of a nine-match unbeaten run during which we took 21 points out of 27 and climbed to fourth spot, just three points off the top two with eight games left. But instead of pushing on we tailed off, winning just one of our remaining matches to finish fifth, making the play-offs. Here we made light of beating Fulham, who had finished one point and one place higher than us, 1-0 at Twerton Park and then 4-0 at Craven Cottage to reach the final against Port Vale.

Sadly there was no trip to Wembley as this was the final season that the play-offs were held on a two-leg, home and away, basis before they were switched to the famous Twin

Towers. Our fans had to wait until the following season for that treat. Instead there was a capacity crowd of 9,042 at Twerton Park to roar us on. We didn't disappoint as Gary Penrice gave us a first-half lead, volleying over goalkeeper Mark Grew after Devon White flicked on a Nigel Martyn goal kick. We knew they were dangerous though and Ron Futcher had an effort disallowed for Vale just before the break. Robbie Earle equalised when he headed home a cross from Futcher with 17 minutes to go to leave it all square going into the return. They could even have won it at the death but Darren Beckford's header was nodded off the line.

On a baking hot evening of June 3, there were more than 17,000 crammed into Vale Park for the second leg and we knew we were going to have to produce something special to silence them. We needed a goal to give ourselves a chance, but sadly it wasn't to be as Robbie Earle was again their hero when he headed home the only goal just after half-time after Darren Beckford flicked on a Simon Mills corner. To be fair to Vale, they had finished third, 10 points ahead of us and only missed out on automatic promotion on goal difference to Sheffield United. They were a very strong side, like us with many players keen to test themselves at the higher level. We were left to reflect on another season of improvement – but our best was yet to come.

We jokingly renamed Twerton Park 'Trumpton Park' because of the seemingly comical nature of the amount of games we had postponed there as it got waterlogged so easily. But there was nothing funny about playing at our place if you were the opposition. And I'm convinced it was playing at Twerton Park that was a massive factor in us wining the Division Three title in 1989-90. When you got inside the ground you had to climb some steps to get on to the pitch and Gerry used to say to me when the away team had a look before the game, 'Go with them and have a listen, to see if they fancy it'. You could hear all their players moaning about the playing surface and I would report their reaction back to our lads. We'd say 'Hey, come on boys, they don't want to play here, they want to get back on the coach and go home'. So you felt like you were 1-0 up before you started and we gained a lot of motivation from the negative reaction of the opposition.

I guess it must have been similar to when teams went to Plough Lane, Wimbledon's old ground, which was very tight and uncompromising with a poor pitch but was probably a big factor in their success in terms of galvanising the home team and putting off the opposition. It might have been less luxurious and slightly uncomfortable for the teams coming to us and we certainly didn't roll out the welcome mat, but we didn't go as far as the likes of John Beck or Wimbledon and serve them cold tea or turn the radiators on full blast on a hot day. We had heard what they had said so we knew they didn't fancy it and we just looked them in the eye and got on with it. Mentally they weren't ready for the challenge and being at that ground helped us a great deal to achieve that success. We ended up going through the whole of that season undefeated at home – one better than Wolves had done the previous year, thanks to us. We had 15 wins and eight draws to become one of only two teams in all four divisions to achieve the feat that season, along with Exeter City, who romped to the Division Four title.

33

From Wembley To Walsall – A Manager At Last

I felt my time at Bristol Rovers was coming to an end as the gaffer Gerry Francis was being lined up to return to Queens Park Rangers, a club he had served so well during his playing days. As it turned out, he ended up staying for another year before moving to QPR in 1991. But either way I had to look very seriously at where I wanted my career to go because it didn't look like I was going to stay at Rovers. I didn't think the club were going to ask me to take over from Gerry if he left. Indeed, I wasn't asked by the chairman or directors if I would be interested. Yet they knew I was looking to step into management at some time. If I was in any doubt as to the feelings towards me from the board, it came at the presentation evening after we had won the Third Division title in 1989-90. The team had been promoted and reached its first Wembley cup final – we were due to play Tranmere in the Leyland DAF Trophy final – so it should have been a momentous occasion for everyone to enjoy the night and start to unwind after the slog of a long, hard season.

All the staff were there with their wives and partners, and Jane and I sat with the players and their other halves. I might have sensed something wasn't quite right when we weren't invited to sit at the top table with the club's hierarchy. That didn't bother me too much as I got on well with the players and we had a good night – until the presentation took place. The awards were handed out to the player of the year and young player of the year. Then Gerry and other staff, right down to the youth team, were introduced on stage and handed a bouquet of flowers each as a token to recognise their efforts. Fair enough. But there were no flowers for my wife and there wasn't a mention of my work as assistant manager. Goodness knows why I had been completely overlooked but I found it unbelievable. I looked at Jane sat across the table from me then at the players around us and they were all stunned. Ian Holloway and the captain Vaughan Jones looked as surprised as Jane and I. I was so angry. We both said together 'Come on, let's go home', and said our goodbyes to the people on our table and left. I don't know whether they just forgot about the flowers but it wasn't nice and I never got an explanation. The next morning before training, Ian Holloway brought in for Jane the biggest bouquet of flowers you have ever seen. It was wonderful to think he had gone out of his way to get them and he said we weren't the only people who felt the disappointment of me and my wife not receiving any recognition from the board of directors or the club. The players felt the way we'd been treated the previous evening was wrong. Ian said 'This is for your wife – we all know what happened last night and that was out of order'. I will never forget what 'Olly' and the boys did for us. It was a wonderful gesture and very much appreciated, but it was still so annoying and disrespectful of the club not to acknowledge the work I had done as assistant manager, not just over that season but over the four years I'd spent with the club. The fans were great to me and they had supported me when I was playing and also when I broke my leg, but I felt the club showed little respect towards me. I didn't take it up with anyone but after that happened, I thought my days were numbered. I was very disappointed and I felt I had no alternative but to get away, the sooner the better.

I certainly don't think I had upset anyone on the board. I got on well with the players and hoped they felt the same way as me; they certainly gave me that impression anyway. Because Gerry lived in Bagshot, Surrey and I was on the doorstep, I took the lads for training sessions whenever he was off. We would share the workload between us, which allowed him the chance to work from home trying to recruit players and doing a bit of scouting around London. But I enjoyed having days alone to work with the players and it also gave them a breather from the manager, so the arrangement worked really well. All the while I was gaining more experience for when the time came to have a crack at management. I worked with Gerry for three years and learnt so much from him. I tried to put all those good things into my management style along with what I had picked up in my 20-odd years playing under other managers. I tended to ignore the traits I didn't like but tried to take on board all the things that appealed to me. For me the main part of the job was man management. I thought by treating players right I would get the best out of them. I decided I wanted to treat them like men and be honest to them.

My chance to be a manager came when John Barnwell was sacked at Walsall. I was sad to see one of my old gaffers lose his job, but I was very interested and thought it was a good opportunity for me. I discussed it with Jane and she agreed I just had to apply for the vacancy. Having lived in the area for almost 20 years, I always had a soft spot for Walsall. I scored on my Bristol Rovers debut against them when we beat them 3-0, a

25-yarder with my left foot that went into the top corner, so I felt I owed them one! They were one of the smallest clubs in the region but were, and, still are, a very well run outfit that were going through difficult times after successive relegations that took them from the old Second Division down to the Fourth. They were a lot of people's second favourite team in the West Midlands and they were a good cup side. When I was at Coventry, they knocked us out of the League Cup in 1984-85, and deservedly so too. The season before they had beaten Arsenal on the way to reaching the semi-final in the same competition, where they narrowly went out to Liverpool after drawing 2-2 at Anfield. I had been really impressed with Walsall at the time and I couldn't believe they had gone down the leagues so quickly. They were in the Second Division (now Championship) when Barnwell took over but he struggled to emulate the success he had enjoyed with Wolves.

I approached Gerry to ask if I could apply for the job and he gave me permission. He would never have stood in my way anyway and we have been friends ever since. Gerry wasn't sure he was going to get the QPR job so it was never really on the agenda for me to have followed him to Loftus Road. So when that chance came for me to manage, I thought I had better take it. Having won the league with Rovers and reached the final of the Leyland DAF Trophy at Wembley, it was a good time to move on, although I would have stayed if the board had shown any interest in me replacing Gerry if he left.

So I applied for the Walsall job and got a reply from the chairman Barrie Blower asking me to attend an interview. The club had several applications so it wasn't going to be easy to land the job. But with my experience of playing for Wolves for so long and with a successful three years working under a top player and manager in Gerry, I hoped it might give me the edge on other candidates.

In the back of my mind, however, I was concerned that they may have been seeking a more experienced manager. Barrie interviewed me for the job at the Friendly Lodge hotel just off the M6 at junction 10 between Walsall and Wolverhampton. I think I'd read in the *Express & Star* that Alistair Robertson, who had just retired from playing after leaving Wolves, was also being spoken to. The interview went as well as it could and I got some positive feedback from the chairman and directors. Whatever I said must have impressed them because they offered me the job after that first discussion. Jane was outside sitting in the car waiting for me. I came out of the hotel, ran straight to her and said 'I've got it!' and we hugged. I was surprised to get it but they seemed to like what they had heard. They liked that I had worked with Gerry. They also knew I had played at the top level and knew me from my days with Wolves and they thought I was ideal for them. The board gave me as much information as they could as regards what they were looking for and what needed to be done. It was going to be a bloody tough job ahead but I was ready for the challenge. Whatever was thrown at me, I would give it my best shot and work hard to achieve their target, which was to stop the rot and build the club back up. But there was no money to spend on players and I would have to wheel and deal in the free transfer market.

But before I could start work at Walsall I had some unfinished business at Bristol Rovers. The clubs agreed for me to go down to Wembley for the Leyland DAF Trophy final with the boys and be part of the day with them. Everybody knew I was leaving – it had been reported in the press, but the Rovers fans were great. It was just a pity that I signed off with a defeat. We went down 2-1 to Tranmere Rovers. Devon White equalised for us after Ian Muir put Tranmere ahead, but it wasn't to be our day and Jim Steel scored the winner for them. But it was a great day out and there were 48,402 at Wembley to see it. The supporters loved Gerry because he was successful but they applauded me for the work I had done over four years there after playing the first season under Bobby Gould. In fact the number four seems to have cropped up throughout my career – I spent four years at Bristol Rovers, four years at Walsall and the same amount of time at Cardiff. Wolves were the only club I spent longer at, but 16 years is four fours so the connection remains! My favourite number is also four, although I played the majority of my games in the number seven shirt.

Less than 24 hours after saying my farewells to Bristol Rovers at Wembley, I started at Walsall. At first, the club offices were still at Fellows Park, their old ground, but the team had played their last game there at the end of the 1989-90 season and they were in the process of moving to a brand new stadium at Bescot, about half a mile away. I was given John Barnwell's car – a Renault automatic that had done about 100,000 miles. As someone who has always been very superstitious, I wasn't too keen on having the car driven by my predecessor who had just been sacked. My foot was going through the floor to get it going. I felt I could run as fast as it would drive, so after two or three weeks I asked them to change it and they gave me a Vauxhall Cavalier. That only had about 60,000 miles on the clock so it was a helluva step up! But I didn't care too much what I was driving, I was just delighted to be taking my first steps in management. Finances were very tight and I was told we could only bring in players on free transfers and I had to reduce the wage bill. This was easier said than done because there were players there on contract so I had to keep them while working on a very small budget. Thankfully, as I had gone in at the end of the previous season, I had all summer to prepare for the new campaign and I managed to bring in some decent players. I was indebted to our general manager, Paul Taylor, who helped me enormously and worked overtime trying to bring in players. Paul gave me an insight into what I'd got and what I might need, and did all the players' contracts working closely with Barrie on the financial side, and helped with scouting.

First we had a pre-season and I needed to get to know the squad so we decided to take the players away. Paul booked us into a holiday camp in the south west. We stayed in caravans and when we used to go down to dinner, we'd say 'Hi-de-hi!', taking off the TV comedy of the time. Before we went on the trip, I signed Chris Hutchings, a right back, after a successful trial, and Charlie Ntamark. He had been studying law at university in Birmingham and came in for treatment during the summer. Charlie was suffering with a groin injury which prevented him playing at the 1990 World Cup, where his country, Cameroon, stunned everybody by reaching the quarter-finals before going out to England after extra-time. Roger Milla was their big star, having scored four goals in Italia 90, and I wondered if it was possible to sign him. Walsall were down in the doldrums at the time and desperately needed a lift, so I thought he would give the place a huge buzz. I asked Charlie if he could have a word with Roger to ask him to come, but he wanted a million dollars. I said 'We're Walsall, not Warsaw!' Charlie proved to be one of my best signings for Walsall and ended up staying for seven years.

Another excellent signing was Tony Grealish. A former Republic of Ireland international, Tony was a gritty midfielder who had captained Brighton in the 1983 FA Cup final. He was 33 at the time and with no money to recruit an assistant manager or coach, he became player-coach. He initially arrived as a player on a short-term deal while he got over a foot operation after leaving Rotherham but when he regained full fitness, we soon promoted him to coaching duties. It was ideal for me because if you're working with 20-odd players and want to work with a specific department, such as the defence, I could do that and Tony would work with the midfield or strikers, or vice-versa. He was a lovely man but two years down the line, he was involved in one of the most difficult conversations I've ever had in management. By then Jeff Bonser had taken over from Barrie Blower as chairman and he told me Tony was too expensive to keep in his dual role. The budget was small but the finances weren't great, and with Paul Taylor as general manager, the chairman didn't want to be paying a coach as well so we had to release him. I could see where the chairman was coming from because it was an excess wage for someone who wasn't playing regularly. I called Tony in and told him he had to go but he was absolutely brilliant about it. He said 'Kenny, I understand'. He accepted my reasons and my admiration for him went through the roof.

To open the new ground, we played Aston Villa in a pre-season friendly, and in front of nearly 9,000 fans, lost 4-0. I had a battle to choose between my two goalkeepers, Ron Green and Fred Barber, after alternating them in pre-season. For the first game of the season, I think Fred was expecting to be picked but I went with Greeny. I used to call big Fred 'Knock Knock' because he was always knocking on my door asking to go on loan somewhere if he wasn't in the team. We also had a goalscorer, Stuart Rimmer, and he saved us in more ways than one. Rimmer, who Barnwell had managed at Notts County, was Walsall's 18-goal top scorer the previous season, and picked up where he had left off. He had the honour of scoring the first competitive goal at Bescot in a 2-2 draw against Torquay United on the opening day of the 1990-91 season. Stuart was a prolific striker who did brilliantly for us but Walsall were in deep financial trouble at the time and we had to sell him to prevent the club from going under, it was that close. We managed to keep him until the February of that season by which time he had registered 19 goals in 35 games before we sold him to Barnsley for £150,000.

After the deal went through, the chairman Barrie Blower thanked me because the money from the sale went directly to keeping the club in business. I had no money to buy a replacement, although earlier in the season I had been allowed to bring in Mike Cecere from Huddersfield and Rod McDonald from non-league Colne Dynamoes. I didn't know much about McDonald – he came on recommendation from Paul Taylor. Rod liked to play off a big man and did well for us, scoring a lot of goals. The only negative about Rod was the difficulty to get him to train on Mondays. He used to ring in, saying he'd got trouble with his car so couldn't travel down from Merseyside. Rod had come from non-league so it was a step up to the pro game, and I think he enjoyed his weekends, hence his Monday calls. But he gave us really good service and was a top lad, so a bit of careful man-management was required there. That same month we sold Rimmer, I was reminded of the pressures of management with a visit of an old foe from my playing days. Billy Bremner, who had been a great midfielder during his long career as captain of Leeds, was now in his second spell managing Doncaster, after helping them to promotion from the Fourth Division during his first spell in charge. That helped earn him a crack at the hotseat at Elland Road.

Anyway, we beat Doncaster 1-0 and, as was customary with all visiting managers whatever the result, I invited Billy into my office for a drink afterwards. I always kept a bottle of Scotch in there – not for me, but to share with guests and visiting managers. So I poured about an inch of whisky into a tumbler and handed it to Billy. He said 'I asked for a f****** Scotch, son' so I poured more in and he said 'Come on then' waving his glass at me to add more, so in the end, I pretty much filled the tumbler and Billy replied 'That's better!' and drank the lot before boarding the coach for the journey home. It was a real pleasure for me to have someone like Billy in my office and I felt honoured to share his company. I had watched him play for Leeds when my brother was there before I had really started my career, I had played against him many times and he had captained his club and country to glory. You knew you were up against a top class player when you faced Billy and Johnny Giles, and Leeds were a top class team, as were Liverpool at the time, so I had no problem with Billy depleting my resources of Scotch!

34

Alas Smith And Moans At Walsall

One of the first jobs I had at Walsall was to sit down with the general manager Paul Taylor and look at the wage structure and bonuses. Some of the senior players were on far more money than the club could now afford to pay operating at the lower level. There was a massive difference in the amounts. So I had a choice: Get rid of some of the senior players or persuade them to accept a pay cut. I decided to call a meeting with the players and explain the situation to them. I told them I couldn't change their basic wage as that was guaranteed as part of their contracts, but I needed to change the bonus system to bring it into line with the Fourth Division.

When I had told the players what I had in mind, one lone voice piped up, saying: 'What happens if we don't agree to it?' It was Dean Smith, then just 18 and still to make the first team and one of the youngest players we had. Fair play, I thought. I admired his guts for speaking out. 'I'll play the youth team,' I replied. I was deadly serious too. We had all these experienced players such as Fred Barber, Graeme Forbes, Alex Taylor and Peter Skipper, all on decent money. In the end, all the players agreed to the revised bonus scheme apart from two – Forbes and Taylor. Taylor claimed I had no right to change it, which was true, but I was hoping they would agree to it. They wouldn't, so unfortunately I couldn't pick two of the better players. Paul Taylor and I explained the situation to them but they wouldn't budge. It was a shame and very sad because they would have strengthened the team, but their minds were made up.

Taylor ended up returning to Scotland where he joined Falkirk and Forbes, another Scot, signed for Dundee. It was sad because they were good lads and decent players, but I had to accept the fact that they were within their rights to go. I had no qualms about it but I couldn't play them because if I did, the other players wouldn't have signed for their revised bonuses. What Dean Smith didn't know at the time was I would have carried out my threat to field the youth team. This was seen as a 'bonus' season, as there was to be no relegation from the Football League for the first time since the trapdoor to the Conference had been introduced several years earlier. Brian Flynn's Wrexham finished bottom of the Football League that season, 1990-91, and he played a lot of youngsters. The following year they finished 14th, one place above us. With Taylor and Forbes out of our plans, the attention turned to replacements and this was where Paul Taylor came into his own.

When I was with the players in training, he was in the office on the phone, trying to beg or borrow players to get us the best deals for the budget we had. We tried to sign Nigel Vaughan, a former Wales international midfielder who had been released by Wolves. But we couldn't agree a deal with him and he ended up signing for Hereford. To supplement the players we had, along with new arrivals Tony Grealish, Chris Hutchings, Charlie Ntamark and Mike Cecere, we had youngsters such as Dean Smith, Chris Marsh, Adrian Littlejohn and Matt Bryant, a 19-year-old central defender on loan from Bristol City.

August 25, 1990 was a landmark day for me – my first game as a manager. With Hutchings, Grealish, Ntamark, Cecere and Marsh in the starting line-up, we fancied our chances against Torquay, but got off to the worst possible start. Poor Bryant had a mixed Football League debut which included the dubious pleasure of scoring the first competitive goal at Bescot Stadium. Sadly for us, it was in our net after he got too much on a back pass. The rule about goalkeepers not being allowed to pick the ball up hadn't been introduced back then and the ball flew past Ron Green and into the top corner of the net. Matt Elliott, who went on to have a great career at Leicester, made it worse for our defence when he doubled Torquay's lead. Thankfully, Stuart Rimmer halved the deficit to claim the honour of scoring Walsall's first goal at the new ground, before a promising youngster, Martin Goldsmith, came off the bench to score with his first touch to equalise with about 10 minutes left. An inspired substitution you might say! Our first win at Bescot duly came three days later with a 4-2 victory over Cambridge in the League Cup when Rimmer bagged another two goals, but there followed an eight-match run without a win in September. Rimmer continued to find the back of the net, but it was clear we needed strengthening elsewhere if we were to improve. By the time new signing Colin Methven made his debut at the start of November, Rimmer had scored his 15th goal in 20 games as we beat high-flying Burnley 1-0. Colin was a lovely man who did fantastically well for me. He was just shy of his 35th birthday when we brought him from Blackpool and he was settled with his family in that area. We came to an arrangement where I allowed him to train on his own at home from Monday to Wednesday if we didn't have a midweek game, then he would travel down the M6 and train with us on a Thursday and a Friday, so he was involved in the preparations for the game on the Saturday. The outcome was he performed tremendously well for me. A lot of managers would not have allowed that to happen but I felt it was good man-management.

I always remember my old Wolves boss Ian Greaves saying that to get the best out of players, you had to treat them like men, and Colin repaid me with loyalty and the level of his performances. I don't think I fell out with any of the players because I tried to treat them all like I did Colin, which was the way I would have wanted to be treated as a player. All of my managers were like that. Something else I did as a manager was always be up front with the fans. I told them what we had got and what we hadn't. I felt it best that way because you can't pull the wool over supporters' eyes. I was always truthful with them and I think they accepted that.

It was a huge challenge at Walsall but after four years at Bristol Rovers, I felt I had the experience to equip me for it. It was a difficult start for me and we finished 16th in that first season, which was probably the toughest of my entire career. Playing and coaching is one thing, but football management drains you mentally and emotionally. I had Paul Taylor as general manager and Tony Grealish helped with the coaching, and both helped me hugely. But I didn't have an assistant manager. I was dealing with the board and the press and having to manage the fans' expectations, things I hadn't had to deal with at Bristol Rovers.

As manager the buck stops with you. But I gave it everything I'd got and although the squad were not what we wanted them to be, they were improving. After that first season in charge, I sat down with Jane and told her it was a big challenge for me. She asked me whether I was happy doing it and I said 'Yes' and I was determined to build the club up. I was driving up and down the motorway and going to games here, there and everywhere to watch players. Sometimes Jane would meet me off the M5 when I was en route somewhere to hand me a flask of coffee and some sandwiches to keep me going. But I got stuck in, I enjoyed it and the players gave me everything. That first summer came probably my only regret from my time at Walsall when I released Adrian Littlejohn. He was a quick, powerful winger who went on to play for Sheffield United – including a season in the Premier League – and went on to have a successful career with spells at Plymouth, Bury and Port Vale and other teams. In hindsight, I should have given him more time and worked with him for longer. Recognising the need for extra quality, plus experience to help the talented crop of youngsters we had, I brought in Derek Statham and Kevin MacDonald that summer. I wanted someone mobile to play down the left-hand side and had tried to sign Micky Adams, who I played with at Coventry. I knew he could get up and down the pitch, but he wanted too much money to come. I also tried to sign Andy Thompson from Wolves as I had been told he was available after refusing to sign a contract and Graham Turner put him on week-to-week terms. But he ended up signing a new deal to stay at Molineux. Derek was a great player who did well for us. He was one of the best left backs I had played against and was part of the exciting West Bromwich Albion team under Ron Atkinson that finished third in the League in 1978-79, going on to win three full England caps. Kevin had won the Double with Liverpool in 1985-86 after a successful time at Leicester City and was very vocal in midfield.

At the opposite end of the age and experience scale to Statham and MacDonald, I also added a goalkeeper, Mark Gayle, and right back Wayne Williams. Gayle gave up his job as a market trader in Handsworth to join us, and I paid £15,000 to Worcester City to take him. They weren't the only ones to put pen to paper as that summer I signed a new two-year contract. I felt we were on the right path towards a better future.

Talking of experience, I also added a bit of my own, dusting off my boots to make an albeit very brief playing comeback that summer. As a favour to an old mate Mike Garland, we took a team down to Somerset to play Radstock Town of the Western League in a pre-season friendly. I was 40 at the time and with us comfortably in the lead (we ended up winning 6-0), I came on and played about 15 minutes near the end. It was enough to counter claims from anyone who says Paul Merson was Walsall's first player-manager!

But there were still difficult times off the field, and with the club losing £8,000 a week, Barrie Blower decided to stand down as chairman. It was a shame as I enjoyed working with Barrie and wished I could have worked with him for longer. Jeff Bonser, a local businessman and fan of Walsall since childhood who had been on the board for three years, replaced Barrie in the chair. He was joined in a new-look board by Clive Welch and Mike Lloyd, fellow lifelong supporters. Despite new blood in the boardroom, the club continued to struggle financially, and with the biting weather hitting us hard, we were left without a home League game for seven weeks from early November to Boxing Day 1991. With a lack of income, the chairman put the entire squad up for sale, and the PFA were called in to provide a loan to help pay players' wages. We had a number of promising youngsters, and one of them, striker Neil Tolson, was sold to Oldham Athletic – then in the top flight – for a six-figure fee after playing just three first-team games. Losing Tolson was a blow, but worse was to follow as Aldershot delivered a reminder of what can happen to clubs in financial peril as they became the first Football League club in 30 years to fold, going bankrupt with debts of £1.2m. It meant their records were expunged and we lost four points as a result. The cost-cutting continued with me forced to release Tony Grealish as injuries meant he wasn't playing enough to justify the wage. We ended the season in 15th place, an improvement of one on my first season.

If we were looking to ride higher the next season, we got lift-off – but in a way I never expected. One day a helicopter landed on the artificial pitch just behind the stadium so I went out to see what was going on. It turns out it was there to pick up the chairman, Jeff Bonser, for a flying lesson. As a few of us were showing interest, he invited us to join him and the pilot. So Tom Bradley, the physio and now kitman, and I agreed to go with them. Very quickly we were high in the air and then I noticed the entire cabin was made of glass so everywhere we looked we could see how far we were off the ground. I felt sick to the stomach, which wasn't helped as we started to lurch up and down rapidly. I think this is where I developed a fear of heights. We ended up flying over Cannock Chase but rather than admire the view, I couldn't bear to look – it was the longest 45 minutes of my life. When we got down I told the chairman to never do that to again to me as it had left me as white as a sheet.

When the squad re-assembled for the start of pre-season training in 1992, optimism was high. Colin Methven, Derek Statham, Mike Cecere and Rod McDonald had all signed new contracts, but I made perhaps my most high profile signing at Walsall that summer. Wayne Clarke was at Manchester City at the time and had had loan spells at Stoke, Shrewsbury and Wolves, but he wanted to move back to the Midlands and start playing regularly again. The youngest of the five famous footballing brothers, Wayne was regarded as a special talent as a kid and played for England at schoolboy and youth level. Like his older brother Allan, who had started his own career at Walsall before going on to become one of the most feared strikers in the game with Fulham, Leicester, Leeds and England, he was a good finisher, but perhaps without his older sibling's devilment. Two of their other brothers, Derek and Kelvin, had also played for the Saddlers, so there was a further connection there. I'd always looked out for Wayne. I remember when he came to Wolves, his dad said to me, 'Will you look after him?' I said, 'Yes of course, no problem'. Wayne did well for Wolves but he had to be sold during the club's financial troubles and moved the same summer I left. He helped Birmingham to promotion back to the First Division before going on to win the League with Everton in 1987. He joined me at Walsall and it was payback time for me, having looked after him all those years earlier!

To mark my 25 years in professional football, the club agreed to award me with a benefit game, and, with Wolves an obvious choice of opposition, their manager Graham Turner kindly supplied a full-strength opposition for a pre-season friendly at Bescot. I was a proud man as I walked out of the tunnel through the guard of honour formed by the teams. John Hendley, my old friend from Wolves who was programme editor there, did a lovely job putting together a match day programme for me. But if I was delighted with the game staged in my honour, then I was also full of hope for the season ahead for Walsall. With my experienced players all signed up and a top-class striker on board, we beat a strong Championship side in Wolves 1-0, before overcoming Oldham, then in the Premier League, 2-1.

Once the season proper started, Wayne did repay me too, as he scored 21 goals in 39 League games that season and 24 in all competitions, which would be the equal highest number of goals he scored in any season of his career. Wayne's goals helped us finish fifth, easily the best campaign we'd enjoyed in my time at Bescot. It meant we were in the play-offs and we had to face Crewe, a team we'd beaten home and away just a few weeks earlier after finishing with a flourish on an eight-match unbeaten run and five straight wins.

One of the main reasons behind that excellent end to the season was one of my best signings for Walsall, Martin O'Connor, who made his debut for us at the end of March 1993. The route to him joining was another unusual one. In the maelstrom of activity that greets a manager after a game – chewing the fat with sponsors, addressing board members, giving a press conference, meeting supporters – you probably speak to dozens of different people and a lot of things are said. On this occasion, someone approached me, saying 'You want to have a look at Martin O'Connor – he's at Crystal Palace but he used to play for Bromsgrove Rovers'. You hear a lot of this type of talk from fans and people claiming to be 'in the know' and the tendency can be to take it with a pinch of salt as you're always getting different names thrown at you. But I thanked the person, remembered the name and spoke to Paul Taylor about him. It turned out Martin was a local lad who lived close to Bescot. I decided to take a look at him and took Jane to Southampton to watch him play for Palace in a reserve game. We almost missed the kick-off as we'd stopped for a bite to eat en route. But we were soon glad we had made it on time. After 20 minutes she turned to me and said 'What do you think?' I said, 'I'm going to take him.' She replied, 'But he hasn't touched the ball yet.' I said, 'Yes, I know, but look at the way he closes down the play, presses opponents and organises people. Look at his energy, his quickness, the spring in his step and the way he moves so well. I need that in my team.'

My mind was made up from that first 20 minutes but we stayed until 20 minutes before the end, during which time he only reinforced my first impression of him that we just had to sign him. He was getting beyond the rest of the midfield and supporting the front men. So on that performance I knew I wanted to take him, but it took quite a while to get him on board permanently because Palace originally wanted £100,000 for him, a price well beyond our means. Initially, we took him on loan to the end of the season and we soon came to appreciate what a good passer of a ball he was too and what a fantastic lad he was. Unfortunately, we didn't get him back until the following February, when he finally signed for us on a permanent basis for a knockdown fee of £40,000. Alan Smith was the Palace manager at the time and there was a lot of haggling before we reached agreement. In the end I think the Walsall supporters club helped to purchase him, but I wasn't bothered where the money came from, I was just relieved and delighted to sign him, this time for keeps. From then on, I tried to build a team around him.

But however good Martin was, he was unable to prevent what happened in the play-offs. The stakes were huge but were cranked up before the first leg at Gresty Road after Crewe manager Dario Gradi had accused us of being 'over physical' in the two League games. But this time we were our own worst enemies. And it was someone we had come to rely on heavily who was unwittingly at fault. Colin Methven, such a rock for

217

us in all the time he had been at the club, made two bad back passes which ended up gifting them a two-goal lead. Unfortunately, it gave them the momentum they needed and knocked us for six really, Crewe winning 5-1. Before the second leg, I got the players in the dressing room and just told them to give it everything and go hell for leather. We started like a train and went ahead in the first five minutes, only to lose 4-2. The lads had given it everything and the fans clapped us off at the end, knowing we'd lost the tie in the first leg.

After losing in the play-offs, expectations among the fans had risen and they expected promotion the next season. But changes were forced upon us. After protracted talks, we ended up losing our top scorer, Wayne Clarke. When it came to re-negotiating his contract at the end of the campaign, I felt he led me up the garden path a bit. There was a lot of haggling and then he ended up signing for Shrewsbury for an extra £50 a week. He did very well there, helping them to the Division Four title, but it left me with a sizeable gap to fill.

Thankfully, we managed to plug the gap with Kyle Lightbourne, who was an unknown trialist from Bermuda who joined us in pre-season from Scarborough. We had to wait until September before he could play so he could gain a work permit, and he started off as a winger as he had so much pace. We used to do a fitness run in training which consisted of sprinting from the goalline to the halfway line and back, then from the goalline to the edge of the 18-yard box and back, then repeat it all and Kyle would always be way out in front. Initially, however, he didn't always show consistency in his play. But he worked at his game and he became one of the best finishers I have ever worked with so we put him up front.

Another player we signed that summer was goalkeeper Jimmy Walker, who had been released from Notts County. 'Wacca' was a great signing for us. He was on his knees at Notts County in terms of his demeanour before he signed for us, because he had suffered knockbacks and couldn't get a game. He turned out to be a fantastic keeper who was a great shotstopper and a superb striker of a ball. Initially, Walker was behind Mark Gayle, who was our player of the year the previous season, but he soon displaced him and we were later able to sell Gayle to Crewe for £35,000, which represented a £20,000 profit. Right back was also a problem area for us as I had released Wayne Williams, so I signed another Wayne – Evans – from Welshpool on a free transfer and he quickly nailed down the place as his own. I also had to replace Martin O'Connor after he returned to Crystal Palace following the expiry of his loan, so we took Dean Peer from Birmingham. Dean's arrival soon proved a profitable one, in more ways than one. Hardly known for his prolific goalscoring during his time at St Andrew's, he arrived having netted eight times in 120 League games for Blues. Around this time, the chairman Jeff Bonser came up with a novel idea to motivate the players to score and help team spirit. As a bit of fun, he started giving out odds on all the players finding the net. Jeff would come into the dressing room before a game and write the odds on a blackboard and it quickly became a popular idea among the players. We were due to play Lincoln and Dean, not known for scoring, was rated well below the favourites to find the net at about 25-1. But he managed to get himself on the scoresheet and after netting, he came running to the dugout shouting he'd pocketed £25. We won 5-2 and Dean ended up with a hat-trick. After each goal he shouted out 'That's another £25 the chairman owes me!' Dean couldn't wait to see the chairman's face when he went to collect his winnings.

The Peer-inspired win against Lincoln came in what turned out to be our best spell of the season, winning five games out of six in November. The other game that month was an FA Cup first round tie away to Wrexham. This was going to be a tough task as they were a division higher than us at the time and on a four-match unbeaten run in mid-table. I was suffering with 'flu but the chairman rang me to say he wanted me there. I was feeling awful but managed to get off my sick bed and travelled on the coach with the squad to north Wales. I tried to rally the players before the game but in doing so almost collapsed. I managed to get to the dugout to watch the match but all the way through I was sweating and I had a high temperature. We ended up drawing 1-1 which meant a replay at Bescot. The chairman knew I was friends with Andy Gray, who was then one of Sky's main pundits, so he asked me if I could try to get them to screen the replay, which I did and they agreed, bringing in some much-needed funds. As a double boost, we managed to win 2-0 with goals from Kyle Lightbourne and Rod McDonald in what was Walsall's first home game broadcast live on TV.

I recovered from the flu, but my health had started to become a concern. I started suffering from heart palpitations, and I was convinced it was down to the stress of the job. I had always got on well with the chairman, in fact he used to say 'You make me laugh' and he praised me for bringing a smile to the club again. I was easy going and I liked to have a laugh but I was serious when I had to be. But I felt a lot of pressure was on me. Jeff wanted me at the club 24-7, but living in the Cotswolds and commuting to Walsall on an almost daily basis, I wasn't prepared to do that. I was working without an assistant, coach or a scouting network and felt I was giving everything to the job as it was. I would be up and down the motorway, scouting to watch a player, getting home in the early hours then be up again the next morning and back up the M5 to the club. Sometimes I would stay overnight with friends in Wolverhampton and on occasions I would stay at the Friendly Lodge hotel off M6 junction 10 near Walsall, just to cut down on the travelling. The hotel manager was a Manchester United fan so I used to get him tickets in return for a free room, and I used to sneak fish and chips in there when I got back late. I stayed there that often and got him so many tickets for Old Trafford that the staff at United must have wondered why Walsall wanted to watch so many of their games!

The problem was that I needed someone alongside me. When I was at Bristol Rovers and Gerry Francis was the manager, he only went in to the club three days a week to reduce the travelling from Surrey. Living locally, I went in the other four days to lessen the burden on him. The pressure of the job at Walsall would have been eased if I'd had some staff around me, for example if I had someone with me, I could have said 'Could you take the players training today?' That would have helped me enormously. I was having to take training, deal with the players and their problems, attend board meetings, and deal with the press, and it all built up.

Despite the growing pressure I was feeling, I thought at the beginning of that fourth season, 1993-94, that we had a squad good enough to win promotion. I'd put in three years of hard graft and felt I'd developed the team I wanted. By the end of the November, we were up to third in the table, just three points behind the leaders, Preston. But we weren't able to sustain that form, and a run of two wins in 12 from the end of December to the start of March prompted calls from the fans chanting 'Sack the board'. We were still in the play-off places at the start of February and won five matches out of seven from the start of March to the beginning of April to lie seventh, but we fell away to eventually finish 10th, four points outside the final play-off place. That was a disappointment after reaching the play-offs the previous season. That close season, I set about trying to strengthen us for that final push and attempted to sign Derek Mountfield, who had been released from Wolves. We had lost the experienced

Colin Methven a year earlier and I'd pinpointed Derek as a strong, competitive centre half who could do really well in both boxes at set-pieces after he'd been there and done it at the top level with Everton and Aston Villa. But he ended up signing for Carlisle for another £150 a week and was part of the team that won our division that season. Whenever I see him now he says he was gutted we couldn't come to an agreement. As it happened, he signed for Walsall the following summer. But despite that blow I said to Jane that for the first time, we'd got enough about us to get promoted. We got off to a reasonable if unspectacular start to the following campaign, 1994-95. After starting with a 1-1 draw away to Fulham, we beat Plymouth 4-0 at home in the League Cup, then got our first League victory of the season, 2-1 at home to Lincoln. We then went down 2-1 at Plymouth in the second leg to go through to the second round of the League Cup and we pulled a glamour tie at home to West Ham. Before we could play the Hammers, we had several League fixtures to concentrate on and drew 0-0 away to Hereford on the Saturday before going down 2-1 at home to Carlisle the following Tuesday. Carlisle were joint top at the time and it was their third win in four games. Despite the result, the fans gave us a standing ovation in response to our performance after a tight game which left us in mid-table.

If we played on a Tuesday, I always gave the players the Wednesday off and took it off myself. I felt I needed to recover as much as they did. Jane would always drive me home afterwards as she knew I was drained from the emotion of the game, as if I had just played every position from one to 11. In fact, one match I was so involved that when the ball came to me in the technical area, I carried on as if I was playing! On the Thursday, I told my general manager, Paul Taylor, that I was playing in an annual Midlands football charity golf day. Virtually all the managers from the area played in it, as I had done for several years. Afterwards I was told I had won an award, but I told them I couldn't stay on because I was going to a Wolves v Manchester United reserve game to watch a player, and I remember being sat in the stand next to Kenny Swain, who was then manager of Wigan.

Friday morning came and I was lacing up a pair of new boots ready to take training as we were preparing to face Northampton at home on the Saturday when the chairman Jeff Bonser kicked open my office door. As soon as he did that, I knew something wasn't right as it was out of character for him to act like that, rather than politely knock. I looked up and said to him: 'I'm just lacing these new boots up in case I'm needed tomorrow'. A few words were exchanged and I think we caught each other on a bad day. He told me to clear my desk. I asked him if he was sacking me. He said 'Yes' and that was it, I was gone. I went outside, rang Jane and said 'You'd better get the kettle on, love'. She asked why and I told her I'd been sacked. Before I left Walsall for the last time, I got the players together in the dressing room. When I walked in to tell them the news, you could have heard a pin drop until one voice said 'F****** hell!' It was Charlie Ntamark. They were just in disbelief. A couple of them said they weren't going to play for the club again. I said 'Look, I've got the best squad I've had in the four years I've been here and you are the players who are going to take this club up because you've got the quality'. I went on to say I would be watching their progress very closely. Later, a few of them wrote to me thanking me for what I had done.

Driving home, I heard about my dismissal on the radio, and also that Kenny Swain, who had sat next to me at Molineux the previous night, had lost his job. Funny old game, eh?! What prompted Bonser to flip like he did I don't know as I had no issues with Jeff and I thought we had a great relationship and got on well. Yes, there were times when he asked me to be somewhere and I couldn't because I couldn't be in two places at once, but I had Paul Taylor to help out. But I didn't get on with all the directors and I sensed someone somewhere had put the boot in for me. I remember saying to Jeff at a board meeting 'I don't want to be sat here for two or three hours discussing every part of the club's business. I'll come in for the football business and then I would like to go and carry on with my work' and he said he didn't have a problem with that. Whether the other directors took a dislike to that, I don't know.

Paul Taylor gave me a budget and I always worked to it. I don't know whether the speculation linking me with a return to Wolves as Graham Taylor's number two – more about that in the next chapter – had affected the relationship with the chairman, as he never asked me about it. I couldn't understand his decision as I'd worked my socks off for over four years and felt we had finally got a team ready to get promoted. There was no reason for the chairman to have a pop at me like that. I couldn't have done any more for Walsall or been any more involved in the club. I loved it there and thought I would be there for a long time because I believed our relationship was stronger than that. These things happen in football, but I must admit, I didn't think it was going to happen to me at that time. Normally if you get the sack you feel sad and aggrieved but I felt none of those emotions. I actually felt relieved – it was like the biggest weight had been lifted off my shoulders. I was knackered. I actually felt it was the right move for me for health reasons. I drove home with a clear mind thinking Bonser had done me a favour as I was still suffering palpitations and they were strong and powerful, but when the games were on, I felt fine. I rang Paul Taylor to tell him what had happened. He tried to get the decision reversed but to no avail. But I didn't mind. I now believe Bonser saved my life in many ways. The decision was a big relief for Jane and me. There was some disappointment because I couldn't see the job through to fruition, but I felt a lot better in myself and healthier as a result, not that I wanted it to happen.

Some time later, there was a telephone call from the club secretary, Roy Whalley. He asked for the Vauxhall Cavalier, the club car I'd been using, to be returned. Jane answered the call and told him if he wanted it, the club had better arrange to collect it themselves. It took three weeks for the car to be collected off our drive and when they came the car's battery was flat. But when my replacement, Chris Nicholl, went in there, they gave him a Jaguar because he said he only drove Jags.

At the time, I felt that was going to be our season, and so it proved as Chris led the team to automatic promotion as runners-up to Carlisle. Full marks to Chris, he didn't change anything, he kept the same team, and when they went up, he didn't brag about what he had achieved, he said 'That's not my team, that's Kenny Hibbitt's team'. That was a lovely thing to say and it sums the man up. I just wish I would have been in his shoes.

I've only once been back to Bescot, which is, of course, now called the Banks's Stadium. Walsall were playing Shrewsbury Town and I was there to summarise the game for local radio. Kevin Ratcliffe was manager of Shrewsbury at the time. I saw Kevin down on the touchline and he came up through the stand and gave me a big hug. Fair play to him, because he knew the kind of job I'd done there. I had so many people say to me they couldn't believe what had happened after the position I had got the club into, but the decision had been made and I had to move on.

35

A Taylor-ed Offer to Return To Wolves

One night during one of my regular stopovers at the Friendly Lodge Hotel near Walsall I was watching television in my room when the phone rang. I was surprised to hear the voice of Graham Taylor. This was the first time he had called me so I was a bit shocked. My first thought was 'Why?' I didn't have to wait long. He said 'Hi Kenny, it's Graham Taylor. I have been watching your progress as manager of Walsall and have been impressed. I am looking to get the manager's job at Wolves and was wondering if you would be interested in coming with me as my assistant if I got the job?' Obviously I said 'Of course, but you will need to approach my chairman first'. He replied, 'That will come later but first I want to have a chat with you. Where can we meet?' We made arrangements to meet up, I put the phone down and did a merry dance round the hotel room clenching my fist shouting 'Yes, yes'. I was so thrilled to think I could be working with an ex-England manager, and at my beloved Wolves. Then the phone went again, this time it was Jane. She asked if Graham Taylor had called so I said yes and asked how she knew. She said he'd rung our home.

Graham and I met at another hotel nearby. In the car on the way to his house in Little Aston, near Sutton Coldfield, Graham seemed keen to pick my brains and he asked me about Steve Bull. I was a bit taken aback and didn't understand what he meant or why he asked it, but I recalled he didn't pick him much for England and sensed this might be his way of assessing me, or my job interview. I said 'Bully is a legend at Wolves and it would be difficult to sell him, if that's what you're thinking'. He just said 'Mmmm, OK'. When we got to his house we spent a good hour chatting over a pot of tea. When I left him as he dropped me back off at the hotel car park his last words were 'OK Ken, if I get the job let me get my feet under the table then I will come and get you'. We shook hands and he left, I got into my car and was absolutely thrilled that maybe an opportunity to work at my beloved Wolves was going to happen. The prospect of this didn't distract me from my job at Walsall. If anything it inspired me and I got on with building my team. I told myself it might not happen and would only happen if Graham got the Wolves job.

I never mentioned it to anyone else, but the prospect of me joining Graham if he was installed as Wolves manager was leaked to the press somehow. Paul Marston, the veteran Walsall correspondent for the *Birmingham Evening Mail*, kept calling me asking what was happening with the Wolves interest. I couldn't believe the story had hit the streets because I hadn't said anything. Graham got the job and was appointed towards the end of March 1994, replacing Graham Turner. From then, the story about me being appointed as his number two seemed to be everywhere. I would be filling my car up with petrol and I'd be getting shouts from Wolves fans leaning out of their cars and trucks shouting 'See you down at Molineux, Kenny'. It was amazing how it had escalated so much.

Back in my room at the Friendly Lodge I was watching the local news on television before I went out scouting and the sports presenter Bob Hall announced I would be joining Wolves the next day as assistant manager to Graham Taylor. I was stunned because I hadn't spoken to Graham or anyone at Wolves since he had dropped me off at that hotel after our meeting. Following the news bulletin I received a call from the wife of the Walsall chairman Jeff Bonser who had also seen it and she asked what was going on. I told her I didn't know but asked to chat with Jeff. She said he wasn't there but added that she would try to contact him and ask him to call me. 'Good' I replied because I needed to speak to him. I thought he knew something I didn't.

Jeff called me and I asked him to come to the hotel because I needed to speak to him. We met and I asked him if he knew anything about Graham Taylor wanting to take me to Wolves. He looked at me and said 'I have no idea what is happening'. I believed him because I trusted him and had no reason to doubt him. It was extraordinary how it had been heavily reported but neither myself nor the chairman knew of any official approach. Anyway we had a pint, he left the hotel and I carried on with my job.

Not long after, I was in Paul Taylor's office at Bescot discussing players when the phone went. He picked it up and said 'Just a minute Graham', then turning to me, whispered 'It's Graham Taylor'. I said I'd take the call in my office. I said 'Hi Graham, how are you?' I hadn't spoken to him since our meeting. He replied 'Hi Kenny, I won't be bringing you to Wolves with me'. I said 'Fine' and put the phone down. That was it. No reasons were given. The only explanation I could come up with was that I thought he had used me to get the Wolves job and can't help feeling he played me like a fiddle.

Graham had taken an awful lot of criticism and personal abuse towards the end of his time as England manager so his return to club football was always going to be a controversial one in the eyes of some fans. As a popular former Wolves player who was still involved in the game as a manager and working locally, I could see how linking my name with a return to Molineux as part of his backroom team could act as a sweetener to any misgivings fans had about him taking charge of their club.

After that I put it to the back of my mind and continued to get on with my job as Walsall manager and it was never mentioned again. But I have often wondered how much a part the speculation played in my sacking at Walsall a few months later. I may never know but I felt my judgement wasn't affected because results were good and the team I had assembled were the best I had put together since I started four years earlier. I was left with a few unanswered questions. Why didn't the chairman speak to me about the speculation about Wolves, as it had been there for some time? Was he disappointed I didn't go there? Was he sitting tight, wanting and expecting compensation from them? Only Jeff Bonser will know the answers.

Sadly, my sacking at Walsall came within a month of losing my brother Terry at the ridiculously young age of just 46. I think I was still grieving when it came. He had been ill with cancer, even though just 12 months earlier we had been celebrating his son Richard's wedding in Newcastle. I can still see him running around, having a drink with him at the bar looking so happy. We had our usual argument about football over a pint. That's all we ever talked about really other than the family.

On the day of the funeral we drove up as a family and were amazed at the reaction from the public of Newcastle. From the car we could see people lining the streets and television cameras following the procession. There must have been thousands of people paying their respects. It was an unbelievable turnout and send-off. All of his old Newcastle team-mates were there and they all said such wonderful things about him, which made me feel so proud of him. He was a cracking player with one of the best left foots I have ever seen. Malcolm Macdonald, who profited most from the partnership with my brother, said he would never have scored all the goals he did but for Terry's brilliant passes and crosses from the left. Losing Terry made me think of all the times we spent together, both on and off the pitch. We played against each other many times when I was at Wolves and he was at Newcastle in his two spells sandwiching his three years at Birmingham. Bearing in mind we lived within 30 miles of each other when he was at Blues, we probably didn't see as much of each other as we should then, although we met up to play golf together at Penn once or twice. We probably never got as close as we could have done, but the affection was always there when we met up. The memories go back much longer than that, to when we were kids in Bradford.

We grew up together playing football and although he was three years older than me, he always included me when his mates were around to have a game. I miss him so much now and keep looking at some of the write-ups on him from his playing days. They still bring tears to my eyes. Having lost my dad when he was just 40 years old and my brother when he was 46, I feel very lucky to be able to be alive to see my children and grandchildren grow up.

At the time of Terry's death, Jeff Bonser told me to take as much time off as I needed. But after the funeral and a week off, I felt I had to get back to work. That was what Terry would have wanted, and just eight days after he passed away on August 5, 1994, I was leading Walsall in their first game of the season away to Fulham. Looking back now I should have given myself more time to grieve. I didn't realise how long it can take to deal with the loss of someone so close. I also think the grief I was suffering may have played a part in my angry reaction to Jeff in the argument that led to my dismissal. I still think of Terry most days. He was a moaning so-and-so but I loved him; I knew him for longer than I had known our dad. He was my inspiration when we lost our father and I looked up to him.

36

Martin Was Smartin'- And So Was I!

I can't recall too many clashes with other managers down the years, but one stands out in my mind – and it was hardly a case of happy new year! On New Year's Day 1994 we were up against Wycombe Wanderers, who at the time were managed by Martin O'Neill. The stakes were pretty high with Wycombe fourth in the table and Walsall one place below. His team were doing pretty well so I knew we were in for a tough game. With a healthy crowd at Bescot, everybody was expecting a strong performance and most of all a win. With the remnants of the festive season still in full flow from the night before, the atmosphere was great and the fans got right behind the team and the players responded really well.

We managed to get in front but O'Neill didn't look too happy in his dugout. Suddenly he jumped out, and, with his fist clenched, I heard him tell one of his players to try to hurt one of ours. I didn't like that one little bit and approached him, saying 'What are you on about Martin? You don't tell your players to hurt anyone.' He just turned to me and said 'F*** off'. I said 'It is totally out of order' and he repeated to me 'F*** off'. I was livid and again told him he was out of order, but he repeated it again twice more before I went back to my place near the substitutes' bench. All I could think about was we had to beat them to shut him up.

We came out 4-2 winners with goals from Chris Marsh, Rod McDonald, Kyle Lightbourne and Jason Lillis. When the final whistle went, I was prepared to forget what happened during the game and I went over to Martin to shake his hand. But he completely ignored me and ran down the tunnel. I was totally shocked at his reaction because, as managers, we all get uptight during games and sometimes say and do things out of character. But when the final whistle goes, whatever has happened during the match should be forgotten, and you shake hands and move on. We had to play the return game at Wycombe in April, four months after we gave them a football lesson at Bescot Stadium. During that time there had been no contact between Martin and me so I was intrigued as to what he was going to say when we met up again. I don't hold

228

grudges so what happened in the first game was forgotten as far as I was concerned. When we arrived at Wycombe's ground we went straight to our dressing room, I named the team and the players went out to inspect the pitch to see what the conditions were like so they could put the correct studs in their boots. I saw Martin in the tunnel area but he made no effort to speak to me before disappearing somewhere. I didn't see him again until the teams and staff departed through the tunnel for the kick-off. Even in the dugout areas he still didn't make any attempt to acknowledge me and we didn't speak throughout the game.

Martin had clearly done his talking elsewhere as his team were certainly wound up for the game. We were ready for them and with 10 or 15 minutes remaining, the score remained 0-0 and we were coping very well. I would have taken that scoreline there and then as Wycombe were a good side. But we collapsed in the final few minutes and conceded three goals to lose 3-0. At full-time I again went to shake hands with Martin but again he refused my hand and marched off down the tunnel. I thought 'F*** you pal'. I wasn't too happy getting beat but it is customary to shake the other manager's hand even if you don't like someone.

I like Martin a helluva lot and used to admire the way he played. He was a hard grafter like myself and worked his socks off for the team. Going back to 1980, we were on opposite sides when Wolves played Nottingham Forest in the League Cup final at Wembley. When the final whistle went I wanted his shirt as a memento, not Trevor Francis's, Gary Birtles or John Robertson's. We did swap shirts and that made my day a very special one indeed, along with picking up the cup and our winners' tankards.

Fast forward 14 years and my emotions couldn't have been more different from what they had been that day at Wembley. After the Wycombe game I was gutted. We had thrown it away in the last few minutes, but it had been a half decent performance so I couldn't be too harsh on the lads. They felt the same as me but in my debrief after the game, I made the point of telling them not to relax at any stage of the game in future. Getting changed, there wasn't any reason to hang around so I went straight out to board the coach ready to leave, allowing the lads half an hour so they could meet up with family or friends who had supported them on the day. It meant I was sitting alone with only the coach driver for company. All of a sudden one of the stadium matchday staff dressed in his uniform approached the bus and clambered aboard. He said 'Mr Hibbitt,

229

Mr O'Neill would like to have a word with you.' I said 'If Mr O'Neill wants a word with me he can f****** come here'. The guy just turned and walked away and I thought nothing more of it. But after about five minutes I caught this figure wandering across the car park. I couldn't see his face until he appeared right in front of the coach and it was Martin.

I thought 'Here we go'. He stepped on to the bus and shook my hand and said he was sorry for his behaviour. I told him 'Not a problem Martin – these things happen' and we hugged each other and he went back inside the club. I thought it took a real man to do that – this was the guy I'd admired so much as a player and here he was showing the same qualities as a manager. I was so pleased when he got the Aston Villa job. He did a terrific job there and in fact that was where I got to meet him in more recent times in my capacity assessing the Premier League elite referees, in one of his first games in charge. Suspecting I might have the fortune to bump into him, I brought along his 1980 League Cup final shirt that we'd swapped all those years ago for him to sign. When I asked him he took me into a private room before the game and signed it for me. 'Brilliant' I thought and he was so nice with it – it was no trouble for him and I still treasure that shirt now. I asked him if he still had mine and said it would 'probably be with the rest of them' he had collected in a big box. Even more recently, we met up at Bournemouth for a Premier League game. He was on scouting duties for the Republic of Ireland but we sat next to each other and had a really enjoyable chat over a coffee at half-time. Great player, great manager and a lovely man.

37

Cardiff calling – and a death threat

After leaving Walsall, I decided I would take a year out. I desperately needed a complete break to recharge my batteries because I was just exhausted. I was on a rolling, one-year contract at Walsall and, thankfully, they were as good as their word and paid every penny due to me so I had an income for the next 12 months. When I got home after leaving Walsall for the last time, I said to Jane, 'That's it, I'm going to take a year out'. It was the first time I'd had an extended break since I was 15, having been player, coach, assistant manager and then manager. And when you're a manager, the summer is the busiest time. You're behind your desk or on the road, trying to get players in to improve your squad. You're less busy during the season because you've got your squad to work with. So I took time out and concentrated on seeing more of Jane and the children, although they were growing up by then. During this time, I didn't watch any football or scout for anybody, but I didn't lose any love or feeling for the game whatsoever, because I knew I wanted to get back involved when I was ready. I received a few calls but I wasn't interested in getting back into it so soon.

One of the advantages of having some free time was having a rare Christmas off because ever since I left school, I had always been playing or managing, apart from 1981 when I was out with a knee injury at Wolves. Now I could take things easier for once and it allowed Jane and I to experience a memorable trip to Sweden at Christmas in 1994. Wolves had always enjoyed a good following in Scandinavia, partly because the first British football match broadcast live on television in both Sweden and Norway featured Wolves in a 1-0 win against Sunderland at Molineux on November 29, 1969. The support for the club in Sweden was no doubt helped by us being fairly successful in the early 1970s and therefore featuring regularly on television. Also, visiting that country more than any other in pre-season during my time there could only have lifted the club's profile. But it still came as some surprise to learn I was featured in a book commemorating 25 years of televised British football in Sweden since that first game was broadcast. The book, called 'Dromelvan' (translated as 'The Dream Eleven' and sub-titled 'They played better football when Charlie George was young') by Swedish author Petter Karlsson, featured the 11 favourite British players in Sweden, including 18 pages on yours truly! I think the reason they picked me was because of my long hair when I played – they said I used to look like a Viking. Well, Robert Plant used to say that to me anyway and I was quite proud of that.

The selected 'team' reads pretty impressively and it would have been interesting to see how we would have fared if we had played together: Pat Jennings; Viv Anderson, Terry Butcher, Emlyn Hughes; Kenny Hibbitt, Alan Hudson, Billy Bremner, Charlie George; Steve Heighway, Peter Osgood, Peter Lorimer. To promote the book, Jane and myself were invited to Gothenburg for the launch and I appeared on an episode of *'Tipsextra'*, their equivalent of *Match of the Day*, the programme which showed that Wolves-Sunderland game all those years ago. We also had to select our own favourite British XI from that period, which had to include yourself but not any of your team-mates. I went for the following team: Gordon Banks, Chris Lawler, Roy McFarland, Bobby Moore, Terry Cooper; Alan Ball, myself, Alan Hudson, George Best; Denis Law and Kevin Keegan. I wanted to have Bobby Charlton in there as he had always been my favourite player but I couldn't because I had to pick myself in that central midfield position and I had always wanted 'Huddy' in my team as well. It was a pity you couldn't have selected anyone from your own club because I would have had Frank Munro, Mike Bailey, Willie Carr, John Richards and Dave Wagstaffe in there.

We had a lovely few days in Gothenburg. I remember walking around seeing the streets all lit up and people skating on the ice. It was wonderful – well, apart from the prices. As a Yorkshireman, I felt being charged £5 for a bottle of Grolsch was a bit steep. On the way back, there were only about six of us on the plane to Heathrow and we were continually offered free drinks and food. My only problem was that I was driving, so unfortunately I had to say no. But it was lovely seeing London all lit up as we flew above – I had never seen that before.

Wolves' popularity in Sweden in particular continues to this day and six of that 1970s team – myself, Phil Parkes, Derek Parkin, Willie Carr, Steve Daley and Norman Bell – have had horses named after us. The animals are used in a sport called harness racing, which is where two-wheeled carts are pulled by horses going at a trot or faster. Mine was the first to be named, in the mid-1990s, by its owner, a big Wolves fan called Bjorn Perrson, who generously says that Derek Parkin and myself are his favourite players. Apparently the horse named after me has won nine out of its 36 races, earning around £36,000.

About six months into my intended year out, Terry Yorath rang me from Cardiff City, where he was director of football. By then I had recharged my batteries and I was on the verge of wanting to get back to work, but I still wanted a bit more time off. Cardiff are a big club, even though they had just been relegated into the then Fourth Division, now League Two, and it was a tempting proposition to awaken a sleeping giant.

When I was at Walsall the players were paid a bonus based on the size of the home crowd, and whenever we played Cardiff, it was always a good attendance because of their away support. It's got a great fan base, so that took my fancy. It was only over the bridge – the Severn Crossing – and 50 miles from where we lived, so that was handy too. Yorath and the directors invited me for an interview in Nottingham as some of the directors had business interests there. No doubt helped by the fact that Terry Yorath knew my brother Terry when they played together at Leeds, the interview went fantastically well. That provided him with an insight into me, but he also said he was astounded that I'd been sacked by Walsall. I told him it wasn't because of results because we'd started that season reasonably well and I knew that was the year we were ready to go up. Terry, who had been manager but was now in an upstairs role, was very keen and they offered me the job there and then.

I said 'When do you want me to start? I'm ready and available now'. They said 'Oh, we've got to sack the present manager, Eddie May'. I replied 'Are you telling me he's still in place?' and they said yes. I told them I couldn't accept it. Other people may have been happy to do so in those circumstances, but I'm not that type of guy. I prefer business to be done straight and properly. I told them if the job became available, I'd be interested, then shook hands with everyone and went home. I suppose that sort of thing happens all of the time and maybe I'm a bit naïve in that sense, but it didn't suit me.

Three months on, Samesh Kumar, who had been owner of Birmingham City, bought Cardiff and so I thought my chance of managing them had gone. But it hadn't. Sam approached me and said he'd watched what I'd done at Bristol Rovers with Gerry Francis and he liked that, said I'd done a great job at Walsall and added he liked the fact my teams played good football. He also liked people who showed a bit of passion adding, 'I'd like you to come and manage my football club'. So I met the new board over the bridge for a coffee and they offered me the job. It was for peanuts mind – less than I had been on at Walsall, but I wanted to get back on the managerial ladder. If we'd have won promotion, I'd have got a bonus, but of course I didn't get that. Anyway I signed a two-year contract.

It was a similar set-up to Walsall in terms of backroom staff; I had no coach or assistant, just a physio and a youth coach, Gavin Tait. Terry Yorath had gone as part of Sam's takeover of the club, but they had a new director of football, Bill Coldwell. As Sam's business was in London, Bill was the guy the chairman and myself liaised with, and he was a fantastic man with whom I got on really well. He supported me in everything I did and gave me a lot of confidence. Our first task was to get rid of the big earners as we needed to slash the wage bill after the club had been relegated – and I soon thought it was a case of out of the frying pan, into the fire.

Similarly to Walsall, their bonus system was based on them being in a division higher but a lot were on contract anyway so I couldn't get rid of them. Some were on as much as £600 a week – more than I was on – and no one could afford to take them. I remember Sammy Chung years before saying the manager should be the highest paid person at a club, but that definitely wasn't the case at Cardiff when I was there. The fans were so enthusiastic at Cardiff, which I couldn't fault, but I felt they expected too much for where the club was at the time. They had enjoyed success, such as winning the FA Cup in 1927 and then when John Charles was there. When they're doing well, it's one of the most passionate fan bases. But I knew it was going to be just as tough a job – if not tougher – than I'd had at Walsall, because expectations at Cardiff were far greater. I'm not saying Walsall haven't got expectations because they have, but they have never been in the top flight or won an FA Cup. Cardiff is the capital of Wales and it's on a much greater scale than Walsall.

Talking of the FA Cup, one of my better memories of managing Cardiff came in the world's oldest knockout competition. We were drawn to play Rushden and Diamonds in the first round. Bankrolled by Max Griggs, the founder of the Dr Martens shoe company, Rushden were making waves to be the next big thing even though they were playing two levels below us, before joining the Conference the following season. So it was a real banana skin tie and there was a big media contingent there anticipating an upset. But we beat them 3-1 and when I addressed the reporters in front of the dugouts afterwards, I told them we'd cocked it up for them because they'd already got their headlines written. It was a bit of fun because I knew what was going to come if we got beat.

On the Monday after the game, Bill Coldwell was going into hospital to have a hip replacement. Beforehand I was trying to keep his spirits up, saying 'Me and you Bill, we'll still take them on in the five-a-sides'. I never saw him again. He died after developing a blood clot. They flew him from the hospital to Hambrook in Bristol to give him specialist treatment but he never came out. He was just 63. I was devastated and we lost a lovely man. On December 9, two days after he passed away, we beat Hartlepool 2-0 and I dedicated the victory to Bill.

Cardiff might have been a different club and in a different country from Walsall, but I soon felt it was a case of deja vu. I was having to get results without a pot to piss in budget-wise and also forced to sell my better players. My centre forward Carl Dale, a big crowd favourite and my best player, eventually went to Yeovil, and Kevin Nugent, my other striker, was injured. After six games without a win, and in the turmoil after Bill's sudden death, one Friday morning, I decided I'd had enough. I rang the chairman, Samesh Kumar, and said 'I can't do this – I can't go through all this again' and I resigned. He asked me to take the team for the game against Rochdale the following day, adding that we would speak over the weekend. I agreed and we won 1-0 and on the Monday he asked me to meet him in Newbury with Joan Hill, who was chief executive.

Sam agreed to my request to stand down but told me he didn't want me to leave the club. We agreed to appoint another manager and Phil Neal was appointed in February 1996. But Sam knew he could trust me and he didn't want me to go. He told me I could stay in any capacity I wanted. I told him that out of respect to Bill, I would take on the director of football role and be the liaison between Phil and Sam.

Phil was their appointment – I'd made my mind up to leave. My remit was to get the club functioning how we wanted it to go. So if Phil had an issue, he'd come to me and I'd sort it out with the chairman or, if that wasn't possible, get back to Phil and tell him he had to get on with it. I was also still doing the scouting and overseeing the youth set-up. The new structure lasted just a few months as Phil left in the October to become

Steve Coppell's assistant at Manchester City. I thought Phil found it a challenge to adapt to working in a different financial climate after such a glittering career with Liverpool and England and it didn't last long. I remember reading in the paper his thoughts about me being director of football and he said something like 'We'll have to see how it goes'. I thought 'I'll soon sort him out if he starts!' What the hell was he on about?

So after he went I went back in as manager. That situation lasted about a month before we appointed another manager, Russell Osman, who we'd initially signed as a player, and I reverted to being director of football. Under Russell, we tried to sign Michael Owen on loan from Liverpool. Russell had worked with one of the England youth squads that Michael had been part of so he knew him. Owen was only on the fringes of things at Liverpool at the time, but they wouldn't let us have him. We had some good results though, including a memorable 4-1 win at Fulham in January 1997. They were going for promotion at the time and it was a live game on Sky. When we got there I was interviewed before the game and I was asked how we were going to approach it. 'Get stuck into them' was my reply and we ended up battering them, making up for them sticking four past us in both games against us the previous season. Simon Haworth, our best player, scored one in between a brace for Steve White after Jason Fowler opened the scoring for us. Micky Adams, who I'd played with at Coventry and later tried to sign for Walsall, was manager of Fulham and I intended joining him for a drink after the game. But Samesh Kumar always liked to hold court after we'd won and he wouldn't let me out of the dressing room. I think Micky held that against me and he must have felt pretty rotten, especially after he'd lost.

I might have been director of football but my passions belonged in the dugout when it came to the team. Those passions boiled over one afternoon away to Darlington in May 1997. We needed a draw to be sure of a play-off place, and when our striker, Carl Dale, equalised in the 77th minute, I thought we had sealed our place. But within a minute, Darren Roberts, the former Wolves striker, headed home the winner from a free kick. I was livid because, try as we might, we couldn't force an equaliser and I thought our chance of reaching the play-offs had gone. At the final whistle I was furious. I was on the pitch and I ordered all of the players to come to me. It was a bit like that scene when Phil Brown kept his Hull City players on the pitch at half-time at Manchester City. Once the players had trooped over, I laid into them, telling them in no uncertain terms how disappointed I was to see them concede as they did. As I ranted away, a policeman tapped me on the shoulder, requesting I leave the pitch immediately. He claimed I could be seen to be inciting a riot among our fans, who were the only ones left in the ground, and asked me to take the players off the pitch. There was only a small contingent of visiting supporters in the 3,686 crowd at Feethams and I asked if he was f*****g joking. He answered, 'I'm sorry, sir, you're going to have to go'. With Russell in charge, we reached the play-offs that season, losing in the semi-finals to the eventual winners, Northampton, 4-2 on aggregate. One-nil down after the first leg at home, we conceded an early goal at their place and their right back Ian Clarkson celebrated right in my face. My first instinct was to draw back my right fist and smack him one but my arm was held back as he ducked away. Apparently their manager, Ian Atkins, had wound them up by claiming that I'd said Clarkson and his fellow full back John Frain were past it and that we would target them. But that was completely untrue – I would never have said anything like that. I loved having experienced players in my teams because of their nous and at Walsall I signed lads such as Derek Statham, Colin Methven, Kevin MacDonald and Wayne Clarke knowing they could do a job for me.

Simon Haworth, our up-and-coming striker, ended the season with 10 goals in 27 games in all competitions, which was an impressive return for an 18-year-old in only his second full season. I didn't want to lose him but he had been attracting attention from other clubs and I knew if the right offer came in, we'd have to sell to help us survive. It was just the same as it had been at Walsall. Coventry, who were then in the Premier League, were willing to pay £500,000 for him. But Norwich were offering the most money up front, so Sam Kumar decided he was going to Norwich. Simon went there for talks, but they also had him training with them, without our permission. As a kid, he had broken his ankle which had left him with a slight hop as he ran. It wasn't a problem, but it was enough for them to pull out of the deal.

In the meantime, I had told Gordon Strachan, the Coventry manager, that Simon was going to Norwich, because of what Sam had said. So when that fell through, Sam told me to ring Gordon again but I refused because I'd told him he was going to Norwich. So I had to ring Gordon again and I told him Norwich couldn't raise the money. I drove him to Coventry myself. All the way there, Simon was reading out a list of things he wanted as part of the deal. I told him not to be greedy because if he asked for too much, they could lose interest and the transfer could have been scuppered. I got him a bloody good contract and I told him to take it. I said 'You've got to go and play, because the incentives are there. You get in the first team and start doing well and you will double your wages'.

That summer, Everton were looking for a manager after the departure of Joe Royle in the March. Dave Watson had taken over as caretaker for the last few games of the season but they wanted a permanent replacement. They spoke to Andy Gray and helooked all set to return to Goodison Park which he had graced so well as a player more than a decade earlier after leaving Wolves. Andy and I were playing in a charity golf tournament somewhere and he asked me if he got a manager's job whether I would join him as his assistant. I said I would and he told me to leave it with him and then I went on holiday to Portugal. I bought a Sunday paper and there was a story saying Andy was favourite to take over at Everton and that he would be taking me as his assistant and Richard Money, who was then at Manchester City, as his first-team coach.

The story even said who he wanted to sign, with Dwight Yorke, then at Aston Villa, top of his wish list. I thought if Samesh Kumar saw it he would go berserk. I didn't know if Sam got to see the story and I don't know if he was expecting compensation if Everton came in for me because he never discussed it with me. I kept quiet and thought if Andy took the job then Everton would go through the proper channels and approach Cardiff in the right way. Around this time Andy rang me and said he'd got a meeting in London with Sky, who he was working for at the time, and that he would ring me on the way home. When he called he said 'Hibby . . .' and I knew from the tone of his voice he wasn't going to take the Everton job. I said 'You're not going to Everton are you?' He said 'No. I feel like I've won the Lottery because they (Sky) wouldn't let me out of the room until I'd signed a deal'. They locked him in. I said 'Well, I feel as if I've just lost the bleeding winning ticket, in more ways than one!' That was a really big disappointment to me. I thought that was my last chance to make it into management ata big club. The next season results didn't go well for Cardiff. Samesh called a meeting for one Monday morning, and as we were walking up the stairs to the boardroom, he said 'Can you just give me five minutes with Russell?' I said 'Yes of course' and had a coffee while I waited. Then he ushered me in and I asked 'Where's Russell?' and he told me he'd sacked him. This was in January 1998 after 14 months in charge You would have thought he would have liaised with me as director of football before making the decision. But he never mentioned anything to me so his dismissal came as much of a surprise to me as it must have done to Russell. I was in the car travelling home and I rang him. I said 'Sorry Russell, I hadn't got a clue about that'. He said 'Are you sure?' and I tried to assure him that was the case. I didn't see him again until a golf day at Cumberwell Park in Wiltshire and I walked straight on to the first tee and said 'Look me in the eye. I can tell you categorically I didn't have a clue about what happened at Cardiff and it's up to you which way you take it. But I'm telling you, eye to eye, that I knew nothing about it'. He shook my hand and we went our separate ways. Ever since then he's been as good as gold but there was a time when he thought I had stitched him up because Sam and I had a good relationship – or so I thought.

After Russell went, there was a demonstration after one game and Sam sent me out there to talk to the disgruntled supporters. I explained the situation to them – I never hid anything from them because you can't pull the wool over their eyes. One of them called out 'Why don't you take over again, Kenny?' And someone else shouted 'Because you wanted him out when he was the manager!' The other guy replied 'No I didn't' so I got them arguing among each other. Sam turned to me and said 'You should have been a politician!' I did take over the reins again but it remained a struggle on the pitch and we weren't helped when we lost Kevin Nugent to injury. I thought we weren't going to win many games without one of our main front men so I decided to shut up shop and we ended up drawing 23 games. In response to the sequence of results, I was pictured in the paper with the phone at my ear saying 'Don't bother coming, we'll call it a draw!'

Without a recognised striker, I looked in the youth team and found a lad who I thought might make the grade. He was so quick and he knew where the goals were. He didn't have the greatest touch at that age but I knew if he worked on that, which he did, we might have a player on our hands. His name was Robert Earnshaw. It wasn't long before the big clubs were sniffing around him and I recall John Gregory, who was Aston Villa manager at the time, ringing me about him. He asked me if 'Earnie' was ready for the Premier League and I had to say I wasn't sure. I felt he lacked something to be a really top player. I was telling the truth, but he eventually moved on to West Bromwich Albion and subsequently got big-money moves to Norwich, Derby and Nottingham Forest, scoring goals wherever he went and he became a Wales international. I had to ban him from doing his somersaults to celebrate his goals because if he put his back out doing that, I hadn't got cover!

Some fans like you and some don't, and in football you will always get criticism as a manager. But one thing I didn't expect – especially having got into the play-offs – was a death threat. It wasn't as if the team were in a relegation battle. I received a letter which said 'If you haven't resigned by a certain date, we will wipe you and your family out'. I told Joan Hill, the chief executive, about it, before tearing it up and putting it in

the bin. I wasn't bothered about being threatened, but when it involved my family, it worried me. Unbeknown to me, Joan went into the bin while I was out training, put all the torn pieces back together and called the police. For the next two weeks, I was followed by a detective. Every time I left Ninian Park, I'd make sure all the doors on my car were locked, thinking 'I'm glad I'm not bottom of the league – think what they might do then'.

Another time I was confronted by about six fans outside the ground so I invited them in with a security guard, sat them down for a chat and a drink and spent an hour with them, telling them exactly what the situation was. Afterwards, they stood up, and said 'Well done Kenny, we appreciate your honesty, we didn't realise how bad it was, so thank you for listening to us. If you have any problems with anyone, let us know and we'll sort them out'. I got them on side and I just wanted them to spread the word because while a lot of fans didn't know what was going on, some didn't want to listen either because all they care about is results. I think they appreciated someone taking the time to talk to them and telling them what the situation was, and I was happy to do it.

Not long before Russell left, on Christmas Eve, I received a phone call from Derek Pavis, who was then the Notts County chairman. We had met a few years earlier at a golf tournament when I was Walsall manager. I had won a prize but couldn't stay for the presentation because I was going to watch a player at a Wolves v Manchester United reserve game at Molineux. He recalled our previous meeting and my early departure clearly worked in my favour because he said he had never forgotten that adding, 'So I want you to come and manage my football club. Would you be interested?' I said I would but told him he had to do it the right way and approach my chairman first. Samesh said 'You're not going there' and offered me a five-year contract. Now I had a dilemma. Should I go to Notts – a much longer journey from where I lived? Or should I stay at Cardiff, an hour from my home doing I job I like and enjoy with the pressure off a little bit? I agreed to stay but it wasn't long before I was manager again when Russell left. In the meantime we looked at all sorts of different options. I wanted to bring in Ian Atkins, whose Northampton side beat us in the play-offs the previous season on their way to securing promotion, but the fans were 100 per cent against him, so I plumped for Frank Burrows. We'd had a young manager in Russell so we decided to go for an experienced one in Frank. He had been coaching at West Ham and had done it at lower levels of the game before, including a successful previous spell at Cardiff a decade earlier when he led the Bluebirds to promotion from the Fourth Division in 1987-88.

But from there it started to go wrong for me. I remember being at the funeral of Jimmy Scoular, who had been player-manager of Bradford Park Avenue just before I joined them and from there managed Cardiff for nine years. I received a text message from Joan Hill asking me to return to the club as there was a letter on my desk. I couldn't imagine what it could be. It turned out to be a letter from the chairman informing me my job title had changed from director of football to director of football (development). In other words, I was to going to be looking after the kids and Frank Burrows didn't want to work with me. I blamed Sam for that; he should have told Frank that he either worked with me or that he would look for somebody else. It was obvious I wasn't wanted. But I had to be careful what I did because I was on a long contract.

They made it hard for me though. No one talked to me and I never got any information. At the time I had been made aware of a group of Welsh people who worked for Cardiff Devils ice hockey team wanting to take over the football club. As things transpired, Sam lost his 100 per cent shareholding and the ownership of the club was split three ways between him and two Cardiff businessmen, Bob Phillips and Paul Guy. Sam was replaced as chairman and Joan Hill lost her position as chief executive. I was stuck on my own in a Portakabin with no one telling me anything. I would arrive for work at 8.30am, have a coffee and go home at 5.30pm. On a Tuesday and a Thursday I would go to the academy to see the youth teams, but I wasn't allowed to get involved in the coaching or anything. They just didn't involve me. This went on for eight or nine months.

I remember Frank once sending me all the way to Cambridge to watch a game in the sleet and snow and I took Jane with me. I was feeling worse and worse about the situation and one night after being soaked to the skin in the rain, I got home and Jane took one look at me and said 'You've had enough' and I told her I had. I didn't deserve that and I couldn't put up with it any more. So I got in touch with the League Managers' Association and they helped me get out. Management is so different from playing. When you manage a team, particularly at the lower levels, you play every player's game. When I drove home after a game, I went through every player's performance in my head, and I knew exactly how many good balls and bad balls they had played. From that I knew who was going to keep their place and who wasn't. I didn't need to write anything down or have someone give me a load of stats. If I had been writing things down, I would have missed something. I accept things have moved on. I'm not sure how much of an advantage all the data that's now available is.

People say to me the game is faster now; certainly the ball moves more quickly and the pitches and facilities are better. The biggest regret I had in management was not being able to have a decent budget to work with in the transfer market. I would have liked to have been able to go out and buy better players, rather than the ones I had to take. Not being disrespectful to those lads, but the time comes when you get frustrated at not being able to get those you want, especially as they weren't that expensive. I think I proved I could spot a bargain.

At Walsall I signed Martin O'Connor and Kyle Lightbourne, who were eventually sold on for £500,000 each. Not bad for a £40,000 overall investment. I never spent significant transfer fees at either Walsall or later at Cardiff but I got both clubs into the play-offs. After I left Cardiff, I did some work for Sky. It was around the time Sam Hammam had taken over at Ninian Park. He brought someone on board who had been a director there in my time and he said to me 'I'll bet you wish you had the money they've got there now'. I agreed with him because I had always had to sell players and didn't have the funds to replace them. When Cardiff reached the Premier League, I went to their new ground and was concerned at how the people were going to react to me. But they were absolutely fantastic and treated me so well. So maybe I did a good job after all, despite the way I was treated before I left.

38

Part-time With The Pitmen

When I eventually left Cardiff City I decided to take a year out to recover from what turned out to be a nightmare end to my time there. I was hurt by the way they treated me. OK, I'd got a bit of stick sometimes from some of the fans, but they were just passionate about their club and wanted to win every game, which was what I wanted. I hated losing at anything, even tiddly winks with my own children, so I knew how they felt. But I thoroughly enjoyed most of my time there. Now I had a bit of space to reflect. In hindsight I should have taken the opportunity to manage Notts County when Derek Pavis came calling. Big Sam Allardyce got the job instead and look what he went on to achieve.

Out of management but still keen to be involved in the game, I started working for the Press Association doing statistics on match days for a couple of years for clubs in the south west region. My spell in the press box came to an end when I was asked if I fancied a return to the dugout.

John Baldwin was my accountant but also a director and former manager of Hednesford Town in non-league. He worked closely with the chairman and owner Steve Price that coincided with the most successful period of the club's history. John led them into the Conference, where they finished third in their first season and in 1996-97 earned a famous FA Cup fourth round tie against a Middlesbrough side containing Juninho and Fabrizio Ravanelli. But they struggled to maintain that momentum and John stepped down as manager in December 2000, before they were relegated at the end of that season.

After a really poor start to the 2001-02 campaign they found themselves at the foot of the table, several points adrift of the safety line and John's replacement, Paul Raynor was sacked, so they needed some help. Paul has since gone on to assist Steve Evans in the Football League at Rotherham, Leeds, Mansfield Town and now Peterborough. I wasn't sure I wanted to manage outside the Football League, but after discussions with Jane – and persuaded by my accountant – I took the job on, with the team battling against a second successive relegation, this time from the Southern League Premier

243

Division. Steve Price and Jane went to the same school – Wednesfield High when it was Wednesfield Grammar – and he has ended up becoming a very wealthy man after setting up his own recruitment agency, Extra Personnel. Steve said Jane was academically brighter than him, so I've asked her why we aren't millionaires – only joking, darling! The club were in a bit of a mess, they had fallen out with the supporters club, morale and confidence were flat as a pancake and they had players earning bloody good money. Some were earning more than players I'd managed at Walsall and Cardiff City. The one thing I wanted most was to have an assistant, something Walsall and Cardiff refused me, because it was bloody hard work working with squads of between 20 and 30 playing staff. So I wanted to bring in someone I knew and had a bit of experience at League and non-league levels. The club agreed and I brought in Barry Powell, a former team-mate at Wolves, and he was a great guy and a good coach.

My first game was against Havant and Waterlooville, a nice easy one to start with at home as they were top of the table and unbeaten. Barry hadn't joined me at the time so I was in familiar territory – on my own again in the dugout. I thought 'Bollocks, why shouldn't we be able to beat them?' I only had a couple of training sessions with the squad but got the message over to them about what I expected – hard work, commitment and to show the fans some passion. In the dressing room before the game you get a feeling for the spirit among the lads. They had had a torrid start to the season and I think after about 13 games they only had seven points. So I felt we had nothing to lose. In contrast, Havant were riding high and arrived full of confidence. So I said to the lads 'Let's get out there and give them a game, go at them early and let's see how they respond'. We got amongst them and managed to turn them over 2-1 in a thrilling game.

Well it was for us with a somewhat fortuitous winner from the former Burnley, Wigan and Rochdale striker Graham Lancashire. He should really have been penalised for a foul on the Havant goalkeeper. The ball was bobbling around two or three yards from the goalline and their keeper tried to grab it only for Graham to give a slight tug on him, which enabled him to get to the ball first and head home. What a result though! The final whistle went and the manager of Havant, Liam Daish, a bloody big fellow who was a big, strong centre half in his day for Cambridge United, Birmingham City and Coventry City, went ballistic at the referee as we came off the pitch and continued his tirade all the way to the dressing rooms. I didn't care two hoots, we had got the three points many thought we wouldn't get. It was a great start but a lot of hard work was ahead. Barry soon came in and one of the first things we did was to arrange a meeting with the supporters club who had been at loggerheads with the club for some reason or another. In fact we held several meetings with them as we needed to try to solve the problems between them and the club so we could all move forward together.

We eventually got both parties together in a reasonably friendly atmosphere but it still wasn't right for the long term. We set out our plans for the future but also explained to the fans we were all going to have to pull together to stay up. This was the first time I had been manager of a team fighting a relegation battle so it was a real test for me. Having been used to the day-to-day involvement professional football brings, the hardest part for me was only seeing the players for two training sessions a week, Tuesday and Thursday nights, which was the norm for non-league clubs. It was the same for all the teams in our league but I did get very frustrated at times as I had only ever worked with players every day. Some players had full-time jobs and would miss some Tuesday sessions. Big Kevin Francis was one of those. He was vastly experienced at League level having had spells with Stockport, Birmingham City, Oxford, Exeter and Hull City and he was one of my main strikers. But he worked as a lorry driver and most Tuesdays I used to get a call from him saying he was caught up on the motorway and couldn't get to training. I didn't know if he was telling me the truth or not – he could have been at home with his feet up for all I knew – but he would always be there for training on Thursdays, ready to be picked for Saturday's game.

I had some good lads who worked their socks off but it was still a very difficult season for us. Barry was brilliant though. He took so much weight off my shoulders by putting on some great training sessions which allowed me time to plan for the game ahead and look at the squad. I was able to watch the attitude of the players, which was first class. I always felt full of energy because of the help I had in Barry. It made me think in hindsight that I should have demanded an assistant at both Walsall and Cardiff. That would have made my job a lot easier because I could have got more rest, had more energy and gone to a lot more games to watch players instead of dashing here, there and everywhere with little time to get to matches after our afternoon training sessions.

At Cardiff Samesh Kumar once rang me at around 3pm during a training session asking me to go to Leeds afterwards to watch a player involved in a game kicking off at 7 pm. I said 'Sam, have you got a jet lined up then because I won't get there on time

245

without one?' That scenario was always happening. Nowadays a lot of managers have got numerous people working with them. What a luxury! I would have loved that.

Back at Hednesford, the season was coming to a close and, having pegged our way out of a no-hope situation, we had a real chance of staying up. We had to win at Newport Isle of Wight to be certain of avoiding relegation and did so with a 1-0 victory. What a bloody relief! It was hard going but, with the help of Barry and the support of the Hednesford Town fans, we made it.

Along with the first team staying up, there was cause for celebration elsewhere within the club, although it was a bitter-sweet experience. Our youth team did well, excelling in the FA Youth Cup where they earned a tie at Oldham Athletic. I was there supporting the youth coaching staff and the kids, who put up a great fight only to lose 4-3 in extra-time. Afterwards one of their staff came up to me to say congratulations on a great game. I agreed and thanked him, adding how our lads were gutted and he went on to say 'It's not about winning, it's about taking part'. Well, having just seen our dressing room in despair, his words were like a red rag to a bull and I confronted him, pointing and shouting 'You want to go down to our dressing room and say that to our players, because some of them are crying'. In the end Tony Philliskirk, one of their coaches who I'd had for three years as a player at Cardiff, got between us to pull us apart and I calmed down.

Playing for us that night was a very good centre back called Ashley Williams, who came to us after being released by West Brom. He was a big, strong boy who could play, in fact he shone every time I watched him. So I wasn't surprised to see him go on to play at the highest level with Swansea City then Everton and Wales. Unfortunately I didn't have much input to his career as my whole energy was spent trying to keep the first team up and he wasn't in the side at that point. Once he did graduate to the first team though, there was no stopping him, and he got his big break in December 2003 at the age of 19 when he moved to Stockport County, who were then in League Two. Ashley made his debut in March 2004 and went on to make over 150 appearances for the Hatters in five years before moving to Swansea City for a then club record fee of £400,000. He continued to impress in South Wales, adding another 350 appearances and helping the Swans to two promotions, from League One to the Premier League prior to his £12m move to Goodison Park in 2016, and he has over 70 full caps for Wales.

246

After the high of keeping Hednesford up came a low. At the end of the season the chairman told us he no longer needed Barry and myself. Barry, feeling disgusted by the way we had been treated, left the room immediately but I stayed a little longer with the chairman before shaking hands and leaving. Had he asked me to stay I would have seriously considered it, because I believed I could have picked the club up and made it a force again. But that opportunity didn't come. It was a shame as I had a really good relationship with the fans and I received some lovely letters thanking me for saving their club and bringing belief back to them for the future. The really annoying thing for me was that the press reported I had been sacked, but I had no contract to be sacked from. I went in there to keep them up, and I achieved that, so it was a case of job done. I was simply paid to keep them up.

I still look for their results even now simply because the fans treated me so well in the short time I was there. I thank them for that and always will be grateful for their support. After Ian Painter replaced me, Barry eventually went back as manager and led them to the FA Trophy final in 2004, where they played Canvey Island. I was asked to summarise the game, which was played at Villa Park, for local radio. Before the match I spoke to Barry to wish him well and I nearly fell over with shock when he said win or lose, he would get the sack. I said 'What the hell do they want?' and concluded nothing had changed. They won the cup in an exciting game, coming from 2-1 down to win 3-2 but it didn't prevent Barry getting the push straight afterwards. What a stupid thing to do to him. It just underlines the sentiment that nothing surprises me in football any more. But that beat the lot.

39

Come On Ref!

In the 2002-03 season I became a Premier League match delegate, or, as we have become known, referees assessor. Along with an insight into the difficulties, scrutiny and pressures match officials are put under, I'm proud to say it has led to me having a hand in Howard Webb officiating at the 2010 World Cup and indeed him earning the honour of taking charge of the final itself between Holland and Spain.

During the season prior to the tournament, 2009-10, he was actually going through an indifferent period of form and I was part of a team asked to analyse him in depth. I watched him in three out of seven games in 2009. At the time I thought he was getting too square to the play and too close to the action, so he didn't get the best overall view of the match and so couldn't form a bigger picture of everything going on. I think Howard appreciated my input and I believe I had some influence in improving his performance.

We developed a good relationship that has continued and I texted him my congratulations when he was awarded the final. Following the final, which was won by Spain by the only goal scored by Andreas Iniesta in extra-time, Howard was accused of failing to send off Nigel de Jong, the Dutch midfielder, for a studs-up kick into the chest of Xabi Alonso in the 28th minute. He thought he had made the right decision at the time but later admitted in interviews that he should have given a straight red card. But he told me he was desperate to keep all the players on the pitch if possible so as not to ruin the biggest spectacle in world football. Ultimately he ended up making 14 bookings, two of which ended up as red cards, but I have to admire, and agree with, Howard's common sense for his desire to keep it 11 versus 11 if possible.

My job as a delegate started when Jane answered a telephone call from the League Managers' Association, whose committee I was on for five years. They asked her if I would be interested in a new initiative working with the match officials. She had to laugh because as a player and manager they weren't my most favourite people, even though I respected them. When I was at Walsall I once locked a referee in his dressing room to 'question' a decision, and when I was manager of Cardiff I told that same ref

248

during a game 'I should have thrown the key away'. We laugh about it now when we see each other. But the role sounded interesting so I contacted them and we had a really good meeting in London. The job was completely different from anything I had done but it kept me involved in the game and at the top level for the first time since I left Coventry City in 1986. I believe I am one of only a few to still be doing the role since they created it, along with the former Hull City and Bradford manager Terry Dolan, John Duncan, the ex-Chesterfield boss and Mick McGuire, who was a PFA-licensed agent for many years after playing for Newcastle and Norwich. Many other former prominent players and managers have tried their hand at it over the last decade and a half, such as Micky Adams, Mick Harford, Keith Burkinshaw, Peter Shreeve, Len Ashurst, Simon Barker, Richard Jobson, Steve Harper, Tony Parkes, Jason Lee, Iffy Onuora, Martin Allen, Paul Allen, Wayne Fereday and Clive Whitehead.

Fans may wonder what the job entails as there wasn't much publicity about it when it was introduced. The Premier League carries huge prestige globally and the money and media coverage it attracts has led to intense and unprecedented scrutiny of decisions, which puts a lot of pressure on officials. To address this, a group of retired footballers were asked to help officials improve the management of the players. There was a time when players used to race towards the referee and shout abuse at them. I know from experience as a former player that that could happen, although we showed far more respect towards the referee and his linesmen (as they were called back then) than players did in more recent times. Thankfully, since the delegates were brought in, the respect towards the officials has improved, largely through hard work from the PFA, Football League and the Professional Game Match Officials (PGMO). On match days there are so many TV cameras at each ground that they can spot somebody picking their nose if they want to. So every decision the officials make is scrutinised very closely, with slow motion and still shots shown to the television viewers. We have about 16-18 delegates nationwide. Mainly I cover matches in the south and the Midlands, but occasionally make a foray to Liverpool and Manchester and I have enjoyed every minute, working with some top officials.

In the last two decades the game has changed incredibly, from the amazing facilities at training grounds to the incredible stadiums, while the global interest in the Premier League is something I never thought would happen. Through the saturation media coverage, transfer fees and players' wages have gone through the roof but good luck to them. The players didn't change the wage structure. The TV companies have effectively done that by paying billions of pounds for the rights to cover matches. It's quite amazing really, and it doesn't look like it is going to change in the next few years. I feel sorry for the fans who have to pay extortionate prices to watch games.

The job of a match delegate starts with the journey to a game selected by the PGMO. I like to get to a ground approximately two and half hours before kick-off to greet the four officials. We share a tea or coffee then make our way to the dressing room, or if it is a pleasant day we walk out on to the pitch for a briefing by the host club's head of security, who says where the away fans will be seated, the nearest first aid point, the emergency procedure and how the officials can reach a safe area as quickly as possible.

Among our more recent tasks are to check the goal-line technology and to check the length of the grass is under 30 millimetres. Most club ground staff keep it to an average 25mm. I take the team sheets to the referee's room at around 1.45pm for a 3pm kick-off and show them to the referee to check all is in order, then at 2pm the managers or coaches and both captains enter the referee's room. The referee introduces his staff, tells the captains and managers what he expects of them and warns them not to over celebrate goals and not to leave the pitch after scoring. Many players get carried away and ignore that, but it brings a cheap caution and puts pressure on the player not to get a second yellow card. The referee asks the captains to work with him, for example if any players lose their temper then it is up to the skipper to calm his team-mate down to help the referee, or expect the consequences. He then wishes both teams good luck and everyone shakes hands, including me. At this stage I take my seat in the directors' box ready for kick-off. We note down what time the referee leads out the teams, the actual time of kick off, then everything noteworthy that happens, such as cautions, advantages, management of players by the officials, how good the teamwork is between the referee and his assistants, all major decisions, whether the referee was right or wrong, plus his positional play. We also have to keep an eye on the fourth official.

After the game we allow the officials about 20 minutes to warm down before conducting a de-brief. We compare all the timings of the cautions with the fourth official and we ask them if there was any trouble from the dugouts. Questions are put to each assistant if needed before we discuss the referee's performance. Our time with them finishes with us either telling them it was a good team performance or an indifferent one with key issues not met. However, I always finish my de-brief on a positive note as they often have a long journey home and I don't want them dwelling on their performance. They know if they have done well or not. For me, they are the best officials in the world. They are honest, they perform with integrity and do the best they can, but they could be helped much more by the players.

One of my pet hates is seeing the fourth official with his or her hands in their pockets. I feel it looks like they're disengaged. I was always told when working with players to have a ball in one hand because it looks more professional and the players will think your mind is on them. I realise the fourth official can't do that but the players are working so the officials should look busy too. When I first started the job I remember having to remind the fourth official that you wouldn't see plumbers or electricians working with their hands stuffed in their overalls would you? Once I was covering a game at Birmingham City and the fourth official, Mark Halsey, bet me a fiver I wouldn't catch him with his hands in his pockets. I accepted the bet and said I'd give the £5 to a charity if I won. It was a really cold night so I was quite confident he would drop his guard – or rather his hands – at some point.

During the second half the game was stopped because of an injury. It looked a bad one so there was going to be at least five minutes' delay before the game resumed. I looked down towards where Mark was standing and he suddenly turned around and caught me pointing at him as he whipped his hands out of his pockets. 'Got you!' I indicated and he raised both his arms in a 'guilty' gesture and laughed his head off. All the fourth officials now are aware I have my eyes on them.

Over the years I have witnessed some interesting scenes involving managers. Having been one myself for the best part of a decade I know how passionate they can get. In the technical area you go through a whole range of emotions and it's difficult not to show your feelings when you play every player's game and kick every ball in your mind. You watch everything every player is doing, not just on the ball but off it, so you notice his positional play and marking, both in general play and on set pieces. It is remarkable that teams spend all week working on formation, set plays and who is marking who but when players run out on to the pitch they can forget what has been asked of them. I suppose I was the same when I played but for a manager it is so frustrating and annoying. Sadly I can't divulge what happens behind the scenes because

251

our contracts prevent us from speaking publicly about that, but anyone with a passion for football would find it absorbing. What the officials have to put up with is amazing. With all the criticism and scrutiny that comes their way, they really have to be thick-skinned to do their job, yet they are so patient and calm, professional, tolerant and honest. It's something I have learned from them after working with them for over 14 years. They are a fantastic bunch of lads who I have the utmost respect for – which is an improvement on my relationship with them I had as a player!

40

A Golfing Family

Like many footballers, I've always enjoyed other sports, particularly with a ball involved. My second love after football was cricket but it wasn't long after I joined Wolves that I was introduced to golf. Bill McGarry, our manager at the time, got myself and a few of the lads interested when he first arrived at the club. If we had played in Europe on a Tuesday, he would invite a lot of us for a round of golf at Brocton near Stafford or Beau Desert on Cannock Chase the following day. I loved it, as did players like Phil Parkes, Geoff Palmer, Derek Parkin, Mike Bailey, John McAlle, John Richards, Dave Wagstaffe, Steve Kindon and Barry Powell. Bill was a very good player who played off a handicap of four and he always hit the ball straight. When I first started I used to hold the club like a baseball bat and would swing the ball out to the left. Bill would go mad because I would always beat him, despite my awkward style of hitting the ball at the time. People think that because I became a scratch golfer I used to practise every day but that wasn't the case. I have just been lucky to be good at sports involving a ball – even now, I only play golf once a week but still play at senior county standard. It was only in between my spells at Walsall and Cardiff did I have the time to play regularly and I took full advantage. My father-in-law Len Clarke was later captain of Penn Golf Club so Jane and I joined and were members for many years. Within a year I was down to a single-figure handicap, and soon after, I was playing off five, which I played off for 12 years. I learned so much from Tony Weston, who was a county player and should have been a professional. We became good friends with Tony and his wife Di.

Golf became my escape. I wasn't a big drinker and I didn't bet or spend my afternoons in snooker halls, so I used my free time to play golf, which I thought was a much healthier way to occupy my leisure time than the other activities I have mentioned. I quickly grew to love the game and it's played a big part in my life ever since. It was a great way to relax away from the pressures of football. I started receiving invitations to tournaments, particularly charity days. I would attend most of them if we didn't have a midweek game. I won a celebrity day at Edgbaston Golf Club with a team from Handsworth. I won a £50 voucher to spend on golf gear and a trophy. But we weren't allowed to play after a Wednesday if we were playing on a Saturday because it would

253

have affected our fitness, while as a manager, golf never interfered with my work. The one time my football and golf mixed, I made sure one of my team-mates paid the price. I captained the Wolves players' golf team and I used to organise a game against a team from Penn, my club. As the captain I was required to welcome everybody, meet and greet people, give a speech thanking various people and make a toast before sitting down to a meal. This happened a number of times and I often noticed Geoff Palmer and Paul Bradshaw standing at the back, laughing and giggling to themselves, which could put me off what I was saying. So on one occasion, I decided to get my own back and show them. As I started to make my speech, they were taking the mickey as usual so I said something like 'Thank you, ladies and gentlemen. As you know, I normally make all the speeches, but tonight, for the first time, we have a willing volunteer who has agreed to speak to you. Please give a warm around of applause to . . . Mr Geoff Palmer!' Geoff went bright red and didn't know what to say. I said 'That will teach you'. Many years later Geoff was made captain of Oxley Golf Club, a role that required him to speak in front of lots of people regularly, so I was quite surprised when I heard about that. But I thought that experience all those years ago at Penn may have stood him in good stead.

As a footballer, I didn't always get chance to play a lot of golf during the season so I tried to make up for it in the summer. With Jane a keen golfer as well it was good to play a few holes together. We played in a lot of mixed competitions and open events with friends. When I was in my golfing heyday playing off scratch – which I was for about 10 years – at one point Jane got down to a handicap of 11. We played in quite a few mixed open tournaments and won some.

When we moved to the Cotswolds I represented the Gloucestershire senior team for five years. We won the South West Counties Championship team event, and I finished second in the South West Counties Senior Championship having led in the first round before trailing on the back nine holes. I have won three Andy Gray Golf Classics and the Phillips tournament for professional footballers at St Pierre near Chepstow, winning £5,000 which I donated to the British Digestive Foundation, the organisation that helped me in my battle against colitis. The following year I finished second and gave my cheque for £2,500 to the BDF again. I beat Clayton Blackmore, who now plays off scratch but then had a handicap of four or five. But for me the biggest honour was winning the La Manga Golf Footballers Classic in 2015. It is by far the most competitive golf tournament for retired footballers, with 40 of us playing each summer. I've been invited for about 16 years in a row, so to get to wear the green jacket for winning was a great thrill and I've still it got it in my wardrobe at home. Wally Downes came second and Lee Hendrie third. I was being chased by those two which isn't a nice feeling because I prefer coming from behind but I managed to par the last hole to win it by six shots. I didn't know that at the time, but Derek Mountfield told me afterwards. Playing off two at the time, I am the lowest handicapper to have won it. I really got my game together and shot one under par to finish with 39 points, which gave me a massive thrill. Andy Gray always claimed I would never win it, and afterwards he texted me, saying as much.

Afterwards, Alan McInally – another previous winner – bowed in front of me. As a scratch golfer, I had finished in the top 10 many times but not got anywhere near winning it. But the year I did it I went there with the intention of winning. I didn't have too much to drink – I still enjoyed a beer with the boys, I wasn't unsociable because that's what it's about, sharing your old stories with the punters – but I made sure I got to bed early so I felt refreshed and ready to play the next day.

Flying out on the Saturday, we come home the following Thursday and it's a great trip. We have lunch with the punters, who just want you to talk football because they're all fans who want to hear us tell stories from when we played. They love it. It's a great do and everybody gets on really well. You have one too many on the night, and get up next morning with a sore head but it's a lovely social occasion. Occasionally I see former team-mates but mostly it's lads I played against. Steve Daley went two years ago and is hoping to be invited back again this year.

We're all well behaved – it might be La Manga, where Stan Collymore infamously let off a fire extinguisher when he was there on a trip with Leicester, but there are no such high jinks with us. Terry Mancini, the former Arsenal and QPR player, who has his own sports events company, organises it and the tournament has been going for 22 years. Terry warns everybody beforehand to behave themselves and to start on time because the punters who pay good money have to tee off with us. Thankfully I have been invited to La Manga again. This year it fell on June 2, my wedding anniversary. I missed the tournament before when it was our 40th anniversary. It wouldn't have been right to miss that. Well I could have, but I probably wouldn't have celebrated a 41st!

Jane was understanding about that. Sadly, though, golf is not like a fine wine – I haven't matured with age. I was a better player 10 or 12 years ago, when I was playing off scratch and regularly hitting under-par scores. Along with meeting lots of people who have become friends and seeing loads of footballers, golf has also allowed me the chance to rub shoulders with the odd celebrity too. Over the years I have played in a lot of charity golf events which have generated a lot of money for worthwhile causes and had a lot of fun. Sir Bruce Forsyth, Dennis Waterman, Bobby Davro and Eddie Large used to have golf days and I played in those.

I'm proud to say the golfing tradition in the family has been passed on to a third and fourth generation. My son Rod is the club professional at Cotswold Edge Golf Club, where Jane and I are long-term members and my 16-year-old grandson Tom has been playing golf since he was a toddler and actually played three holes in his nappy! There was a par five in that as well and I had to carry him in because he was knackered, bless him. When he had his first golf set we were pictured together, with him on my shoulders, on the front page of the *Express & Star*. Rod's son Jasper is also a keen golfer. We went to a presentation night last year and he and Tom won trophies. Jasper is also a good rugby player. It's lovely that we can all play golf together. We're looking forward to that this summer as they both improve. Hopefully we can all play together for many years to come because you can play golf until you're 80 or 90, as long as you can walk and swing a club. Tom is a real sporting all-rounder. I'm happy to say, though, all of our grandchildren enjoy sport and we watch them in various activities apart from football and golf, including rugby, hockey and long distance running for the boys, and horse riding and gymnastics for Kelly's daughters Ella and Lucy. I am proud of them all.

41

Extra Time

Looking back on my life, I feel I have been blessed for many reasons. I was lucky to be born with a talent and the work ethic to play sport for a living, and to have had a professional playing career spanning 21 years. I feel I dredged every last drop out of my time on the field, which for the overwhelmingly large part was hugely enjoyable. Those 21 years form part of half a century's involvement in football, from apprentice to professional, to coach, to assistant manager, manager, director of football and match delegate assessing referees. I was fortunate enough to be on the winning side in two major cup finals at Wembley – scoring a goal in one of them – and played in a European final, having played against and beaten some of the best teams on the continent. Honoured to play for 16 years at my beloved Wolves, one of the best teams and biggest clubs in the country, I featured alongside some top players in what I consider to be the toughest league in the world, and got to represent my country, albeit at Under-23 level and only once. Travelling the world, I visited and played in places that as a kid you can only dream about. I am proud to have been a Football League manager for almost a decade, building teams at two clubs that reached the play-offs on small budgets. If Lady Luck shone on me in any way as a player, I don't feel I received the same good fortune in management.

But if I felt I could have had a better crack at being a gaffer, then I certainly could not have wished for more support from the team that has always been there for me – my family. I simply could not have achieved all I have without the love and support of Jane, who has been alongside me in good times and bad throughout our 45 years of marriage. We have two wonderful children in Kelly and Rod, who have given us beautiful grandchildren in Tom, Jasper, Ella and Lucy. We are so lucky to have such a lovely daughter-in-law in Katie and our son-in-law Ed.

Life hasn't always been a bed of roses, though, and, like any family, we have endured our fair share of ups and downs. Our daughter Kelly's life has been turned upside down in the last two years after she was suddenly diagnosed with type 1 diabetes. Her son Tom, our grandson, has developed scoliosis, a severe rotation in the spine and will need surgery. His sister Ella was born with a serious heart condition. In addition, in

257

2016, we lost Ricky, Jane's brother, after he tragically died of cancer. Jane in particular has found it very hard coping with the premature loss. Len and Hetty, their parents, lived with us for 10 years but sadly they both suffered with different forms of dementia, Len with Alzheimer's which was a tragedy to see unfold. But we have slowly come to terms with it and are getting on with our lives.

Sadly I lost my mother in 2008 and it wasn't just the grief of her death that I had to deal with. A row broke out after I discovered that in my mother's will, which was made in 1982, there was no mention of Terry and I. The only name included was that of my sister. I was not seeking any financial inheritance, but the fact I had been directly responsible for helping to keep a roof over my mother's head by sending money towards paying the mortgage from 1966 when I was an apprentice to well after Kelly was born, hurt me to the point of feeling sick. All I wanted was for her to acknowledge me. We travelled up to Bradford to see my mother whenever we could, both during the season when I was playing and in the summer, partly because of her reluctance to travel to the Midlands. I also continued to help her out financially over the years.

But there is plenty to be proud of in the family as well and I am not the only one to have enjoyed a spell in the limelight. Our niece Emilia Clarke – the daughter of Jane's brother Ricky and wife Jenny – has played Daenerys Targaryen in the American fantasy drama television series *Game of Thrones* since it first hit the screens in 2011. It will premiere its eighth season next year. But that is only one of a host of roles she has played. As well as acting the female lead in a romantic film *'Me Before You'*, she played Sarah Connor in *Terminator Genisys* opposite Arnold Schwarzenegger. Emilia has also been cast as the female lead in the latest *Star Wars* Anthology film: *'Solo – A Star Wars Story'*, which has just been released and we were lucky enough recently to attend a private screening in London as a family, with her. But to us she's just our Emilia. She's still part of the family and we've enjoyed Christmas dinners together with her wearing her party hat.

Jane's family were a firm connection to my adopted home, Wolverhampton. My unbreakable tie to the area – Wolves – will always be there. Often on a Saturday, I will be working at a Premier League game so I don't get chance to see them play much. I watch them when they're live on television when I'm not working and I was very impressed by them in the season just gone. I was invited by the supporters club Tatter

Travels on one of their coaches for the game at Aston Villa and gained a thoroughly fascinating insight into the life of a dedicated fan. Wolves were well beaten 4-1 and it was impossible to escape the frustration and disappointment everywhere afterwards. There was no doubting the fans' passion or loyalty. It's always a pleasure to be invited back to my spiritual home and I loved being back on the hallowed turf for the game against Derby towards the end of the season. With the introduction of the Hall of Fame and the museum, they have strengthened the links to the club's golden past. I still keep in touch with several of my old Wolves team-mates and I stay in close contact with John Richards, Willie Carr, Steve Daley and others. Whenever we visit the area, we always stay with John Pam or Willie and his wife Tessa.

Sadly we all lost a good friend in John Hendley, who died on New Year's Day. Foz, as he was universally known, was Wolves' long-term programme editor but was also a good friend to many of the former players. He always helped me out with anything I needed from Wolves, from tickets for matches to kits for the grandchildren. Looking ahead, I think the current team could become arguably one of the club's best ever, certainly it's the most stylish football I can remember seeing from a Wolves team for many years. The owners Fosun seem keen to build the club back up to be what it used to be and hopefully the good times are on the way back. At the time of writing, they have just clinched the Championship title, which is fantastic. I think the owners will pump serious investment into the club which will hopefully bring the success the supporters crave and that would be great for the area as a whole.

They look like they are really going to compete in the Premier League. We had a good team in the early 1970s and when we won the League Cup in 1980. We had a couple of disappointments with two relegations but we bounced back at the first attempt on both occasions and it was only when we went down again, in 1984, that the rot really set in and the depth of the club's financial problems became apparent. Thankfully those dark days now seem like a distant memory. I think the current squad will establish themselves in the top flight very quickly and they are looking at staying there, which is great. The ground has changed a lot since my playing days but it's always wonderful to go back to Molineux. I loved my 16 years there and have a great affection for the club and the area. My wife is Wednesfield born and bred, and my two kids were born in Wolverhampton, so I have some brilliant memories of my time at Wolves. We still have friends and family in the area, as do Kelly and Rod, who are frequent visitors.

Football has changed a lot in the 50-odd years that I have been involved in it. It's now a billion- pound industry and quite rightly, there is huge scrutiny on every game with so much at stake. That means there is more pressure than ever on officials to get decisions right. Their cause is not helped by players willing to go down at the slightest touch in the box, and we have some very clever players around only too willing to test the resolve of referees, while defenders are afraid to make a challenge in case they concede a penalty. Going back to my playing days, attacking players have always tried to win penalties but nowhere near as much as now. Decisions were more accepted – you didn't find managers rushing to see referees after the game to debate why they had made them.

There is now a lot of talk about eradicating the errors made by officials in games by introducing Video Assistant Referees, or VAR. With the speed of the game now and the way players bend the rules trying to win penalties, officials need all the help they can get. But while the delays caused by technology are an accepted part of rugby, cricket and American sports, the time lapses we currently see with VAR are alien to our football. In this country we have always enjoyed the spontaneity of the game and the talking points that incidents and the decisions that are given from them throw up. They fuel the debates in the pubs and clubs after matches and if we take those away with VAR, what will folk be left to talk about? There will always be controversial decisions. Officials will make errors, just the same as you will always get managers making mistakes on tactics. Referees and their staff work very hard on their fitness during the week to get themselves into the best positions to make their decisions and they watch lots of clips of incidents. Whether having so much information helps modern-day managers, I don't know because for me, there is now too much analysis in football. I have always felt uncomfortable watching a studio full of pundits dissecting a manager's decisions made in the heat of the moment. Who is to say anyone in a studio can comment on a decision made by a vastly experienced manager when he hasn't done the job himself, or knows the circumstances behind it? It doesn't sit right with me.

But there is no doubt football has become bigger in my five decades involved in the game and I think it is only a matter of time – maybe in the next five years – before we see a European league made up of the top teams from the major nations. I dread to think what will happen to the rest of the competitions, such as the rest of the Premier League, if that happens, but when you see clubs paying £75m for a defender, there is no doubt that football is now a game where only the extremely wealthy succeed. It's not the players' fault, it's a symptom of the huge amounts of money sloshing around in the game at the very top levels now.

As you get older and hopefully wiser, you tend to become more reflective. I have a few regrets from my time in the game. There have been occasions in management when I was too accommodating to people I worked for and should have taken a few more risks by putting myself first a bit more. I certainly don't begrudge the top players earning the riches they are paid nowadays. Of course I wouldn't mind the salaries they get, but I wouldn't like the scrutiny they are under. I had my time and we were well paid for what was a bloody enjoyable job, and it felt like we had more fun than they have now. One of the greatest golfers Gary Player once said the harder you work, the luckier you get. I always gave my best and supporters acknowledged that.

These days when I'm not travelling up and down the country working as a Premier League match delegate, I enjoy spending time with my family and playing golf. But at this point I must mention my all-time favourite comedy actor. David Jason has given me so many laughs down the years and I love watching him in TV shows, particularly *'Only Fools And Horses'* but even before that, when he appeared in *'Porridge'* and *'Open All Hours'*. When Wolves supporters come up to me and say that I gave them so much pleasure from watching me play, I feel the same way about David Jason. I was reminded of that affection last year. It was a nasty, horrible night and I had been invited to open a pub in Willenhall. Unfortunately, I left my lights on in my car so when I returned afterwards, my battery was flat. Just what you need on a freezing wet evening with a two-hour drive ahead of you! Anyway, a Wolves fan arranged to get a set of jump leads and got my car going again. Afterwards I asked him if I could give him anything for his trouble. He said 'Kenny, you've given me so much pleasure down the years, you don't owe me anything.' That was a lovely thing to say and left me with a wonderful feeling at the end of the night.

Reflecting on my life now, I eat healthily, I'm not overweight and feel I'm fit for my age. I go for regular power walks and play golf once a week. The power walking started off with some of the mums from our local village school a decade or so ago and continues to this day. A few years ago some of the mums surprised me – we all met up and they turned up with T-shirts emblazoned with 'Kenny's Angels' with a full action photo of me from my Wolves playing days on the front and we walked to the next village for Christmas lunch. As you get older you're bound to suffer aches and pains occasionally and when I go to La Manga the old players joke about our 'footballing wounds'. In my case, it's arthritis in my left leg which has caused it to bow slightly. I get the odd sharp pain, especially if I turn quickly, but having heard what they do to correct it, I can live with the odd ache at the moment. I'm quite happy with my lot, and am looking forward to many more seasons of my life yet.

Statistics

Bradford Park Avenue

	League		FA Cup		League Cup		Others		Total	
	A	G	A	G	A	G	A	G	A	G
1967-68	8	0	-		-	-	-	-	8	0
1968-69	5 (1)	0	-		-	-	1	0	6 (1)	0
Totals	13 (1)	0	-		1	0	-	-	14 (1)	0

Wolverhampton Wanderers

	League		FA Cup		League Cup		Others		Total	
	A	G	A	G	A	G	A	G	A	G
1968-69	0 (1)	0	-		-	-	-	-	0 (1)	0
1969-70	-	-	-	-	-	-	-	-	-	-
1970-71	30 (2)	2	2	1	-	-	5	0	35 (2)	3
1971-72	33 (1)	7	2	0	1	0	9 (1)	2	45 (2)	9
1972-73	31	6	4	1	6	2	3	0	45	9
1973-74	29 (4)	2	2	0	5 (1)	3	4 (1)	1	40 (6)	6
1974-75	41	17	1	0	1	0	2	0	45	17
1975-76	39 (2)	8	5	1	4	3	-	-	49	12
1976-77	40 (1)	17	5	1	1	0	-	-	46	18
1977-78	23	6	3	2	-	-	-	-	26	8
1978-79	37	6	7	1	1	0	-	-	45	7
1979-80	32	9	4	0	11	4	-	-	47	13
1980-81	33	3	9	2	1	0	1	0	44	5
1981-82	33	4	-	-	1	0	-	-	34	4
1982-83	27 (4)	2	2	1	1	0	-	-	30 (4)	3
1983-84	19 (4)	0	-	-	2	0	-	-	21 (4)	0
Totals	447 (19)	89	46	10	35 (1)	12	24 (2)	3	552 (22)	114

Others for Wolves: 1970-71 Texaco Cup; 1971-72 UEFA Cup; 1972-73Texaco Cup; 1973-74 UEFA CUP, FA Cup third place match;1974-75 UEFA Cup.1980-81 UEFA Cup.

263

Coventry City

	League		FA Cup		League Cup		Others		Total	
	A	G	A	G	A	G	A	G	A	G
1984-85	31 (2)	3	2	0	1	0	-	-	34 (2)	3
1985-86	11 (3)	1	-	-	0 (1)	0	-	-	11 (4)	1
Totals	42 (5)	4	2	0	1 (1)	0	-	-	45 (6)	4

Bristol Rovers

	League		FA Cup		League Cup		Others		Total	
	A	G	A	G	A	G	A	G	A	G
1986-87	27 (1)	3	2	-	2	0	-	-	31	3
1987-88	24	2	3	0	2	0	-	-	28	2
1988-89	(1)	-	-	-	-	-	-	-	(1)	0
Totals	51 (1)	5	5	0	4	0	-	-	60 (2)	5

Career Totals

League		FA Cup		League Cup		Others		Total	
A	G	A	G	A	G	A	G	A	G
553 (26)	98	53	10	41 (2)	12	24 (2)	3	671 (30)	123

In addition, Kenny Hibbitt played for Seattle Sounders in the summer of 1982, playing 14 games and scoring four goals for the NASL side.

Bradford Park Avenue first game (manager Jack Rowley).
Chesterfield 2 Bradford Park Avenue 0, March 23, 1968, Fourth Division. Position: 24th
Chesterfield: Roberts; Holmes, Lumsden, Clarke, Neale, Phelan, Moore, Randall, Hollett, Kettleborough, Curry.
Goals: Hollett, Randall pen
Bradford Park Avenue: Hardie; Hart, Rowley, Drury, Lyons, Tanner, Draper, Giles, Down, **Hibbitt,** Robinson.
Attendance: 7,337.

Bradford Park Avenue last game (manager Don McCalman).
Bradford Park Avenue 0 Chesterfield 1, October 26, 1968, Fourth Division. Position: 24th.
Bradford Park Avenue: Hardie; Hudson, Singleton, Tanner, Gibson, Darfield, Robinson, **Hibbitt** (Clancy), Draper, Brannan, Cockburn.
Chesterfield: Humphreys; Holmes, Lumsden, Kettleborough, Finnigan, Phelan, Moore, Randall, Moss, Bell, Bishop.
Goal: Randall.
Attendance: 3,088.

Wolves first game (manager Bill McGarry).
Wolves 0 West Bromwich Albion 1, April 12 1969, First Division. Position: 15th.
Wolves: Parkes; Taylor, Parkin, Wilson, Holsgrove, McAlle, Farrington **(Hibbitt 70),** Knowles, Dougan, Munro, Lutton.
West Bromwich Albion: Osborne; Fraser, Wilson, Brown, Talbut, Kaye, Krzywicki (Clark 25), Lovett, Martin, Hope, Hartford.
Goal: Clark 25.
Attendance: 37,920

Wolves last game (caretaker manager Jim Barron).
Watford 0 Wolves 0, May 5, 1984. First Division. Position: 22nd.
Watford: Sherwood; Gibbs, Jackett, Taylor, Terry, Sinnott, Callaghan, Johnston, Sterling (Gilligan), Atkinson. Rostron.
Wolves: Burridge, Humphrey, Smith, Bayly, Pender, Dodd, Towner, **Hibbitt,** McGarvey, Eves (Crainie), Dougherty. Attendance: 13,534.

265

Coventry City first game (manager Bobby Gould).
Aston Villa 1 Coventry City 0, August 25, 1984, First Division. Position: 17th.
Aston Villa: Day; Williams, Gibson, Evans, Foster, McMahon, Bremner, Walters, Withe, Cowans, Mortimer.
Goal: Bremner 53.
Coventry City: Ogrizovic; Stephens, Pearce, Jol, Kilcline, Peake, Bennett, Platnauer, Withey **(Hibbitt),** Gibson, Gynn.
Attendance: 20,970.

Coventry City last game (manager: Don Mackay).
Ipswich Town 1 Coventry City 0, March 31, 1986, First Division. Position: 16th.
Ipswich Town: Hallworth; Parkin, McCall, Atkins, Cranson, Butcher, Gleghorn, Brennan, Cole, Wilson, Dozzell (D'Avray).
Goal: Brennan 78.
Coventry City: Ogrizovic; Borrows, Downs, McGrath, Kilcline, Peake, McInally (Bennett), Brazil, Regis, Pickering, **Hibbitt.**
Attendance: 13,817.

Bristol Rovers first game (manager Bobby Gould).
Walsall 0 Bristol Rovers 3, August 23, 1986, Third Division. Position: 1st.
Walsall: Prudhoe; Dornan, Mower, Shakespeare, Hawker, Hart, Taylor (Jones), Cross, Kelly, Jones, Naughton.
Bristol Rovers: Carter; Scales, Tanner, Jones, Smalley, **Hibbitt**, Alexander, Penrice, Morgan, Mehew, Micallef.
Goals: Hibbitt 22, Morgan, 25 63.
Attendance: 6,269.

Bristol Rovers last game (manager Gerry Francis).
Bristol Rovers 2 Chesterfield 1, March 11, 1989, Third Division. Position 6th.
Bristol Rovers: Martyn, Alexander, Twentyman, Yates, Hazel **(Hibbitt),** Jones, Mehew, Bailey, McLean, Penrice, Purnell.
Goals: Bailey 27, Penrice 30.
Chesterfield: Leonard; Bloomer, Prindiville, Arnott, Brien, Rogers, Rolph (Hewitt), Shaw, Waller, Eley (Alleyne), Morris.
Goal: Shaw 60. Attendance: 4,691.

Top 10 Wolves appearances

609 Derek Parkin
574 Kenny Hibbitt
561 Steve Bull
541 Billy Wright
512 Ron Flowers
509 John McAlle
497 Peter Broadbent
496 Geoff Palmer
487 John Richards
486 Jimmy Mullen

Top 10 Wolves goals

306 Steve Bull
194 John Richards
167 Johnny Hancocks
166 Jimmy Murray
145 Peter Broadbent
126 Harry Wood
124 Dennis Westcott
123 Derek Dougan
114 Kenny Hibbitt, Roy Swinbourne
113 Dennis Wilshaw

Index

270

275

279